digital *Essentials*

the quilt maker's must-have guide to images, files, and more!

Gloria Hansen

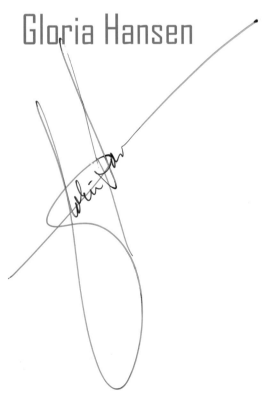

THE ELECTRIC QUILT COMPANY

Notice of Trademarks:

Adobe® Photoshop®, Adobe® Bridge, Adobe® Flash®, Adobe® Gamma®, Adobe® RGB (1998), Adobe® RGB, Creative Suite®, Distiller®, Illustrator®, InDesign® and Photoshop® Elements and Acrobat® Reader are either registered trademarks or trademarks of Adobe Systems Incorporated in the United States and/or other countries.

CorelDRAW® and Corel® Paint Shop Pro® are trademarks or registered trademarks of Corel Corporation and/or its subsidiaries in Canada, the United States and/or other countries.

Apple®, ColorSync®, Keynote®, Leopard®, Macintosh®, iTunes®, iPhoto® and Mac® are trademarks of Apple Inc., registered in the U.S. and other countries.

UNIX® is a registered trademark of The Open Group.

AutoSketch® and AutoDesk® are registered trademarks or trademarks of Autodesk, Inc., in the USA and/or other countries.

Electric Quilt® is a registered trademark of The Electric Quilt Company.

Windows®, Microsoft®, Microsoft® Office, Microsoft® Word, Windows Vista® and PowerPoint® are registered trademarks of Microsoft Corporation in the United States and other countries.

DURABrite® is a registered trademark of Epson America Inc. in the United States and other countries.

EPSON® and Epson UltraChrome® are registered trademarks of Seiko Epson Corporation in the United States and other countries.

Spyder® is a registered trademark of Datacolor.

Digimarc® is a registered trademark of Digimarc Corporation.

Many titles used by manufacturers and sellers to distinguish their products are claimed as trademarks. Where The Electric Quilt Company was aware of these trademarks, the trademark symbol was printed beside the trademarked title or product name the first time it was mentioned in this book.

Hansen, Gloria
Digital Essentials: The Quilt Maker's Must-Have Guide to Images, Files, and More!
Gloria Hansen
p. cm.
ISBN 1-893824-64-0

Published by The Electric Quilt Company
419 Gould Street, Suite 2
Bowling Green, Ohio 43402 USA

www.electricquilt.com

Printed in Malaysia

Credits:

Editors: Penny McMorris and Sara Seuberling
Book and cover design: Sara Seuberling
Editorial assistant: Sara Woodward

Dedication

I dedicate this book to Penny McMorris for approaching me with the idea to write the book, and to my business partner, Derry Thompson, for encouraging me to agree. Thank you both for the needed push to take this project from an idea to a reality.

Table of Contents

the fundamentals

working with images

saving for the web

reference

Acknowledgements

First and foremost I thank Derry Thompson. Derry lives in the beautiful town of Bewdley located in England and is the person I continually question, pushing for clarifications and explanations of what often seems contradictory information. He read every word in this book, often several times, confirming that they are technically accurate or correcting them where needed. His vast wealth of knowledge is a continual godsend to me. He is a gentleman and a scholar, and I have and continue to benefit enormously from the confidence he shows in me and his continual encouragement that pushes me farther than I think I'm capable.

I thank Andrew Frazier for his clarification of certain PC issues and both Andrew and Anita Truswell for answering E-mail that I forwarded to them to take care of while I was busy working on the book. Both Andrew and Anita also reside in England.

I also thank Margaret Tuchman of Princeton, New Jersey for being a light in my life at a time when I needed it most.

I thank my family—Mike Chiravalle, MaryAnn Burns, and Bob Patrowicz; my wonderful mother, Theresa Patrowicz; and my dad, who I like to think is watching over me. I am grateful to them all.

I thank everyone at The Electric Quilt Company for polishing my words and Sara Seuberling for creating the beautiful cover and layout of this book. I especially thank Penny McMorris, a woman I have admired long before Electric Quilt came along. Penny is a beautiful mix of grace and talent, and she has a quiet strength that epitomizes the woman I aspire to be.

For nearly two decades I have been active in various online communities since I first logged onto the Internet via a bulletin board service. Being connected has introduced me to countless talented quilt artists and has resulted in a range of opportunities that have changed my life. I thank all of the people that I have met through these communities.

And finally, I thank my husband, Rich. He watched me graduate high school, college, and has witnessed my every achievement since with patience, love, and pride.

About the Author

Digital Essentials is the 14th book that Gloria has authored or co-authored on quilting/computer and Internet-related topics. She regularly contributes freelance articles to a variety of magazines, and has written a tech column for *The Professional Quilter* magazine since 1996.

Gloria's passion for digital design began in the late 1980s. With no instruction available for using a computer as a quilt design tool, she began using early programs to develop digital designs. She also experimented with various methods of printing on fabric using early inkjet printers, laser printers, and photocopy machines. She helped develop an early recipe for making inkjet ink water resistant (this prior to today's pretreatment solution).

As the personal computer, design programs, and inkjet printing technologies grew, so too did Gloria's expertise in using them and applying the skills to her quilt making. Since she had studied photography and was an early user of Photoshop, she embraced digital photography early on. Gloria is also a regular on many Internet mailing lists and is happy to answer digital-related questions.

Gloria's quilts have been exhibited throughout the country and abroad for over two decades. Her dual passions for the arts of quilt making and digital design blend perfectly, as evidenced by her one-woman exhibition, "Advanced Geometry: Gloria Hansen" (April 1 - June 8, 2008), at the San Jose Museum of Quilts & Textiles in California. In a short blurb written for the show, Museum Curator Deborah Corsini described Gloria as "one of the world's foremost experts on computer-generated quilt design."

She's won over 150 awards for her quilts, including the Master of Innovative Artistry award at the 2007 IQA show in Houston, Texas and the Best Wall Quilt at the 2008 AQS show in Paducah, Kentucky. The wall quilt is now part of the AQS Museum's permanent collection. Her quilts have appeared on television, on the cover of magazines and her books, a college textbook, as well as within numerous books and magazine articles. She has also taught and lectured on quilt making, computer-generated design, and fabric painting.

Gloria (in New Jersey) and business partner, Derry Thompson (in the U.K.) together operate GloDerWorks, a full-service Web design company founded in 2001. Gloria lives in East Windsor, New Jersey, and invites you to her Web site at www.gloriahansen.com.

Introduction

It's a digital maze out there. The terminology gets confusing, the tools overwhelming, and asking questions can result in conflicting answers. Why can't someone just explain how to resize a digital image for a show—or how to get good color from a printer—or how to cut a quilt image from a background so it doesn't look like it's been done with hedge clippers? And does it all have to take so much time?

This book guides you through the maze. And since I am a quilt maker, I'm writing specifically with quilt makers in mind. I'll share techniques I've learned—often the hard way—and tricks I've discovered. And I'll explain the **whys** behind everything. There is a way out of the maze, and this book gets you on your way.

The Fundamentals

the digital journey

The digital world is an odd one. Filled with seemingly foreign terms like bitmaps, vectors, and JPEGs, it's easy to feel overwhelmed and frustrated over the whole mess of it. And just when did quilt shows start requesting digital entries rather than slides, and is it true that slide projectors aren't even being made anymore? If you feel like it's all passing you by, I'm here to guide you down the digital path. As you make your journey, take your time, stop to absorb and experiment, and have fun with it. Soon the exciting world of digital possibilities will open before you. Let's begin.

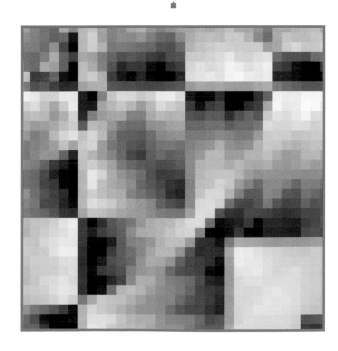

Metafiles, Bitmap and Vector Images

A **METAFILE** is a general term for a file format that can store various types of information, including **raster** or **vector** information. Understanding the difference between raster (also called bitmap) images and vector images is important when you're making images.

BITMAP IMAGES, the better-known name for raster images, are made from **pixels** (the smallest element in any digital image). Each pixel is individually described as a particular color. While not technically correct, you can think of pixels as the dots of color that create the image on your computer monitor. Photographs from your digital camera and scanned images are examples of bitmap images.

Poor quality bitmap images, such as "dotty" photographs or "stairstep" edges of a design, are the result of not enough pixels. I'll talk more about pixels in Chapter 4 "Resolution—It's the Pixels" (page 21).

> **Note:** The more pixels in a bitmap image, the higher the quality of that image. This is sometimes referred to as **pixel density**.

A single pixel

In the larger circle, notice how the image starts to look "pixelated" as we zoom in close. In the smaller circle, we've zoomed in so much that we now begin to see the individual pixels.

VECTOR IMAGES, also called object-orientated graphics, are made from a series of mathematical geometric objects such as polygons and curves. No need to panic! All the mathematical calculations are done behind the scenes by the software program you are using.

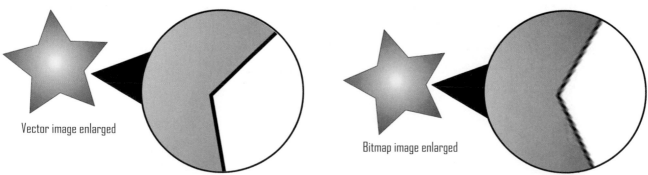

Vector image enlarged

Bitmap image enlarged

The vector image is "resolution independent," meaning you can enlarge the image without quality loss. Zooming in shows the edges are crisp. When zooming in on a bitmap image, it degrades in quality and becomes blurry. This is why enlarging a photograph above its original size can result in a poor quality image.

Note: Vector images can be enlarged to any size without any quality loss. This means, for example, that you can create a logo as a vector image and use that logo on everything from a business card to a poster or even a billboard.

Vector images are the ideal format for line drawings. Programs such as CorelDRAW® and Adobe® Illustrator® create vector images, and programs such as Electric Quilt® can create vector line drawings. Other programs, such as Photoshop® Elements, which is primarily a bitmap application, include simple vector elements such as shape-based objects and text.

So, Why Not Use Vector Programs for All Images?

In order for a photograph to look its best, thousands, even millions, of pixels in various values of color (or gray) are required. At this point in time, vectors cannot give the beautiful photographic quality that bitmaps can without creating a massively huge file requiring very powerful computer processing just to open the file. The key is using the best of both: **bitmap (image-editing) programs for photographs** and **vector (drawing) programs for flat art** such as logos, quilt pattern drawings, and text. Some programs allow both! Chapter 3 "Quilt Designing on the Computer" (page 17) will tell you more about bitmap and vector programs.

Quick Review

Metafile: A general digital file. It can have either vector or bitmap information.

Bitmap (raster) files: A pixel-based file. Used for photographs and photo-realistic images.
- Advantage: Supports millions of colors.
- Disadvantage: Cannot be enlarged without sufficient resolution or specialized programs.
- Programs: Adobe® Photoshop®, Adobe Photoshop Elements, Corel® Paint Shop Pro®, and any other photo-editing software.

Vector (object-orientated) files: A math-based file. Used for flat line art, text, and other illustrations.
- Advantage: Can be enlarged without any degradation of quality.
- Disadvantage: Unless a bitmap image is embedded in a vector, it is not practical to use the vector for images, such as photos, that contain millions of colors.
- Programs: Adobe Illustrator, CorelDRAW, Electric Quilt 6, and any other drawing software.

digital file formats

The digital world is riddled with acronyms: PSD, EPS, JPEG, and PDF. There are so many bewildering digital file names and terms.

Some file types can work in a variety of programs; others only work in the particular program in which the file was created. Some file formats are compressed, others are not. Some are geared towards the Web, others for print. The good news? You don't need to learn them all. For most graphic applications, you only need to be aware of a handful of formats.

```
IFF/LBM - Amiga Interchange File Format
IMG - GEM Raster Files
JP2 - JPEG2000 File Format
JPG/JPEG - JPG Files
JPM - JPM Files
KDC - Kodak Digital Camera Files
LDF - LuraDocument Format
LWF - LuraWave Format
MED - MED/OctaMED Audio Files
MNG/JNG - Multiple Network Graphics
MP3 - MPEG Audio Files
MOV - Apple QuickTime Movie
MPG/MPEG/DAT - MPEG Files
NLM/NOL/NGG/GSM - Nokia LogoManager Files
OGG - Ogg Vorbis Audio Files
PBM/PGM/PPM - Portable Bitmaps
PCD - Kodak Photo CD
PCX/DCX - Zsoft Paintbrush
PNG - Portable Network Graphics
PSD - Adobe Photoshop Files
PSP - Paint Shop Pro Files
RA - Real Audio Files
RAS - Sun Raster Files
RAW - RAW/YUV Image Data
RLE - Utah RLE Files
SFF - Structured Fax Files
SFW - Seattle Film Works Files
SGI - Silicon Graphics Files
SID - LizardTech MrSID Files
SWF - Macromedia Flash/Shockwave Files
```

Common File Formats

JPEG, JPG (.jpg)

Joint Photographic Experts Group (JPEG) – bitmap

JPEG files are primarily used for photographs and continuous tone images (images that have a virtually unlimited range of colors) rather than images with flat colors, such as drawings. For example, the JPEG is the most widely used format for saving photographs and continuous tone images for the Internet.

A JPEG file (jpg for short) uses "lossy" compression to compact the data within the image file. A lossy compression replaces individual pixels with blocks of color. This means that while the file format takes up less memory than most other image file formats, quality can be lost. The higher the level of compression, the lower the quality of the image.

> **Note:** To maintain the highest image quality, always save a JPEG at the lowest compression setting.

When saving a JPEG image for the Internet, you can get by with a middle- to middle-high compression, depending on the size of the image and the quality desired.

Always keep the original digital image file that you saved as a JPEG. Each time you open a JPEG, make changes, and resave, the quality of the image drops—especially if you compress it at less than the maximum setting. So if you ever need to make changes to a JPEG image, start by opening the original JPEG, work with it, and resave it as a new file with a new name. That way, the image quality of your original JPEG and your new file will both be maintained.

TIFF (.tif)

Tagged Image File Format (TIFF) – bitmap

The TIFF image may be the most widely used and supported printing format across both the PC and Mac® worlds. It doesn't support vector artwork. And it doesn't support "lossy" compression. But it does support multiple layers in Photoshop. TIFF is the preferred format for publishing, and for saving photographs without compression.

GIF (.gif)

Graphics Interchange Format (GIF) – bitmap

The GIF file format is generally only used on the Internet, for images that contain flat colors, such as logos and line art. It supports only 256 colors, but it also supports transparencies and animation. Its low resolution makes it unsuitable for printing.

PDF (.pdf)

Portable Document Format

A PDF is a page description language developed by Adobe. It describes how a page is to be displayed or printed. A PDF packs everything into the document—text, fonts, and graphics—and displays the document exactly as it was originally laid out, even if the recipient doesn't have the software or fonts used to create the original document. To open a PDF file, you need a "PDF reader" (free from Adobe). A PDF can be viewed on Mac, PC, and Linux/Unix® machines.

Saving your document as a PDF and including it on your Web site is an excellent way to allow viewers to print your information exactly as you intend for them to see it. This option is great for teachers who want their students to have a particular classroom handout. For more details on using and creating PDFs, see Chapter 18 "The Power of PDF Files" (page 187).

PNG (.png)

Portable Network Graphic (PNG) – bitmap

The PNG format allows compression with no data loss. This means you can save and resave the same PNG file over and over with no quality loss (unlike a JPEG). The PNG format supports 48-bit color, transparencies and can be used for both photographs and line art. As browsers evolve and fully support PNG files, it will most likely replace most GIF and JPEG files.

RAW

RAW – bitmap

Raw is a file format that is uncompressed and completely unprocessed.

Camera RAW

Camera RAW – bitmap

Camera RAW is an uncompressed and unprocessed file format used in higher-end cameras. The moment a camera's shutter is opened, the sensor captures the most pixel information of any digital camera format and stores a mirror of that capture on a memory card. Because the file is untouched, Camera RAW can be considered the negative, with the image-editing software that supports it being considered the darkroom.

EPS (.eps)

Encapsulated Postscript (EPS) – vector

EPS files are generally used to save an illustration created in a drawing program. In other words, a vector format. The file can then be imported into a page layout program such as InDesign®. Within a page layout program, the illustration can be resized without any quality loss.

EPS is a vector file that can contain bitmap images. (hence "Encapsulated"). If the file contains a bitmap it's possible that it cannot be enlarged without losing quality—depending on the size of the bitmap. However, you can shrink it without losing quality.

BMP (.bmp)

Microsoft Paint's BMP (BMP) – bitmap

BMP is Microsoft's original bitmap file format.

PICT (.pic or .pict)

Apple's PICT (PICT) – vector

PICT is an original vector file format from Apple®, which can also contain embedded bitmaps.

PSD (.psd)

Photoshop Document (PSD)

PSD is the default format for Adobe Photoshop documents. It can contain both vector and bitmap images.

PSP (.psp)

Paint Shop Pro document

PSP is the default format for Paint Shop Pro documents. It can contain both vector and bitmap images.

Exporting or Converting from One File Format to Another

Many graphic programs, such as Electric Quilt, save images in their own unique format (also referred to as **native files**). Such images generally cannot be opened in another program. For example, an Electric Quilt file cannot be opened in Photoshop. However, many programs, such as Electric Quilt, can change their own native files to other formats. (For example, Electric Quilt 6 can export its block and quilt images as .jpg, .gif, .tif, .bmp, or .png files and also export blocks as metafiles.) This is known as **exporting a file**. And many graphic programs can change one file format into another. This is known as **converting a file**.

There are programs developed specifically to open one file format and convert it to another. IrfanView (www.irfanview.com) is a free program for the Windows® platform. GraphicConverter (www.lemkesoft.com) is a low-cost shareware for Macintosh®. (Check your Mac's Applications folder, as some Macintosh computers ship with GraphicConverter already installed). Converting an image is generally as simple as doing a Save As and selecting the file format. (Doing a Save As, and renaming the file will keep your original file intact.)

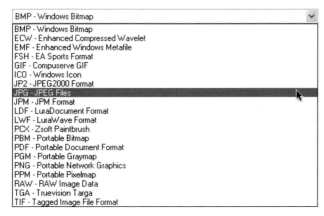

By going to File > Save As, you'll find a list of file formats that you can save to.

IrfanView also allows you to open a variety of different image formats.

If you're planning to download IrfanView, use this address: http://www.irfanview.com/main_download_engl.htm and also install the free plug-ins for IrfanView. Once you launch the plug-ins, it will automatically install itself into the program and give you a larger selection of file formats to work with.

Depending on what format you start with and what format you convert to, you may degrade the quality of your image. For example, **if you convert a JPEG with thousands of colors to a GIF, the photo will degrade** because a GIF is only capable of displaying 256 colors. Additionally, some graphic programs contain their own unique properties and may lose something in the translation. For example, while a conversion program may be able to open a PSD file, it may not retain all of the layers saved within the original document.

On another note, while you can convert one bitmap image to another, and you can convert a vector image to a bitmap format, **you cannot convert a bitmap image to a vector image**. Depending on the complexity of the bitmap image, you can open the image as a layer in a drawing program and trace it using drawing tools to create the vector image.

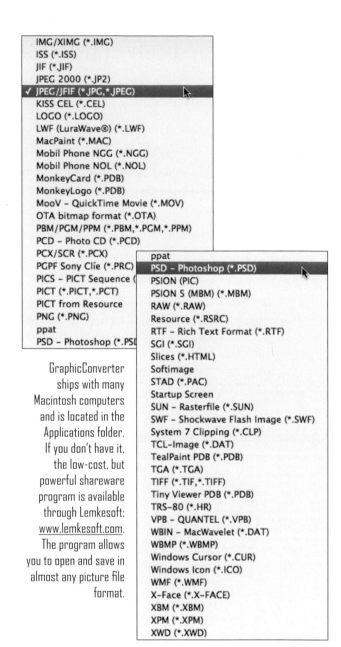

GraphicConverter ships with many Macintosh computers and is located in the Applications folder. If you don't have it, the low-cost, but powerful shareware program is available through Lemkesoft: www.lemkesoft.com. The program allows you to open and save in almost any picture file format.

Question for the expert

Q: Is there any benefit in using the converter programs versus just doing a Save As in any other program? Or do both perform the exact same function as the other without affecting the original file?

A: The benefit would be that you can open native files in IrfanView or GraphicConverter and save them as another, usable file format. For example, you can open a Photoshop PSD file and resave it as a JPEG even if you don't have Photoshop.

chapter --- ③

quilt designing on the computer

Remember when using a rotary cutter was revolutionary? That simple tool is now a quilt making staple. Using a computer program to help design a quilt is much the same. Designing on a computer can save time, increase accuracy, and inspire us to push tradition into a wider arena of possibilities. A quilt design program can quickly allow us to experiment with layouts, color, and a variety of design possibilities—all before cutting a single piece of fabric. And while the prospect of starting on the digital path may seem daunting, the journey starts with a single step.

Bitmaps and Vectors—Is it Time to Draw?

There are two basic types of programs suitable for quilt designing. The big difference between the two program types is how data within the file is stored.

Bitmap-Based Programs

Image-editing or paint programs are bitmap-based (also referred to as raster-based or pixel-based). Any time you work with a photograph, you are working with pixels. In other words, if you open your digital camera image to edit it on your computer, chances are you're in a bitmap program. On the plus side, bitmap programs allow a file to have millions of beautiful colors. But, unlike a vector drawing, an image with pixels cannot be enlarged without sacrificing quality. In simple terms, the more pixels, the greater the potential image quality.

Bitmap-based programs are good for:
Photographs, fabric fills—any image containing continuous color tones. ("Continuous tone color" means the subtle gradation of shades and color that can be of photographic quality.)

Bitmap-based programs include:
- Photoshop
- Photoshop Elements
- Paint Shop Pro

Vector-Based Programs

Drawing programs are vector-based. A vector is based on XY coordinates. It sounds like complicated math, but the program does all the math for you. This allows the drawing to be enlarged to any size you desire without degrading the image.

Vector-based programs are good for:
Drawings, quilt patterns, logos—lines unfilled, or filled with any type of flat color or simple color graduation. ("Flat color" means a solid color or any non-continuous color tones.)

Vector-based programs include:
- Adobe Illustrator
- CorelDRAW

Questions for the expert

Q: When it comes time to print, what happens to vectors? Can a printer print them?

A: No. A printer cannot print a vector, it can only print dots. Whether you're printing a photograph or a vector line drawing, the information from the digital file gets converted to dots. Yes, this may be an over simplification, and I could ramble about RIP for those that understand the term, but the key idea is this: **a printer can only print dots**.

Q: If the vectors will turn into dots, why not just start with a bitmap image?

A: Because vector-based images can be scaled to any size within your program. In other words, vector-based images do not depend on resolution like bitmap images do. (This is why vector images can be referred to as "resolution independent".) Once your drawing is sized to your output needs, and you send the file to the printer, the printer driver takes the information from the program, turns that information into dots and prints a beautiful sharp image. The drawing program doesn't care how large or small you scale your image. It will always look great.

Vector-Based Programs That Use Bitmaps

Why not just use a drawing program? You can. But who can resist working with photographs? Or experimenting with beautiful fabric fills?

Adobe Illustrator and Flash® are two examples of vector programs that use bitmaps. However, note that while you cannot edit the pixels, you can in some cases apply effects to them.

Electric Quilt—The Best of Both Worlds:

Electric Quilt is an example of a vector-based program that also uses bitmaps. EQ line drawings, unfilled or filled with solid colors, are vector files. You can print them from EQ at any size, or export them and use them in other programs such as Word or InDesign, to create whatever professional output that you need.

But EQ also has a large library of scanned fabrics. Scanned fabrics are bitmaps. While EQ's flat color fills (solid colors) can scale to any size, the fabric fills can only be printed so large in Electric Quilt 5 (EQ5) before they start to degrade and look dotty. But EQ's newer version, Electric Quilt 6 (EQ6) has a different functionality that accurately rescales the fabric bitmap image "on the fly" dithering so the fabric bitmap looks good no matter what size it's printed.

EQ allows you the precision needed for quilt design, the accurate printing of patterns, and export for professional use, but it also gives you the opportunity to experiment, seeing real fabrics (or photographs) in your quilt.

Quick Guide

EQ line drawings of blocks and quilts = vector = can scale to any size
EQ block or quilt images filled with solid colors = vector = can scale to any size
EQ5 block or quilt images filled with fabric = fabric is bitmap = fabric images will get "dotty" if enlarged too much
EQ6 block or quilt images filled with fabric = fabric is bitmap = but program rescales and printing functionality dithers the bitmaps, so fabric images do not get "dotty' when enlarged

You can export designs from Electric Quilt 6 as **.tiff**, **.jpg**, **.gif**, **.png** and **.bmp** files in the following resolutions: **75 dpi**, **150 dpi**, **300 dpi** and **600 dpi**. This allows you to use your completed EQ6 design for everything from images for your Web site to classroom overlay projections to a high resolution image for your print portfolio or even a book.

By importing one high resolution EQ6 image into an image-editing program, you can quickly create all of the image sizes that you may need. Here's how:

1   Start with your original exported EQ6 TIFF at 600 dpi (highest resolution).
2   Open it within your image-editing program.
3   Using the Image Size/Resize box, check "resample" and downsample to the highest resolution needed.
4   Save with a new name.
5   Downsample again to the second-highest resolution that you need.
6   Save it with a new name.
7   Continue this way, working from largest size to smallest size, until you have all of the needed images sizes.

Questions for the expert

Q: Wouldn't it be great if a photograph could be vector-based?

A: That technology, while in all likelihood is possible somewhere on some supercomputer, it currently is not available for everyday computers. However, today's image-editing programs are reaching into the vector arena just as drawing programs are crossing into the pixel world. This crossover has been going on for several years and is more apparent with each subsequent program release. Will one program fully replace the other? Not anytime soon, but some vector tools included with pixel-based programs are surprisingly quite capable.

Q: Are image-editing programs good for quilt designing?

A: At one time I only used drawing programs to design quilts. That was back in the days when color wasn't yet available and paint programs were limited. Today, I often use Photoshop, a bitmap program, to experiment with colors, to create digital paintings, and to incorporate photographs into my work. I also use its vector tools.

However, as good as some vector tools are within bitmap programs, they can be very limited when compared to a full-scale drawing program. Additionally, if you are designing with a goal of print publication, you need the quality of vector drawings. You don't want your illustrations to have a jagged edge, which can scream amateur.

Additionally—and this is very important—in order for the shapes and text to remain vector, a file created in Photoshop, Elements, Paint Shop Pro, or another bitmap program that offers vector tools, must be saved in its native format, as an EPS or as a PDF, if available. The seemingly perfect union of pixels and vectors living together ends the instant the file is saved into another format, such as a JPEG, TIFF, PNG, BMP, and so on. At that moment, all vector information converts into bitmaps and is never to be seen again. The text is no longer editable, and the shapes cannot be enlarged without seriously degrading the quality of the image.

BUT, this can be fine if you first save your file in its native format, and then resave the document in the necessary resolution (which should be the same or less than the native file) for whatever output is required. **Remember, vector information has infinite resolution while bitmap resolution information is defined**. Thus, define the resolution size of the document you need, and fill that document with the vector information. Once the document is saved in another format, it has been rasterized—all turned to pixels—but in the resolution size you need, meaning no ragged edges. If you plan to have your document printed by a print house for publication, contact them for their recommended resolution. Often you can supply the original native file allowing the printer to output directly from it.

Q: Would it be best to stick with a dedicated drawing program to design quilts?

A: It depends. If when working with vector tools in a bitmap program you find yourself continually pushing those tools to their limits, it's time to for something more. Once again, the type of drawing program will depend on your needs. I know many people who have paid big dollars for Adobe Illustrator or CorelDRAW only to use it for basic shapes that could be done using a far less expensive program or end up not using it at all because of the steep learning curve. If you do need something high-end like Adobe Illustrator or CorelDraw, visit the Web site of each to download a free 30-day trial. Then use the program and see if it works for you. Rather than a high-end program, you may want to try a less-complex, yet fully capable drawing program such as EQ6, AutoSketch® (from AutoDesk® for Windows) or Lineform (from Freeverse for the Mac). These programs are far less expensive, and have a lower learning curve, too.

chapter ---- (4)

resolution—it's all about the pixels

Now that you know how important pixels are to the quality of bitmap images, how do you determine how many pixels are needed for good images? And just how do pixels relate to resolution?

The Building Blocks of Resolution

Pixel

Some call it a dot; others a square. But a pixel, short for **PIC**ture (or "pix") and **EL**ement, is actually a single point in a graphic image—or a single piece of information. The number of pixels that make up an image is referred to as the **Resolution**.

In other words, **resolution is simply the number of pixels in a digital file**. It is measured by **width and height**, and stated in terms of that ratio, such as 800 x 600. For example, an 800 x 600 pixel image = 800 x 600 = for a total of 480,000 pixels.

> **Very Important!**
> Pixels are not dots. Dots refer to print. When printing, it often takes several dots of ink to represent one pixel of color. More on that in the next few pages.

Bitmap (or raster) images are made up thousands, even millions of tiny pixels. As we zoom into the photo, you can start to see the individual pixels.

Megapixel

The term megapixel is short for **one million pixels**. This term commonly describes both the number of pixels in a digital image and the sensor elements of a digital camera. However, while a megapixel is short for one million pixels, it is actually 1,048,576 pixels, not a million.

Calculating megapixels is easy: **Multiply your pixel width by the height**.
> **For example:** A 1200 by 1800 pixel image is 1200 x 1800 = **2,160,000 pixels**. Rounded down, that would be an approximate **2 megapixel image**. Thus, the best quality photo a 2 megapixel camera can take is one with any width x height equaling approximately 2 million pixels.

Most cameras today are at least 5 megapixels, meaning an excellent amount of image resolution. Remember, referring to megapixels is referring to the actual pixels in an image, not the physical size of the document.

Question for the expert

Q: How many megapixels do you need in a camera?

A: Most people will not need more than a 5 megapixel camera unless they intend to crop small sections of their images. It takes more than megapixel number to create a good image—lens quality, image stabilization, and, most importantly, picture-taking skills are all key. No number of megapixels will make up for a poorly taken image.

How Does a Pixel Relate to the Physical Size of an Image?

The **physical size of an image is generally stated in megabytes**. The easiest way to determine your image size is by opening your Image Size dialog box (or Resize dialog box) in your image-editing program and looking at the size given next to Pixel Dimensions. In this example, the Image Size box defines the document as 1800 x 1200 pixels, and it indicates 6.18M in the upper-left. The "M" can be confusing, as you might think it stands for megapixels. However, it stands for <u>megabytes</u>. A **byte** is a unit of file size.

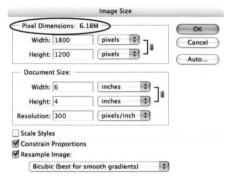

Here's some terminology associated with file size:

    1 bit = a single digit, either 0 or 1 (the smallest unit of electronic data)

    8 bits = 1 byte, which is a combination of 0s and 1s

    1,024 bytes = 1 kilobyte

    1,024 kilobytes = 1 megabyte (MB)

    1,024 megabytes = 1 gigabyte (GB)

    1,024 gigabytes = 1 terabyte (TB)

Image Size box in Photoshop

If you want to know the math behind the example—that is, calculating the physical space of a 1800 x 1200 pixel document—read on:

- Image resolution: **1800 x 1200 = 2,160,000 pixels**
- **2,160,000 x 3 = 6,480,000 bytes**

   (The 3 is for the three color channels in an RGB image. A CMYK document would be multiplied by 4.)
- **6,480,000 ÷ 1,024 twice = 6.179 megabytes**

   Or, rounding up, 6.18M. The 6.18 megabytes defines how much space your digital document takes up. (We divided twice by 1,024 to convert bytes to megabytes: to get bytes to kilobytes divide by 1,024; for kilobytes to megabytes divide again by 1,024.)

If you're anything like me, you'll find yourself loving the Image Size dialog box. It does all the math for you!

Do all images need high resolution? Although more resolution (or pixels) generally equals better quality, it's a common misconception that all digital images need high resolution. Not so. It all depends on how you intend to output your image. Will you print it with your home inkjet printer? Or will you send it to a printing house to be printed on an offset press? Or is the image only intended for display on a Web site?

For a Web image, too much resolution and your Web image may display far larger than you want. Too little resolution and the beautiful image on your monitor may print poorly. **The goal is to have your image resolution match your output device.**

Resolution for Various Outputs

Monitor Resolution

WEB SITE IMAGES

Images meant for display on computer monitors require less resolution than images that will be printed. While 72 ppi (pixels per inch) has become a kind of shorthand for screen resolution, do not perpetuate this. Get in the habit of thinking in terms of **pixel dimensions** instead.

Most of today's monitors have a display of 1024 pixels wide or greater. But many people still use monitors displaying only 800 pixels wide. So what happens if you make Web images wider than 800 pixels? Those viewing your images on an 800 pixel wide monitor will need to scroll horizontally to see your whole image. Unless you have a specific reason to do otherwise, you should **consider the lower monitor resolution that is still being used by a number of people and create your image accordingly.**

> **Note:** Currently images should be created less than 800 pixels wide until most people are using larger monitor resolution.

As people update or buy new monitors, higher resolution will become the norm, and your images will need more resolution to properly display. But for now, when creating images for the Web, consider your whole audience and think in terms of their resolution.

To simplify:

Monitor resolution has a direct impact on the size at which an image is displayed. The greater the monitor resolution, the more compact the pixels. In other words:

- large monitor resolution = smaller image
- small monitor resolution = larger image

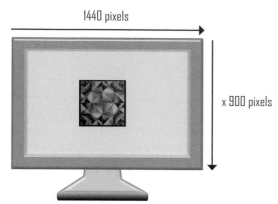

The larger your monitor resolution, the smaller your image will appear.

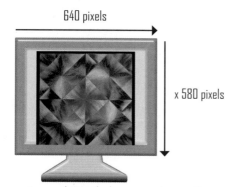

The smaller your monitor resolution, the larger your image will appear.

DIGITAL PROJECTION, INCLUDING POWERPOINT® PRESENTATIONS

The same rules for creating Web images also apply to images for projectors. Projectors have no standard screen size in inches. You cannot specify a ppi because it is meaningless in relation to a digital projector.

If ppi is meaningless, then how do you know what resolution to use? It depends on several factors:

- What is your projector's resolution?
- What is the distance between the projector and the screen.

First, **find out the resolution of your digital projector**. You'll find that information in your projector manual. Then, try to **match it to your monitor's resolution**. For example, an XGA projector uses a 1024 x 768 resolution. In that case, your images should fit within that measurement.

However, if your projector's resolution is 1024 x 768 and your monitor's resolution is smaller, make the image fit within the smaller resolution. If your projector's resolution is 1024 x 768 and your monitor's resolution is larger, make the image fit within the 1024 size.

> **Important:**
>
> - While a Web browser lets you scroll down a page to see a long image, a Microsoft PowerPoint presentation cannot scroll down the page. So if you cannot create your image in a size that fits within your resolution measurement (and therefore scrolling will be necessary), create your document as a PDF or for use within a Web browser.
>
> - When creating images, keep in mind that small details will not show up in the rear of the viewing room. Standing back from your computer monitor can simulate how "readable" your presentation will be to back-row viewers. Sharpness also plays a role, so make sure your images are as sharp as possible.
>
> - Anything imported into PowerPoint, Keynote®, or any other presentation program, will import at the resolution of that document. But it will display at the resolution of the monitor. In other words, if you start with a document that is intended to print at 6 x 4 inches at 300 dpi, it will only display at the resolution of the monitor.

Question for the expert

Q: What happens if you do import a document that is sized for print? In other words, if it has far more pixels than are needed.

A: The program needs to recalculate the image and will randomly drop pixels. Ouch! That means your images (or presentation) can seriously degrade. It also will take longer for the image to display and will take more file space.

To recap:

- Find out the resolution of your digital projector.
- Then try to match your image to your monitor's resolution.
- If your monitor's resolution is greater than the resolution of the projector, fit the image within the projector's resolution.
- If your monitor's resolution is less than the resolution of your projector, fit the image within the monitor's resolution.

Print Resolution

INKJET PRINTING

When it comes to printing, **resolution tells the printer how large or small to make an individual droplet of ink on a printed page**.

Each pixel of a digital document is a particular color. In order for your printer to create that color, it needs to mix ink from the various ink cartridges in your printer. The **dpi** of an image tells the printer how much ink to use to create the image. For example, if an image is printed at 150 dpi, each ink droplet is 1/150 of a square inch. Depending on what color the printer is trying to create, and the dpi of the printed document, the droplets can be larger or smaller or several dots can be placed in the same spot to create a particular color. Thus, the dpi of your image defines how many dots per square inch that the printer will print.

Here's where some confusion comes in: When printing, you insert the final dpi that you want the document to print in the Image Size box, but it's next to a window that says "**pixels/inch" (or ppi)**. That could imply that ppi and dpi are the same thing. But they are not because one pixel doesn't equal one dot of ink.

Let's break it down:

- While an image resides in your computer, it is digital; it contains pixels, not dots.

- Before you can print, you must first define how those pixels will be output for print. This is done by going to the Image Size dialog box and entering a set of instructions into the Document Size area.

- First you define the dimensions for the printed document (e.g., 6 x 4 inches).

- Then you define how many dots per square inch the document should print at (e.g., 300 dpi). To define, you enter 300 into the field, for example, next to the area called pixels/inch. <u>This area is called pixels/inch (ppi) because the document is still in its digital pixel form.</u>

- When you give the print command, the software takes the information you defined in the Document Size area and sends it to the printer driver.

- The printer driver interprets the ppi information and tells the printer how many dots of ink (dpi) to print, and how large to make the document (e.g. 6 x 4 inches).

> **Remember:**
> - A printer cannot print pixels; it can only print dots.
> - Pixels are not one-to-one with printed dots.
> - To recreate one pixel's color at a particular print dimension and resolution, the printer will spray dots of ink. The dots can be in different sizes or overlap, depending on the instructions given.
> - The more pixels, the smaller in size they are; the fewer pixels, the larger in size they are. More pixels generally results in a higher quality image; fewer pixels generally results in a lower quality image.

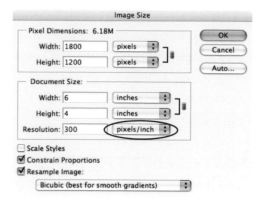

In the Document Size area, the dimension size and pixels/inch resolution are the instructions sent to the printer to interpret those pixels into dots per inch at a particular print size.

Whew! That does get confusing. Just remember that ppi within the Document Size area of the Image Size box is actually referring to <u>an interpretation of ppi to dpi for print</u>. Thus, while it's common for people to say "I want a 6 x 4 inch at 300 dpi image," what is really being asked for is a digital document set up to print at a particular print dimension and resolution. In other words, it describes the end product. The starting product is your digital image made up of pixels, and your instructions in the Document Size area are the recipe for taking those pixels and outputting them to a printer for the end product.

With that being said, since we are now talking about a digital document to print, I'll refer to the print resolution, or dpi. When printing, it's helpful to know **the optimal—or best—image resolution of your printer**.

Optimal printer resolution = Approximately 1/3rd of the printer's rated resolution.

However, most people will not need anything over 300 dpi (or at the most 360 dpi). In fact, unless you are printing very high-end work on certain media, anything over that number is a waste of ink.

While 300 dpi has become the accepted standard for printing photographic images, many people are surprised to discover that their home inkjet printers can offer a wide assortment of resolutions.

For example, say you found an article, including images, on a Web site. You decide to print it for your own personal use. If you print directly from the Web site, the monitor resolution will translate to a much lower than 300 dpi image. Yet the article will in all likelihood print just fine on everyday paper. If you print a 300 dpi photograph on everyday paper, however, you'll often find that there is so much ink on the paper that it makes the paper buckle and makes some colors look muddy.

In other words, **you need to balance dpi and media—balancing how much dpi is needed with what the image will be printed on**. Generally, photographic paper will require a 300 dpi image (some media may require more resolution, but you'll know this as the resolution needed is generally listed on the package). You may find, however, that 280 or 240 dpi also works just fine. (If you discover this, use the lower number. The document will print faster and you'll save ink.) **As you learn what dpi setting works with what media, keep notes so you save time next time you print**.

Unless you are printing on a specific medium that requires a specific resolution, exceeding your printer's optimal resolution will not improve your image. It wastes ink, and can actually make your image look worse because the additional ink that is not absorbed or adhered to the paper can smear. For this reason, resolution that is good on photographic paper is not necessarily good on typing-quality paper.

How to Calculate the BEST (Optimal) Resolution for your Printer

First, check the user manual for your printer's maximum resolution. (Our example printer uses a maximum 5760 x 1440 dpi.) Next, take the lower number (which is the true resolution) and divide it by four.

1440 ÷ 4 = 360 dpi (best resolution)

Why divide by four? There are four colors used to create a print—black, magenta, cyan, and yellow.

What if your printer uses more than four colors? Ahh, here is where people will differ. Most say the "divide by four" rule still applies. (That's because the extra colors generally only "fill in" for one of the standard four colors to enhance highlight or shadow detail.) Others say it's better to divide by the number of separate ink cartridges the printer uses. (This is why some people will use 240 for best quality printing if they have 6 ink cartridges.) **It's best to test out different resolutions on a particular media and write down what settings look best to your eye**.

WHAT ABOUT PRINTING ON FABRIC?

Several factors come into play when printing on fabric. They include the **type of ink** you are using and the **type of fabric** you are printing onto. How ink sits on and reacts with whatever media you are printing on affects the quality of the print. This is why the same print using the same ink can look different depending on what it is printed on.

Important to know:

Using 300 dpi is generally too much ink for fabric to handle. It wastes ink, especially when using a printer with dye-based inks.

How to Calculate OTHER Resolutions for your Printer

Divide your best printer resolution by 2 or 4 for printing that does not require the maximum resolution. For example, if your printer's "best" resolution is 360 dpi, divide that by 2 or 4 to determine printer resolution sufficient for printing average or everyday quality.

If 360 = best quality printing

360 ÷ 2 = 180 dpi for better than average printing

180 ÷ 2 = 90 dpi for everyday printing on typing-quality paper

If 300 = best quality printing

300 ÷ 2 = 150 dpi for better than average printing

150 ÷ 2 = 75 dpi for everyday printing on typing-quality paper

If 240 = best quality printing

240 ÷ 2 = 120 dpi for better than average printing

120 ÷ 2 = 60 dpi for everyday printing on typing-quality paper

I have never needed to print more than 360 dpi. And I tend to use 180 dpi, which also works well for printing on fabric. However, I do know some people using very unusual media, and their output resolution is double. But this is rare. So if you are working with a very specific medium, requiring higher resolution (generally the manufacturer of that medium will tell you), multiply your optimum printer resolution number by two.

360 x 2 = 720 dpi

300 x 2 = 600 dpi

If you plan on sending your images for professional printing, create your image using at least 300 dpi. If you know the required line resolution, or lpi, from the print shop, multiple that number by 1.5 or 2 to find the target resolution.

Dye-based inkjet ink

Dye-based ink is not waterfast. So the fabric you print on must be pretreated before printing, or the ink will run the moment water touches it. Dye-based ink gets absorbed into the fibers of the fabric. The fabric can only hold so much ink. After a print is made, the fabric must be rinsed to remove the excess ink. This must be done prior to using in a quilt, even if you don't plan on washing the quilt. Otherwise, the excess ink will migrate onto other areas of the fabric. Thus, the higher the dpi, the more ink on the fabric. The more ink on the fabric, the more that may be wasted as it rinses off from the fabric.

Pigment-based inkjet ink

Pigment-based ink is waterfast. This makes the ink sit on the fibers, rather than soaking into them. While you should not rinse after printing, too much ink can create an image that loses the shadow and highlight detail. In other words, your printout could look muddier than it should. Pigment ink on fabric does not need heat setting. The image simply needs to dry. (In fact, putting a hot iron to it before the image is completely dry will degrade it.) After the printout has dried, if you need to use an iron, use a hot, dry one and press down rather than drag across. Because pigment ink is waterfast, it does not require pretreated fabric. However, using a fabric with a pretreatment can, depending on the fabric you are starting with, produce a better-looking image. The slight coating on the fabric affects the spread of the ink droplets. The less the spread, the sharper the image.

Dye-based or Pigment-based

If you're not sure whether your printer uses dye-based or pigment-based inks, go to the printer manufacturer's Web site. Epson® currently has the most models that use pigment inks. Look for DURAbrite® or UltraChrome® in the name. Most HP printers use dye-based inks (although some of their blacks are pigment). One exception is HP's Vivera pigment inks. There are also some new Canon® printers that use pigment ink. Again, check the Web site of the manufacturer.

Display vs. Print

The amount of resolution you need depends on what you're going to do with the image.

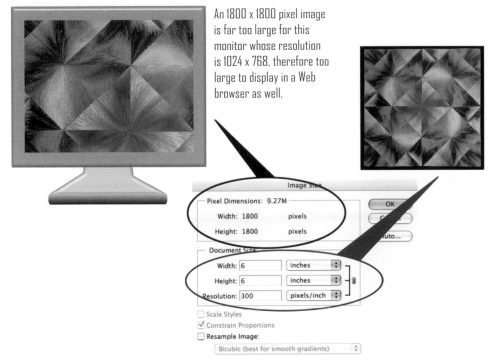

An 1800 x 1800 pixel image is far too large for this monitor whose resolution is 1024 x 768, therefore too large to display in a Web browser as well.

The same 1800 x 1800 pixel image will print a high quality photo at 6" x 6" and 300 dpi.

Scanning

Good quality home/small business scanners are quite affordable these days. And many of today's all-in-one printers include a flatbed scanner. The software that accompanies the scanners often offers easy, one-click scanning options. By clicking around on various customize tabs, you can find options to help tailor your scanning resolution based on your needs. Look for these: "document type" and "resolution."

Images for scanning generally fall into two types:
- **Line art** (such as logos)
- **Continuous tone** (such as photographs)

SCANNING LINE ART

If you've been reading along, you know that most line art is first created in a vector format. Vector images can be enlarged as much as needed within the software program without degrading in quality. To print that vector image, the printer driver converts the file into the dots that the printer will spray onto the paper. In other words, **the vector image becomes a bitmap image when printed**.

To maintain crisp edges and solid blocks of color, **you will get the best quality by scanning line art at the scanner's maximum resolution**. Then reduce the image to your needed size within your image-editing program.

Best quality scan of line art = scan at scanner's maximum resolution.

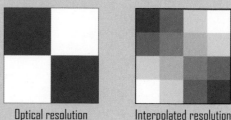
SCANNING CONTINUOUS TONE IMAGES

When scanning continuous tone images like photographs, maximum resolution is not needed.

To scan an image that you want the same size you started with:

- For output to a **Web image** (or other image that will appear on a computer monitor), scan at **85 dpi**.
- For output to a **printer**, scan it at the **dpi of your printer** (generally 300 or 360).

Question for the expert

Q: Why scan at 85 and not 72 or 75 like mentioned earlier for other monitor resolutions?

A: 85 ppi is an average monitor measurement for pixel density. So that will give the best general results.

To scan an image you want to enlarge:

Whenever possible, **enlarge the image through the scanning software**. Most scanning software allows you to enter the resolution directly. In that case, **use the optimum dpi of your printer and double it**. Other software gives you the ability to scan at percentages. With most of today's home scanners:

> Scanning at 100% = basically the same size as your image at 300 dpi
> Scanning at 50% = half of the 300 dpi value or 150 dpi
> Scanning at 200% = twice the 300 dpi value or 600 dpi
> And so on...

It's generally better to scan with more pixels than you need, to give you more to work with. You can always decrease the size of your image through your image-editing software later.

While today's affordable scanners are great for most purposes, if you require the absolute highest quality scan from a print or transparency, you need a professional drum scan. Drum scanners are very expensive, costing several thousand dollars. Contact your local printer for assistance.

Copyright Alert:

If you plan on scanning photographs or other images that you didn't create, be sure it's only for your personal use. For information on copyright law, fair use, and visual artist rights, see:

- http://whatiscopyright.org/   What is copyright protection?
- http://fairuse.stanford.edu/   Copyright and Fair Use - includes a large range of informative and useful articles
- http://www.copyright.gov/   The United States Copyright Office

Quick Resolution Guide for Images

Web Site Resolution:

A pixel width and height that is smaller than the average monitor resolution.

Digital Projection Resolution:

A pixel width and height that fits within the resolution of the projector unless your monitor's resolution is less than the projector's. In that case, fit the document within the resolution of your monitor.

Inkjet Printing Resolution:

- Photographic paper = 240 or 300 to 360 dpi (depending on your printer) for images on photographic paper (higher resolution may be required for a specific photographic medium, but the packaging will give this information)
- Everyday plain paper = 150 or 180 dpi
- Fabric = Lower than 300 dpi – anything from 240 down. Experiment on the fabric you intend to print on. Silk and cotton will vary.

Commercial Press Resolution:

At least 300 dpi, but ask your printer.

Scanning Resolution:

- Simple flat art; (i.e. outline) = One-half of the optical resolution of your scanner. Also use the black/white mode to scan to avoid getting shadows in the background. Consider a Levels adjustment layer to darken the line. See Chapter 10 "Easy Photo Fixes and Beyond" on page 101.
- Flat art = Maximum optical resolution of your scanner
- Photographs for Web images = 85 dpi
- Photographs for print = 100% or 300/360 dpi for 1 to 1; 200% or 600/720 dpi for doubling the size, etc.

clarifying the dpi, ppi, and pixel resolution confusion

Q: **What should I call the measurements of a pixel image? DPI or PPI?**

A: Neither. While it is common to see DPI or PPI in relation to resolution sizes (I still catch myself doing it), it is not correct. DPI is a printing term. It stands for dots per inch. A dot, however, is not equal to a pixel. A pixel is not a unit of measurement. It is a unit of resolution. Thus, when referring to resolution, stick with width x height.

Q: **I hear people say a document is so many pixels per inch all the time. Why is this wrong?**

A: The key reason: Pixels are variable in size. A pixel will be larger or smaller depending on the output device.

Q: **Is there ever a time when pixels per inch is correct to use?**

A: Only when talking about a monitor. However, remember, pixels can vary in size. Your monitor's resolution determines the size of the pixel being displayed. (Different resolutions will display the same image larger or smaller.) That means if you put an actual ruler against a monitor and look at the image underneath it, one inch of image on my monitor at my resolution will display that image at a different size than one inch on your monitor if your resolution is different than mine.

Here's an example that may help this concept click: Have you ever shopped for a flat screen TV? The TV resolution always indicates the quality. The higher the resolution (meaning more pixels crunched in per inch), the sharper the picture (and more expensive the TV). A physical inch on the TV is always an inch. But the pixels within the inch can be larger or smaller depending on the resolution of the device (in this case the TV). Even though those pixels fill inches, you will not see the monitor described as ppi. You will, however, see it described as 1280 x 720, or 1920 x 1080, or 1024 x 1024, and so on. Why? Again, because pixels are variable in size.

Q: **What about the ppi dimensions in the Document Size area of an Image Size dialog box? Logic says it means the document has so many pixels per inch. Since that area defines a print size, shouldn't it say dpi (dots per inch) instead of ppi (pixels per inch)?**

A: No. The ppi within the document size area is only relevant because it tells the printer driver how many dots per inch to print. Pixels are not one-to-one with dots. In other words, one pixel doesn't equal one dot of ink. For more on this, see the Inkjet Printing section on page 25.

Q: **Then why do people ask, for example, for a 300 dpi document instead of a 300 ppi document?**

A: Old habit. If you start with a digital document, you are starting with pixels. When you output that digital document to a printer, your image-editing software takes the pixel dimensions of your document and pours them into the print area allowing you to define how much resolution you want for a particular print size. Then the software takes care of sending that information to the printer.

Q: **Why do people ask for a 72 dpi document when referring to images on the Web?**

A: Again, it's just a habit. Remember, since pixels are variable in size, you need to define how those pixels will display on a monitor (i.e. 1200 x 1800 pixels), not how they will display for print.

Q: **Why is it an old habit? Where did 72 dpi come from?**

A: When the first Macintosh was launched, 72 ppi was the original screen resolution. A point is approximately a 72nd of an inch, and, on that early Mac monitor, one point equaled one pixel. During that time, most other monitor manufacturers adopted the 72 ppi resolution, which is why people began equating 72 dpi with a Web image. However, that is no longer the case. Most of today's monitors are not only "multi-synch," meaning they can operate at multiple resolutions, but can operate at much higher resolutions than earlier models. One of my monitors can display at six different resolutions! Typically monitors display at anything from 65 ppi to 200 ppi, depending on the resolution settings.

In the early days of Web site design, many graphic artists were coming from print backgrounds. The 72 dpi stuck because it was a way (at that time) to conceptualize an approximate size on screen. Today, those in the know understand that you never ask for an image in dpi when the image is intended for display on a monitor.

What really doesn't work is someone asking only for a 72 dpi image. Imagine I sent an image that was 5000 x 5000 pixels, and set the print resolution to 72. The resulting image would be huge on the average monitor. But, I could say, "Well, you asked for a 72 dpi image." <smile>

The next time someone asks you for a 72 dpi image for use on the Web, reply with this question: "Can you tell me the pixel dimensions that you'd like for the image?"

Q: **So, I should always use the pixel resolution to describe the size of a digital document and not worry about the dpi or ppi?**

A: Yes. Defining your document by its pixel height and width gives an absolute size. This size can be translated to any output device, such as a printer, monitor, projector, slide maker, and so on.

Q: **What if a magazine or book publisher asks, "What is the resolution of your photo?" Should I give the pixel dimensions, such as "800 x 600", instead of giving them the dpi?**

A: Yes. Regardless of how it's going to be used—printed, shown on a Web page, etc.— give the pixel dimensions.

Q: **What if a publisher asks for a 300 dpi image? Is the publisher wrong to ask for it that way?**

A: First, a magazine editor will not say "send me a 300 dpi image," because that request does not give you enough information. You'd need to know if they meant a 1" x 1" document at 300 dpi or a 20" x 20" document at 300 dpi. Instead, they should be specific: "Send me an image that is 5" x 6" at 300 dpi." While they should ask for it in pixel dimensions, it is very common for publishers to ask for an image in print terms. They are asking for what they want as an end result printed image.

chapter · · · (5)

the keys to color management

Have you ever printed a photo and thought, "That doesn't look like what I see on my monitor"? Well not only do two people see the same color differently, but your monitor and printer probably do too. If what you see doesn't look like what you print, it's because your monitor and printer don't communicate with each other. The computer does it all. It tells the monitor what colors to make, and it tells the printer what colors to make. And you're the one who controls the computer.

So how do you make your printer's color match your monitor's color? The solution is color management. To me, successful color management comes down to one thing: hitting the print button and knowing that what comes out of the printer will look darn close to what I see on the monitor.

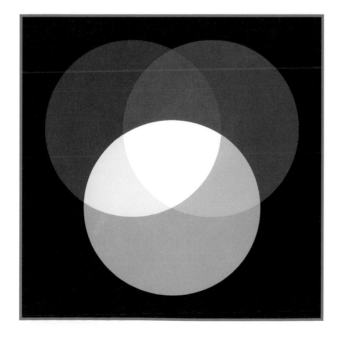

Color Management 101

Color management can be incredibly complex. There are books and classes (I've taken many) on the subject. But many of us don't have time or patience to get deeply involved with computer color management. We just want nice color printouts. But by understanding some core digital color management issues you will be able to do just that. If you're new to this topic, grab a cup of coffee and read on. This chapter may seem tedious, or even overwhelming. But applying these recommendations will make a valuable difference in the color quality of your work. Here we go!

Digital color management is a process in which the numeric scales of particular color characteristics are defined for various devices so that color reproduction among them is consistent. In other words, **it defines a color so your printer and monitor both "read" the same color in the same way**.

The Three Essential Components to Color Management

1   Using Color Management Software

Color management software orchestrates the matching of color from device (e.g. monitor) to device (e.g. printer). You can use color calibration tools already in your computer. Or you can buy a separate color calibration device. The calibration for a particular device is then "saved to a profile."

2   Selecting a Color Space

A color space generally represents a range of colors within the visible spectrum. However, a digital color space also defines the type of scale used to define the numeric value of a particular range of colors.

3   Selecting a Profile

A profile can be device dependent, meaning the color information is specific to a device (such as a particular printer or monitor). A profile can also be device independent, meaning the profile describes color in an absolute way (such as a color profile embedded with a photo when you take a picture.)

The key to successful color management is getting all three of these components to work together.

COLOR MANAGEMENT BACKGROUND

The International Color Consortium (ICC) was established in 1993 to promote the use of an open, standardized system of color management. An ICC-compliant profile (or ICC profile for short) is a set of instructions that converts color data between the profile of a color dependent device and that of a color independent device based on a standardized system. Today ICC profiles are widely used and considered the standard.

1: Using Color Management Software

There is something for every budget to help you improve your color management. If color is not critical, you can simply use the tools installed within your operating system. It doesn't take much time and can make quite a difference.

If color is critical to your work, consider investing in calibration tools (available for both Windows and Mac computers). Calibration systems generally include a measuring device (spectrophotometer) that is placed directly on a monitor, printer, or other output device to read color information, plus software that interprets that information and creates a profile for it. The sophistication and sensitivity of the tools, along with the range of devices it can read and profile, affect the price tag. Two popular systems are **Spyder®3** from Datacolor at http://spyder.datacolor.com/index_us.php and **i1Display** from X-Rite at http://www.xrite.com/. In early 2008, X-Rite introduced **ColorMunki** (http://www.colormunki.com), an affordable monitor and printer calibrator with multipurpose spectrophotometer. I couldn't resist this product and am very happy with it. It even calibrates digital projectors! I suspect other companies will follow and begin offering multi-purpose calibration tools at more affordable prices. To locate additional tools, search online for "color calibration tools."

Color Management Tools

These are the tools that come already installed in your computer. They all require you to calibrate by eye. (And remember, everyone sees color differently.) Calibrating by eye will not be as accurate as using a precision tool specifically designed for calibration such as i1Display or Spyder3, mentioned just above.

MACINTOSH—COLORSYNC®

The Macintosh operating system has long had an advantage in color calibration over other operating systems. It includes **ColorSync**, an ICC-compliant color management system that has been a part of its operating system since 1993. This technology integrates all output devices connected to the computer, and provides tools for calibration and creating ICC profiles. Even if a Mac user didn't initially calibrate her or his monitor, for example, the operating system automatically creates a default ICC profile whenever a new device is connected to the computer. Thus you would have a monitor profile even if you didn't set it up. This is a huge plus because it helps ensure that you're going to get good color between devices right from the start. The ColorSync color management system was one important differentiating feature between the Macintosh and Windows operating systems and one reason that many creative professionals, such as those in the publishing and design industries, began using the Macintosh operating system.

WINDOWS—IMAGE COLOR MANAGEMENT (ICM)

There is no centralized control panel that provides system-based monitor calibration on XP (and earlier) PC systems. However, you can calibrate your monitor and create a profile of it using a graphic program that supports ICM. That profile is then applied to any other graphics applications that support ICM.

If you don't calibrate your monitor and create a profile, the Windows operating system depends on the driver that is installed with an output device (such as a printer driver that you install when you hook up a new printer). The driver provides instruction to the operating system on its color space. When the operating system needs to send color data to that particular device (e.g. your printer), the operating system converts its color space to coincide with that of the device.

Letting something like your printer driver handle your computer's color may seem easy, because then you do not need to calibrate. But this leaves more room for inconsistencies. Additionally, part of the success depends on the driver. For that reason, **it is very important to periodically check to confirm you are using the latest drivers for your output equipment**. Do this by visiting the Web site of the device's manufacturer.

Windows XP users can download a free Color Settings image color management control panel applet. It provides the tools to help calibrate your monitor, create ICC profiles, and manage your various output devices. You can download the applet here and find instructions: http://www.microsoft.com/windowsxp/using/digitalphotography/prophoto/colorcontrol.mspx.

WINDOWS COLOR SYSTEM

The good news for Windows® Vista® users is that Microsoft and Canon have joined to create a color management system called the Windows Color System. This much-welcomed control panel system is specifically designed to address consistent color between output devices by providing system-level tools for calibrating, creating ICC profiles, and managing various output devices.

Monitor Calibration and Characterization

The first thing you should do is calibrate and characterize your monitor. If your monitor colors are off, colors from your printer and other output devices will be off too.

Calibration involves setting the controls of the monitor—such as the lightness and color temperature. **Characterization** is saving that information as a profile.

See the steps below, or follow the instructions that come with the calibration device, such as Spyder, that you purchase.

General Monitor Calibration Preparation Tips

*   Before calibrating your monitor, clean it with display cleaner (a product specially made for cleaning your monitor).
*   If you wear glasses, put them on.
*   Consider the room light. Use the same lighting while calibrating that you normally use when working.
*   For purposes of calibration, change the desktop background color to a neutral gray. (See instructions on the next page.) A colored background will affect your color perception. (If color accuracy is more critical to your work, consider leaving that neutral gray as your background.)
*   If you're using a CRT (cathode ray tube) monitor, have it on for at least an hour before calibrating. LCD (liquid crystal display) monitors can be calibrated as soon as you turn them on.

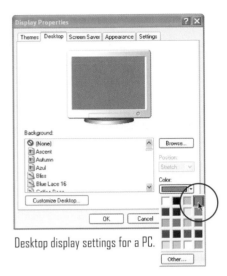

Desktop display settings for a PC.

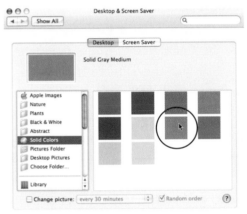

Desktop display settings for a Mac.

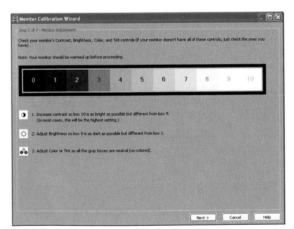

Follow the instructions in the Wizard to calibrate your monitor correctly.

CREATING A NEUTRAL BACKGROUND

For calibration purposes, set a neutral gray background desktop color. If color work is primary, consider leaving that neutral gray on your desktop.

Windows

1   Go to **Start > Control Panel > Display**.
2   In the Display Properties box, click the **Desktop** tab.
3   In Background, scroll to the top and select **None**.
4   Under Color, select the **top-right neutral gray**.
5   Click **OK**.

Macintosh

1   Go to **Apple > System Preferences > Desktop & Screen Saver**.
2   Select **Solid Colors** from the list on the left, then select the **fourth gray** (third gray on right in the second row). Close the box to save.

Windows Monitor Calibration

IMAGE COLOR MANAGEMENT (ICM)

Start by opening a graphics program that supports Windows Image Color Management, such as Paint Shop Pro. (The instructions below are for Paint Shop Pro 9 and higher.)

1   Go to **File > Color Management > Monitor Calibration**.
2   Follow the instructions in the Monitor Calibration Wizard. This system allows you to increase contrast, adjust brightness, and adjust color and tint.
3   Give the profile a name, such as "July 2008 monitor calibration". Make sure the **Enable Color Management** box is checked. The profile can then be applied to other programs that support ICM.

NOTE TO VISTA USERS:

Here's how to add a color profile to various devices.

1   Go to **Start > Control Panel > Color Management**.

2   Click on the **Devices** tab to select the device that you'd like to add a profile to. Generally profiles are added during the installation of a new device. Otherwise, if you need to install a profile that you don't see, click the **Add** button on the left, then locate and select the new profile.

> **Note:** The color selections you use within a graphic or image-editing program will override what is selected here, but will only work with that particular program.

Macintosh Monitor Calibration

MACINTOSH COLORSYNC

1   Go to **Apple > System Preferences > Displays**. Click the **Color** tab. Click the **Calibrate** button. Note that you can click to display the profiles associated with that particular display only.

2   The **Welcome to the Display Calibrator Assistant** launches. The Assistant will walk you through the steps to calibrate and characterize your monitor. The first five windows determine the display's native luminance or brightness. The target gamma adjusts the overall contrast for the display. If your audience is both Mac and Windows users, compromise and select 2.0. When naming these settings, consider adding the date to the suggested default name.

TIPS FOR USING THE WINDOWS COLOR CALIBRATION WIZARD AND THE MACINTOSH DISPLAY CALIBRATION ASSISTANT

- Give your calibration characterization a name, such as "July 2008 monitor calibration."
- Leave the Phosphors at the default setting.
- Under Gamma, squint your eyes and move the slider until the center square blurs into the background. Uncheck the View Single Gamma Only box to calibrate the separate red, blue, and green colors. The gamma controls the overall brightness of your monitor.
- Note that the Windows default gamma is 2.2, and the Macintosh default is 1.8. However, color on a Windows 2.2 gamma displays darker than on the Macintosh default 1.8. If your audience is a mix of both PC and Mac users, compromise and insert 2.0. Unless you understand White Point, leave it at the defaults.
- Save it at the end with the name, such as "July 2008 monitor calibration."

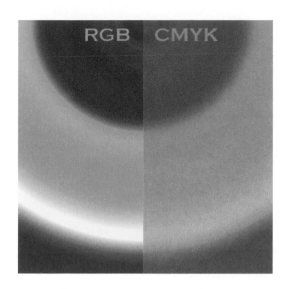

2: Selecting a Color Space

Selecting a color space is the second essential component of color management. **Our own color space—a color model with a specific range of colors—is RGB**, in that the human eye breaks light into red, green, and blue elements. Our brains then zip them back together resulting in our perceived colors.

A **computer monitor** also uses light to project color, and, like us, uses the RGB color space—although it uses a digital numerically-based equivalent of it. The RGB color space is an **additive** system. This means that **r**ed, **g**reen, **b**lue (RGB) and black are combined using light, and mixing them all in equal amounts produces white.

In the digital RGB system, each pixel within an image is assigned an intensity value ranging from 0 (black) to 255 (white)—in a three dimensional space—with the full range of colors (over 16.7 million) represented in the middle.

Any **printer**, on the other hand, uses **c**yan, **m**agenta, **y**ellow, and black (CMYK) to create colors. (The standard symbol for black is always K.) CMYK is known as a **subtractive** color system. Colors are created by light absorption, or subtraction, and the part of light not absorbed produces the color we see. In theory, equal amounts of cyan, magenta, and yellow will result in black. Realistically it results in a dark, muddy color. In CMYK color space, magenta plus yellow produces red, magenta plus cyan makes blue and cyan plus yellow generates green. It's important to understand that **there are far fewer colors available in the CMYK color system than in the RGB color system**.

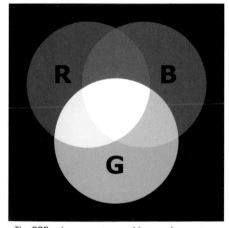

The RGB color space is an additive color system.
All computer monitors use RGB.

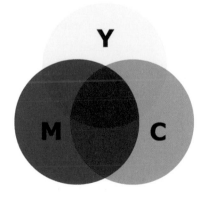

The CMYK color space is a subtractive color system.
All printers use CMYK for output.

RGB and CMYK are two basic types of **color spaces**. Like anything color related, you can find piles of information devoted to color spaces. While there are several different types of RGB color spaces, I am focusing on two—**sRGB** and **Adobe RGB**®—because they are presently the most commonly used.

sRGB is **s**tandard **r**ed, **g**reen, and **b**lue. It is the preferred color space for Web graphics. Many consider this a universal space in that it was designed to match the color space of an average monitor, and because it is the default space of some Windows operating systems and many Windows programs. However, with the introduction of Adobe RGB in 1998 and its increased range of color, Adobe RGB has bumped up in rank and is considered by many to be the preferred RGB standard.

Adobe RGB contains a larger field of colors than sRGB, especially in the blue to green range. The color space was designed to include not only almost all the colors that can be created using CMYK commercial four-color presses, but additional colors that your inkjet printer can print and your monitor can display.

Question for the expert

Q: What color space does my digital camera use?

A: While early digital cameras used the sRGB color space to capture images, many of today's digital cameras are using Adobe RGB. If you are not sure what color space your camera uses, check your manual. If you are taking pictures in the Adobe RGB color space, you should be viewing them on your monitor using the Adobe RGB color space. Otherwise, you can cheat yourself out of seeing and working with all of the colors the camera captured.

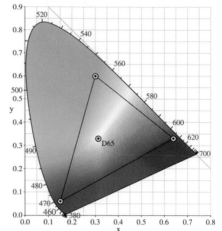

sRGB is the preferred color space for Web graphics.**

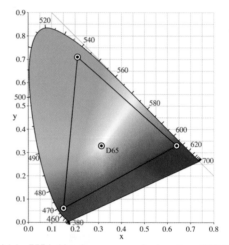

Adobe RGB holds a larger range of colors than sRGB. *

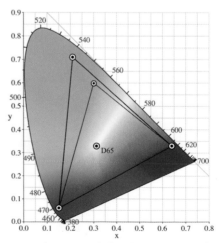

By overlaying one color space with the other, you can see that the Adobe RGB space is larger, especially in the blues and greens.

----DIGITAL ESSENTIALS: A Quilt Maker's Must-Have Guide to Images, Files, and More!

Which RGB color space to select depends on the work you do. Some people have happily used the sRGB default for years. Others want the larger range of colors Adobe RGB offers. (Although, those who really want a larger range of colors use ProRGB. Its color space is larger than what a monitor can display. Now that is tricky!) I generally use sRGB for any Web-destined artwork and Adobe RGB for everything else.

Question for the expert

Q: Since my home printer uses four colors of ink (in other words, it is CMYK), should I work in CMYK to get the best color in my documents?

A: No. Generally, only use CMYK when work will be output on a commercial, four-color press. Even then, you should work in RGB until you are finished, then convert to CMYK as the last step before proofing. In fact, I find that many printers now prefer digital files supplied in the RGB color space with ICC profiles attached. However, always ask the printer for recommendations on what color space to use.

Why work in RGB? First, RGB is a larger color space than CMYK. Second, an inkjet printer is capable of printing more colors than a four-color press. Third, the printer driver will take your RGB document and convert it to the CMYK specifications of the printer so that you can get maximum color quality. Thus, if you start by using CMYK, you are immediately cutting colors out of your document. Then, when you send the document to the printer, it's quite possible it will degrade more.

3: Selecting a Profile

As mentioned earlier, a color space can be independent of a device, meaning it describes color in an absolute way. Such color information can be embedded with your image (I'll show you how). Then, when the color profile meets with a profile-dependent device, the color data from one is better handled in the other. For example, embedding a color profile in your image will help tell your printer the colors to use when printing.

A word of caution: If you embed a color profile with a wider range of colors than the device is capable of handling, you can run into problems. In this case, the device tries to create whatever colors it can based on its data. The resulting image (depending on how many colors are outside its range), is adjusted to the number of colors the device (such as a printer) can handle. The out-of-range colors are considered lost or clipped. This happens when a CMYK device is trying to print an RGB document. This is why if you need to create a CMYK document for commercial printing you should first talk to your printer to learn what particular settings you should use when converting your RGB document to CMYK.

Embedding a Color Profile

I recommend that you always embed a color profile in your image file (unless you have a good reason not to). Otherwise, the numbers that define the pixel colors in your document are open to wide interpretation.

PHOTOSHOP

1   Go to **Edit > Assign Profile**.
2   Select a profile and **OK**.

PHOTOSHOP ELEMENTS

1   Go to **Image > Convert Color Profile**.
2   Select a color profile.

PAINT SHOP PRO

1   Go to **File > Color Management > Color Management**.
2   The recommended color space for Paint Shop Pro is **sRGB**. If you need to change it, select the **Enable Color Management** box.
3   Select **Basic Color Management**.
4   In the **Monitor Profile** drop-down list, choose the monitor profile that you want to use. In the **Printer Profile** drop-down list, select your printer.
5   In the **Rendering Intent** drop-down list, select the setting that matches your intended output.
6   Click **OK**.

Unless you are instructed otherwise, if you are providing an image for display—like a digital image for display on a monitor or projector—use the sRGB setting because many devices use this color space as a default. If the document is for print, use sRGB or Adobe RGB. It's your choice. I use Adobe RGB.

Handling an Image with a Non-Matching Profile or No Profile at All

Have you ever opened an image and got the message: "The color profile does not match the existing color space"? This message appears when you open an image that has embedded information that doesn't match your defined working color space. The best thing to do is to choose the option of using the embedded profile. This way you'll see the image the way the person providing the image intended. Additionally, when you save the image, the profile will be saved with it. But what if the document has no embedded profile? Then, rather than viewing it with no profile, use the profile of your current working space. (You will get a message telling you there is no profile and asking you if you want to use the current working space.) However, when you save your document be sure to assign a profile to it; otherwise you're right back where you started.

It is important to note that assigning a profile does not convert the pixel information in the image. Assigning a profile provides the image-editing program with a description of how you want to view and edit the image. In other words, it changes the type of scale that interprets the pixel color numbers of the image to maintain its appearance.

Color Working Space and Management Policies

A color **Working Space** is a profile (non-device dependent) of a particular range of colors you select to work with in an image-editing program. If you don't select a particular working space when viewing or editing your image, the program will use its default, which is often sRGB. A **Color Management Policy** is a set of instructions that determines how your application handles the color data when you open (or import) a document.

PHOTOSHOP

If you haven't seen a Photoshop Color Settings dialog box, brace yourself. There are a lot of options that can look darn intimidating. Here's what I use and why.

1 Go to **Edit > Color Settings**. As you invest more time in color working spaces, you may discover other settings in the Color Settings box that are better suited for your needs. However, the following is a good start:

   • The Color Settings box displaying the North America General settings, which is calibrated throughout my work applications and uses the sRGB color space.

   • Click on the **RGB Working Spaces** drop-down list to select a different setting. After you have selected your favorite setting, click the **Save** button, and give it a name. Those settings are saved in the **Settings** drop-down menu which you can access at any time.

Select the Working Space you want to use for your profile.

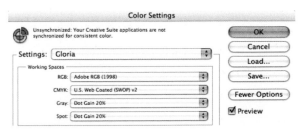

Name and save the profile. The profile will be saved for future use with the selected settings.

Working Spaces:

For the most part, your concern will be with the RGB space. The others can remain at their default. In the drop-down menu next to RGB, you'll see a range of choices. I primarily use Adobe RGB or sRGB. Select the space best for your needs.

Color Management Policies:

• Turn on the **Preserve Embedded Profiles** under the Color Management Policies.

• Turn off the **Profile Mismatches and Missing Profiles** warning boxes. Since you have defined your working space, and since you are preserving the embedded profile when opening a mismatch, you don't need any warning boxes interrupting you.

Photoshop also offers a selection of defined workspaces. They are accessible under **Window > Workspace**. By selecting a particular workspace, various menu items will be disabled. When you are finished, return to **Window > Workspace** and select **Default Workspace**.

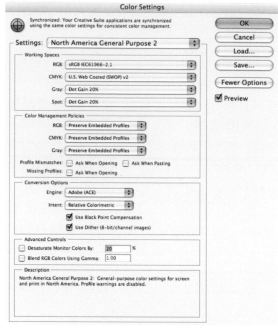

Photoshop Color Settings dialog box

PHOTOSHOP ELEMENTS

1   Go to **Edit > Color Settings**.
2   **Always Optimize for Printing** uses the Adobe RGB color space. **Always Optimize for Computer Screens** uses the sRGB space. **Allow me to choose** gives you a choice. Select the one most suited for your purposes.

PAINT SHOP PRO

1   Go to **File > Color Management > Color Working Space**.
2   Select from the drop-down list which RGB color space you'd like to work in. (If you need to work in CMYK, first talk to your printer and ask what settings they recommend, plus instructions.)
3   Check **Use Embedded Profiles**.

Soft Proofing Your Color

Soft proofing is a method of using your calibrated monitor to preview what your document could look like on your printer (or other output device. The soft proofing feature is not available in the current version of Photoshop Elements.)

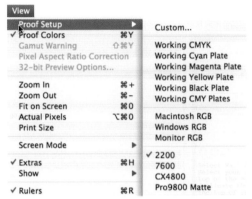

Select Proof Setup > Custom to see more profile options.

Change the options next to Device to Simulate and notice how your proof changes. Choose the option that best fits your needs.

PHOTOSHOP

1 Go to **View > Proof Setup**.

2 In this area you can view approximations of your document in a CMYK environment (again, talk to your printer so you have all settings correct before soft proofing), in a Mac or Windows environment, and for a specific inkjet printer (or other device for which you installed a profile), or for a specific media type.

a The same list of printer profiles available in your Print Media dialog box are also available for you to use as a soft proof. To select one, go to **View > Proof Setup** and click **Custom**.

b In the Customize Proof Condition dialog box, next to **Device to Simulate**, use the drop-down menu to select your device or specific media type. Keep the **Preview** button checked. Then experiment with various settings to see how they affect your proof. (It's eye-opening to see how turning off Preserve RGB numbers and experimenting with the Rendering Intent and the Display Options affect the proof.)

c To save a device or media type (for example, a specific printer make and modelor a specific media type such as a custom profile created for a particular paper) for easy access the next time you want to use it, click the **Save** button, name it, and it will be available at the bottom of your Proof Setup selection drop-down. If you want to experiment with the proofing conditions that are different from those saved for a particular printer, click **Custom**, select the profile, and experiment with it again.

PAINT SHOP PRO

1 Go to **File > Color Management > Color Management**.

2 Check **Enable Color Management** and select **Proofing**.

3 Select a device in the **Emulated Device** profile drop-down, and select a **Rendering Intent** of pictures, proofs, graphics, or match in the drop-down. Click **OK**.

4 When finished, return and click off **Proofing** and click back on **Basic color management**.

Use the Color Management dialog box to change the proofing settings.

Device Profiles

Each printer or other output device that you install on your computer requires a profile. Usually it's as simple as installing the software that comes with the device, and following its instructions.

For example, when you connect a printer to your computer, you'll also install software with it. That software is the printer driver (the printer profile) and the profiles of a variety of media (paper, card stock, transparency etc.) that the printer can print on. For example, your Epson printer will list general paper types, such as "plain paper" but may also list specific Epson papers, such as "Ultra Premium Photo Paper—Luster." If you purchase paper from a different manufacturer, that manufacturer's Web site will often offer free profiles for its paper. These include detailed installation instructions.

Question for the expert

Q: Why does a printer need a profile for a specific paper?

A: Different papers have different display characteristics and different ink absorption rates. The profile tells the printer how much ink to lay down for the surface it will print on. Printing on matte photo paper, or fabric, both absorbent, would require more ink than printing on glossy photo paper, which does not absorb.

If you are shopping for a specific type of paper or other media, and don't want to create a profile for the media yourself, look to see if the manufacturer offers a profile of the media that works with your particular printer or ink set. Installing and using it will save you time and money (no wasted ink or media trying to get good color).

Get into the habit of periodically checking your printer manufacturer's Web site for printer driver updates. Also, if your printer starts misbehaving and you cannot seem to resolve it, go the manufacturer's Web site, download the printer driver for your particular printer, and install it. Generally that fixes printer problems.

Every time you print a document, you're using profiles. You're selecting the printer and the type of paper you're printing on. The print dialog box also offers color profiles that are generally found under the Color Management option on your print driver. When it comes time to select your printer and media profiles, it's generally done directly in the Print dialog box. If you have one printer connected to your computer, it should appear by default after you install the driver. If you have more than one installed, you will select the printer that you want to use from a drop-down menu or list.

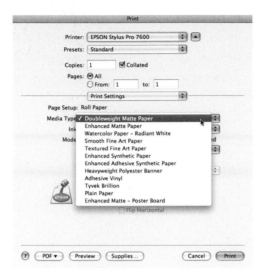

Select the appropriate media type from the drop-down menu.

Selecting the media type is also done in the Print dialog box. For example, in the Epson Print box, select **Print Settings > Media Type** and then select the media. Some printers include more media selections than others. Additionally, any profiles that you install will appear in that area. The Print dialog box also includes profiles for handling color, such as a vivid or a realistic setting. They are generally found in the Color Management option of your print driver.

To select a media type in an Epson printer, after the Print command, select **Print Settings > Media Type**, and then select the desired media.

Photoshop CS2 print dialog box.

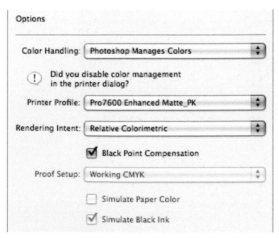

Photoshop CS3 print dialog box.

Managing Printer Profiles within Photoshop CS2 and CS3

If you allow Photoshop to manage your colors, you can also select your printer profile and media profile directly in Photoshop.

In Photoshop CS2, with your document open,

1   Go to **File > Print with Preview**.
2   Next to Color Handling, select **Let Photoshop Determine the Colors**. This will turn on the options for selecting from a list of profiles.

In Photoshop CS3, with your document open,

1   Go to **File > Print**.
2   Next to Color Handling, select **Photoshop Manages Color**. This will turn on the options for selecting from a list of profiles.

Avoid Double Profiling and Avoid the Magenta Color Cast

A magenta cast on your image generally indicates that a color profile is being applied twice. For example, if you allow Photoshop to manage your colors, but also allow your printer to manage your colors—say you select "vivid" under color management—you are double profiling.

Double printer profiles fight, often resulting in a magenta color cast. This problem is so common that Photoshop CS3 includes text right next to the Color Management area to remind you not to "double-proof"—meaning not to apply a color profile twice. Depending on the option you select, one of the following messages will appear:

- If Photoshop Manages Colors, turn off color management in the printer dialog box.
- If Printer Manages Colors, turn on the color management in the printer dialog box.

In short, if your printer driver is anxious to manage your colors but you're working within a program that is also managing your print output colors, turn one of them off.

In Conclusion

To get good color out of your printer or other device, you need to provide good instructions to it. To review:

1 Calibrate and profile your monitor.
2 Install and use the proper drivers and profiles for your devices and media.
3 Use system-wide color management software to manage the color spaces of your devices.
4 In your image-editing program, select a working color space. Select a color policy that embeds images with a specific color profile on the way out, and instructs how to handle images on the way in.

You made it, which brings us back to the opening question. Is what you see what you get? It's all in the eye of the beholder, so you tell me.

---

* This image has been (or is hereby) released into the public domain by its creator, Entirety. This applies worldwide. (Image on page 42)

** Permission is granted to copy, distribute and/or modify this document under the terms of the GNU Free Documentation License, Version 1.2 or any later version published by the Free Software Foundation; with no Invariant Sections, no Front-Cover Texts, and no Back-Cover Texts. A copy of the license is included in the section entitled "GNU Free Documentation License". (Image on page 42)

Working with Images

6 — chapter

resizing and resampling images

Did you ever print a photo that looked great on your screen but awful in print? Or end up with a teeny print of an image that looked plenty large on your screen? You're not alone.

Print size is a combination of the print dimension and the image's resolution. The two are inter-connected. Understanding the difference between resizing an image and resampling an image (changing the number of pixels in the image), and when to use each, will make all the difference in the quality of your print and Web images. Plus you'll feel like a whiz because you'll learn how to let your software calculate the math for you.

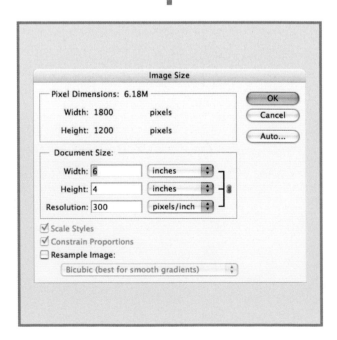

Resizing and Resampling Basics

In most image-editing programs, there is an option called Image Size, Image Resample, or Image Resize.

To resize or resample an image in Photoshop, open the Image Size dialog box by going to Image > Image Size.

In Paint Shop Pro, open the Resize dialog box by going to Image > Resize.

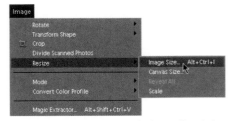

In Photoshop Elements, open the Image Size dialog box by going to Image > Resize > Image Size.

There are two distinct areas in both the Photoshop and Photoshop Elements Image Size dialog box and Paint Shop Pro's Resize box. The **Pixel Dimension** area defines the resolution of your document. The **Document Size** box defines how the image's resolution can be used in a printed document.

To Simplify:

Pixel Dimension area = Image size for Web/Monitor

Document Size area = Image size for print

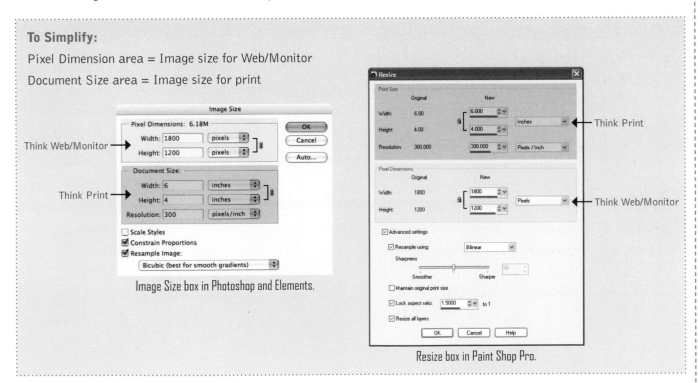

Image Size box in Photoshop and Elements.

Resize box in Paint Shop Pro.

Understanding Resizing

To resize an image, the resampling box must be turned off. Once this box is turned off, you can no longer change the actual pixel dimensions of the document. Only the bottom area is active.

This means that when you change the size of your print, you are not adding or subtracting pixels. Instead, you are making the pixels larger or smaller when printing. The resolution remains exactly the same.

Unchecking the Resample Image box in any image-editing software turns off the ability to alter the information with the Pixel Dimensions area. That means you cannot increase or decrease the pixels in your document.

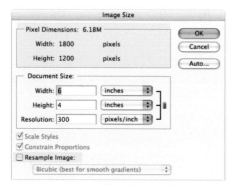

The Image Size dialog box in Photoshop and Photoshop Elements.

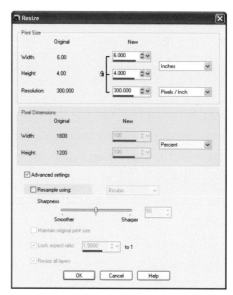

The Resize dialog box in Paint Shop Pro.

Increasing the print size makes the resolution smaller. Conversely, decreasing the print size makes the resolution larger. However, the number of pixels in the image remains exactly the same. That means the smaller the print dimensions, the smaller the pixels are. And the larger the print dimensions, the larger the pixels are.

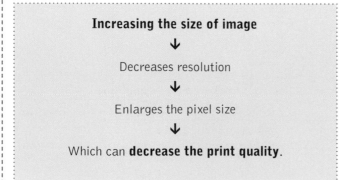

Increasing the size of image
↓
Decreases resolution
↓
Enlarges the pixel size
↓
Which can **decrease the print quality**.

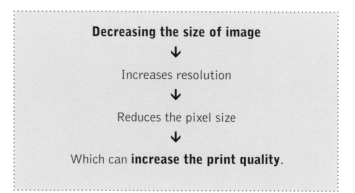

Decreasing the size of image
↓
Increases resolution
↓
Reduces the pixel size
↓
Which can **increase the print quality**.

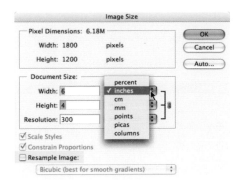

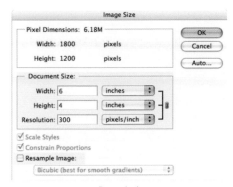

Example A

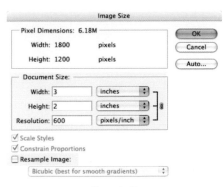

Example B

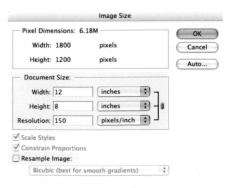

Example C

Resizing an Image in Photoshop or Photoshop Elements

With the Image Size dialog box open:

1 Turn off the **Resample Image** box.

2 Use the drop-down menu to select a unit of measurement, such as **inches**.

3 Type in the new print dimensions. The program will calculate the math and generate the corresponding resolution.

Example A: In the top section of the box, the pixel dimension is 6.18M. The size is 1800 pixels wide and 1200 pixels high. The document size—the size the document will print at—is 6″ x 4″ at 300 pixels per inch.

Example B: Decreasing the image size to 3″ wide x 2″ high increases the resolution (the program automatically does it for you) to 600 pixels per inch.

Example C: Increasing the image size to 12″ wide x 8″ high decreases the resolution to 150 pixels per inch.

Notice how the pixel dimension in all three examples remains 6.18M or 1800 pixels by 1200 pixels. Your print size will change, but the pixel resolution remains the same. **The image in each of the examples will appear exactly the same on a computer monitor**.

Resizing an Image in Paint Shop Pro

With the Resize dialog box open:

1 Turn off the **Resample using** box. (Make sure **Advanced Settings** is checked first to see this option.)

2 Use the drop-down menu to select a unit of measurement, such as **inches**.

3 Type in the new print dimensions. The program will calculate the math and generate the corresponding resolution.

Example A: Decreasing the image size to 3 inches wide x 2 inches high increases the resolution to 600 pixels per inch.

Example B: Increasing the image size to 12 inches wide x 8 inches high decreases the resolution to 150 pixels per inch.

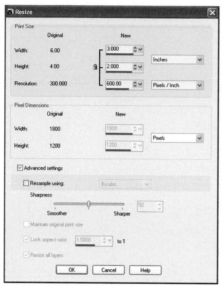

Example A

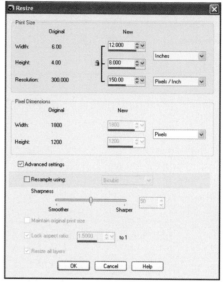

Example B

Questions for the expert

Q: If I know the print resolution I want, how can I find out how large I can print my image?

A: 1 Turn off the Resample Image option.

2 Type in the resolution you want (e.g. 150 dpi).

3 Look at the Width and Height to see the print size.

Q: How can I know how large (in inches) I can print my image before it starts to degrade (get "dotty")?

A: 1 Turn off the Resample Image option.

2 Type in the desired Width and Height in the Document Size box (e.g. 8" x 10"). Look at the resolution. If it's too low, make your image dimensions smaller. (See Chapter 4 "Resolution—It's the Pixels" on page 21 to learn about resolution requirements.)

Be sure to print some samples and note your print settings. You may be surprised to find that your printed image may still look great printed at less resolution that you might think necessary. A large print, for example, often requires less resolution than a small one. Why? Because it is generally viewed from farther away than a small image. For example, billboards are designed to be viewed from a distance. However, when viewed up close, they appear to be low quality, similar to looking at a TV screen from six inches away.

Understanding Resampling

Resampling an image changes the actual number of pixels within the image. Adding pixels is known as **upsampling** an image; subtracting pixels is known as **downsampling** an image. Unlike resizing a document, **resampling an image changes both the pixel dimensions and the file size**.

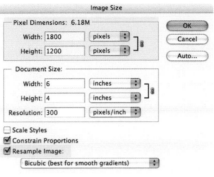

Checking the Resample Image option in the Photoshop and Photoshop Elements Image Resize dialog box turns on the Pixel Dimension area, allowing you to make changes to it.

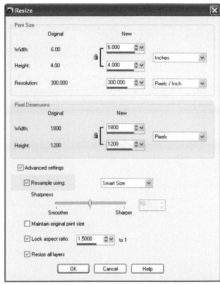

Checking the Resample Using option in the Paint Shop Pro Resize dialog box turns on the Pixel Dimensions area, allowing you to make changes to it.

Key Fact: Upsampling an image not only spreads the pixels apart, it also creates new color pixels from the surrounding pixels. The new colors created when upsampling an image (making it larger) can result in quality and detail loss.

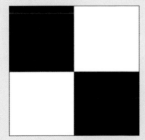

This image shows a 2 pixel by 2 pixel grid consisting of two black and two white pixels.

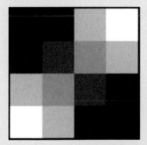

Resampling the image to 4 pixels by 4 pixels (doubling the size), automatically creates new pixels from surrounding pixels. Rather than making additional black and white pixels, the software you're working in blends the surrounding pixels, creating various shades of gray. This is called "interpolation."

Image Interpolation

Interpolation is the term for creating new color pixels by blending the surrounding pixels. Most image-editing programs offer a selection of different mathematical algorithms that blend the surrounding pixel colors in different ways. For most purposes, the defaults are acceptable. However, some options may work better for specific purposes.

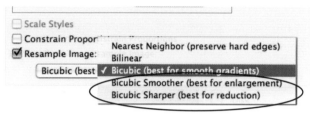

The Resampling Image Interpolation options in Photoshop/Elements. (In Photoshop CS3, the options make more sense as each tells you what it is best for.)

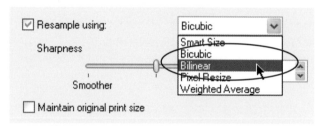

The Resampling Image Interpolation options in Paint Shop Pro.

GENERAL RULE OF THUMB:

In Photoshop and Photoshop Elements, the default is **Bicubic**.

- Select **Bicubic Smoother** when adding pixels to the image (or making the image larger).
- Select **Bicubic Sharper** when subtracting pixels from the image (or making the image smaller).

In Paint Shop Pro, the default is **Bicubic**.

- Select **Bicubic** resample when adding pixels to the image (or making the image larger)
- Select **Bilinear** resample when subtracting pixels from the image (or making the image smaller)

Generally it is not a good idea to upsample your image, because the resulting image can look very blurry. However, there are some options. One is to use a third-party plug-in specifically designed to enlarge images. There are several commercial and shareware plug-ins available. To locate them, do a Web search on "image enlarging software" and you'll find many options.

Another is a method I learned from famed digital photographer Vincent Versace. When working in Photoshop/Elements, change the Resample Image to Bicubic Sharper and enlarge the image in 10% increments. Be sure to work on your document at 100% so you can see what you are doing. Paint Shop Pro users can also try this, but select Bilinear Resample.

Downsampling (Removing Pixels) to Create a Web Site Image

The only measurement that matters for a Web image is its pixel dimension (width and height) or resolution. Since most images from today's digital cameras are far too large for a Web site, pixels need to be removed. To convert your image for use on a Web site, either use the specific Web image optimization tools your image-editing program offers (see Chapter 14 "Saving Photographs for the Web" on page 146) or simply downsample your image.

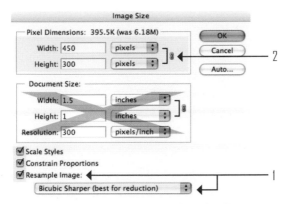

Resampling an image in Photoshop and Photoshop Elements.

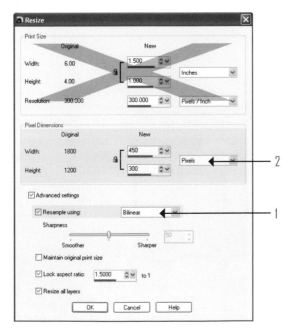

Resampling an image in Paint Shop Pro.

In Photoshop and Photoshop Elements, with the Image Size dialog box open:

1 Check the **Resample Image** option. Since pixels are being removed, select **Bicubic Sharper**. Keep the **Constrain Proportions** box checked so that your image is not distorted.

2 Type in the new pixel width and allow the program to calculate the height (or type in the new pixel height and allow the program to calculate the width). Remember, ignore the Document Size area. This area matters for print only.

3 Click **OK** to resample/reduce the document.

4 To save the image, use the **Save As** command and give your document a new name (different than your original name) so that the original remains untouched.

In Paint Shop Pro, with the Resize dialog box open:

1 Check the **Resample using** option and select **Bilinear**. Keep the **Lock aspect ratio** box checked so that your image is not distorted.

2 Type in the new pixel width and allow the program to calculate the height (or type in the new pixel height and allow the program to calculate the width). Remember, ignore the Print Size area.

3 Click **OK** to resample/reduce the document.

4 To save the image, use the **Save As** command and give your document a different name than your original.

Changing the horizontal measurement is generally all that is required for resizing an image for the Web. Be sure to keep the image width smaller than the width of the body area of your Web site. A size between 450-475 is a generally good pixel width.

increasing and decreasing the canvas

Imagine you appliqué a design onto a piece of fabric. Think of that fabric base as the "canvas size." And consider the appliqué design as the "image." If, later, you think you have too much fabric around your appliqué patches, you may want to trim some of your fabric base away. Think of this as "decreasing your canvas size." On the other hand, what if your appliqué design is very close to the edges of your fabric. Then you may consider adding more fabric to the edges, to give the appliqué design more breathing room. Think of this as "increasing your canvas size."

When an image is opened within an image-editing program, the canvas size for that document is defined by the image size. While the image size may be fine as is, you may find yourself wanting to increase the canvas size. For example, you might want to add space for a caption beneath a photo. Or, if you add an image to a document and want to reduce the amount of white space around the image, you can reduce the canvas size.

The Canvas Size dialog box can give you precise control over the amount of space around an image.

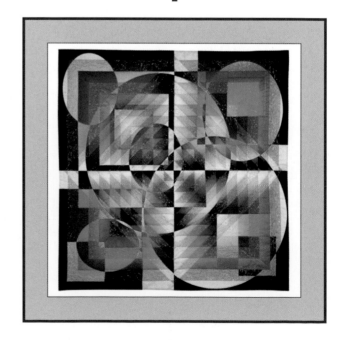

Canvas Size in Photoshop and Photoshop Elements

1 In Photoshop, go to **Image > Canvas Size**. In Photoshop Elements, go to **Image > Resize > Canvas Size**.

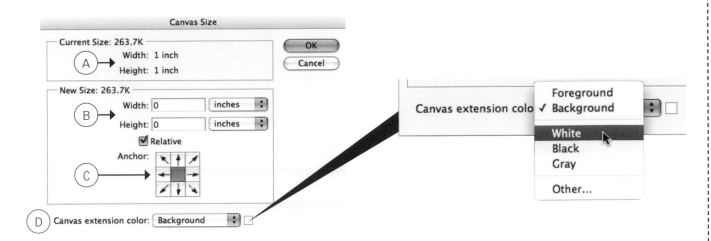

2 The Canvas Size dialog box will open.

A The top section of the box displays the <u>document's current size</u>.

B The top-central area of the box allows you to either <u>increase or decrease the width and height</u> of the document in a specific unit of measurement including pixels, inches, and percentage.

Checking the **Relative** box lets you <u>add or remove space</u> from around the image. The program does the math for you. Note that you need to type in both width and height. The Canvas Size dialog box will not recalculate proportions for you.

C The bottom-central area of the box is the **Anchor grid**. This lets you <u>reposition the image</u> on the resized canvas. The default is center, which centers the image on the canvas. Clicking on a side or corner adds or subtracts pixels in the opposite side or corner of the canvas. The arrows give visual information on how the canvas will change. Outward pointing arrows indicate increasing the canvas size; inward pointing arrows indicate decreasing the canvas.

D The **Canvas extension color** lets you <u>select the color of the expanded canvas size</u>.

Selecting **Other** brings up the Select canvas extension color dialog box allowing you to select a new color. Then, select the **Eyedropper** tool to sample a color from your document.

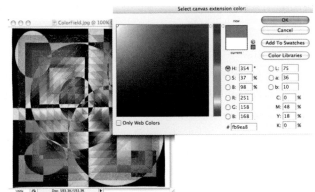

Increasing Equal Canvas Dimension

To increase the canvas size equally around the image, so the resulting image is 600 x 600 pixels (or a 2.0" x 2.0" at 300 ppi document), do the following:

1 Go to **Image > Canvas Size** to open the dialog box. In Elements, go to **Image > Resize > Canvas Size**.

2 Confirm or select the **Canvas extension color**.

3 Check the **Relative** box. This allows you to simply enter the number by which you want the canvas to increase (i.e. increase by 0.50").

4 Type **0.50** inches in the width and height fields.

5 Click **OK**. The canvas size is now increased by 0.50" around the image.

Increasing Unequal Canvas Dimension

An unequal amount of canvas can also be added to your document. In this case, I am increasing my original document to include an extra 0.25" of canvas space underneath the image.

1 Go to **Image > Canvas Size** to open the dialog box. In Elements, go to **Image > Resize > Canvas Size**.

2 Confirm the background color is white, unless you want a different background color, next to the **Canvas extension color**.

3 Uncheck the **Relative** box. This requires you to enter the added size PLUS the original size in the width and/or height boxes (i.e. 1.5 + 0.25 = 1.75").

4 Since the goal is to add 0.25" underneath the image, keep the width the same (1.5"), but change the height to **1.75**.

5 Since we want the 0.25" to be underneath the image (not centered around the image), click the Anchor grid arrow to indicate the direction to add the extra canvas space.

6 Click **OK**. The canvas size is now increased by 0.25" under the image.

The current canvas size is 450 x 450 pixels or 1.5" x 1.5" at 300 ppi.

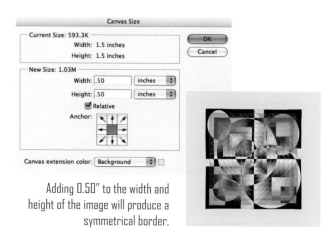

Adding 0.50" to the width and height of the image will produce a symmetrical border.

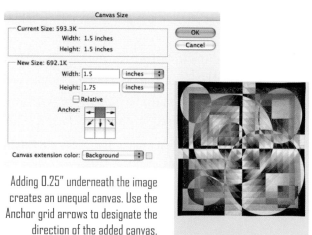

Adding 0.25" underneath the image creates an unequal canvas. Use the Anchor grid arrows to designate the direction of the added canvas.

First place the Eyedropper tool into your document, and then, while continuing to hold the mouse button down, drag the Eyedropper tool. You'll find you can drag the Eyedropper right off of your document and sample any color on your monitor. This is especially helpful in trying to sample the color on something else; e.g., the background color of a Web page.

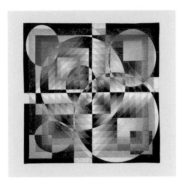

The current canvas size is 1.75" x 1.75" at 300 ppi document.

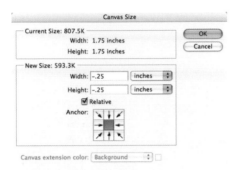

With the Relative box checked, change the width and height to -0.25 to decrease the canvas size.

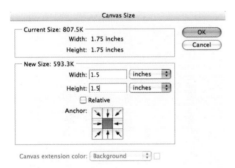

OR, uncheck the Relative box, and change the dimensions to 1.5 and 1.5 to perform the same action.

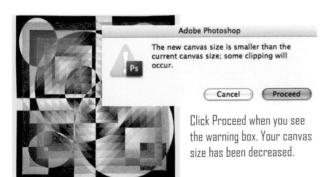

Click Proceed when you see the warning box. Your canvas size has been decreased.

Decreasing Equal Canvas Dimension

To decrease the canvas size using the Canvas Size dialog box, simply type in the decreased dimension size into the New Dimensions box. In the following example, I am starting with the document in which canvas size was added. To remove 0.25″ equally around the image, do the following:

1   In Photoshop, go to **Image > Canvas Size**. In Photoshop Elements, go to **Image > Resize > Canvas Size**.

2   Check the **Relative** box. This allows you to simply enter the number by which you want the canvas to decrease (i.e. decrease by -0.25″).

3   Type **-0.25** (negative 0.25″) in the width and height fields. Or, you can also <u>uncheck the Relative box</u> and type in the new width and height numbers. In this case, the document measures 1.75 by 1.75 inches. To change the canvas size to **1.5** by **1.5** inches, type those dimensions into the New Size width and height fields.

4   Click **OK**.

5   A warning box will appear alerting you that you are about to clip, or cut pixels away, from your document. Click **Proceed**. The canvas size is now decreased equally in size.

In Photoshop or Photoshop Elements, you can return to the default settings of any dialog box by holding the **Alt** key on Windows, or the **Option** key on a Mac, and then mouse-hover over the Cancel button. The Cancel button will turn into a Reset button.

Decreasing Unequal Canvas Dimension

In the following example, I am starting with a document that includes an extra 0.25″ of canvas space under the image. To remove the extra space, do the following:

1 In Photoshop, go to **Image > Canvas Size**. In Photoshop Elements, go to **Image > Resize > Canvas Size**.

2 Uncheck the **Relative** box. This requires you to enter the subtracted size PLUS the original size in the width and/or height boxes (i.e. 1.75 - 0.25 = 1.5″).

3 The current size of the document is 1.5″ by 1.75″. To remove 0.25″ from the canvas, keep the width at 1.5″ and change the height to **1.5**.

4 To remove the space from the bottom of the canvas, click the **Anchor grid** arrow to indicate the direction to remove the extra canvas space.

5 Click **OK**.

6 A warning box will appear alerting you that you are about to clip, or cut pixels away. Click **Proceed**. The canvas size is now decreased under the image.

If you make a mistake when decreasing the canvas size, remember to use the **Ctrl+Z** (**Command+Z** on a Mac) to undo. Then you can give it another try.

The current canvas size is 1.5″ x 1.75″ at 300 ppi document.

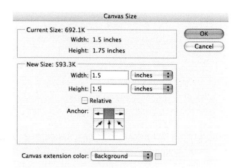

With the Relative box unchecked, change the dimensions to 1.5 and select the Anchor grid to decrease the canvas size underneath the image.

Click Proceed when you see the warning box. Your canvas size has been decreased.

Canvas Size in Paint Shop Pro

1 Go to **Image > Canvas Size**.

2 The Canvas Size dialog box will open.

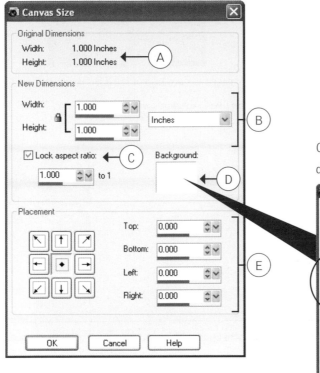

Clicking on the **Background** box brings up the Color dialog box.

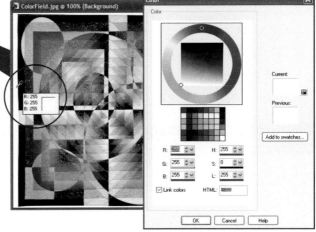

A The **Original Dimensions** displays the document's current size. That size is displayed in the unit of measurement selected in the New Dimensions area.

B The **New Dimensions** area lets you increase or decrease the width and height of the canvas area based on the unit of measurement you select.

C The **Lock aspect ratio** button lets you increase or decrease the canvas size while constraining the proportions of the canvas.

D The **Background** color is the color that will surround your image if you enlarge the canvas.

E The **Placement** area lets you increase or decrease the size of the canvas either on the top, bottom, left, or right sides. Be sure the Lock aspect ratio button is unchecked.

In addition to selecting a color from the palette, the **Eyedropper** tool allows you to sample any color, including color from any open image. This is particularly handy if you want to match the background color to another color. Click the **OK** button to insert that color into the Background field on the Canvas Size dialog box. In this case, I have selected white.

Increasing Equal Canvas Dimension

To increase the canvas size equally around the image so that the resulting image is 600 x 600 pixels, or a 2.0" x 2.0" at 300 ppi document, do the following:

1   Go to **Image > Canvas Size.**

2   Confirm your background color.

3   Check the **Lock aspect ratio** box. Type **2.0** in the width. The height will automatically adjust to 2.0 inches. Notice that the **Placement** values in the bottom portion change to 0.250 on the top, bottom, left, and right. This also indicates that the additional background will go evenly around the image.

4   Click **OK.** The canvas size is now increased by 0.50" around the image.

Increasing Unequal Canvas Dimension

An unequal amount of canvas can also be added to your document. In this case, I am increasing my original document to include an extra 0.25" of canvas space underneath the image.

1   Go to **Image > Canvas Size**.

2   Confirm your background color.

3   Uncheck the **Lock aspect ratio** box.

4   Since the goal is to add 0.25" underneath the image, leave the width at 1.5" but change the height to **1.75**.

5   Since we want the 0.25" to be underneath the image and not centered around the image, click the top-center arrow in the grid. This will add the extra canvas to the bottom of the document as indicated by the 0.250 being added to the bottom field box.

6   Click **OK.** The canvas size is now increased under the image.

The current canvas size is 450 x 450 pixels or 1.5" x 1.5" at 300 ppi.

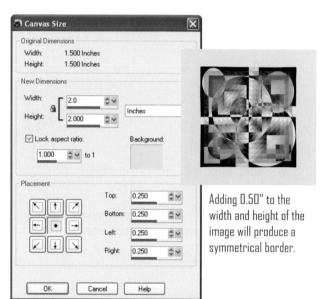

Adding 0.50" to the width and height of the image will produce a symmetrical border.

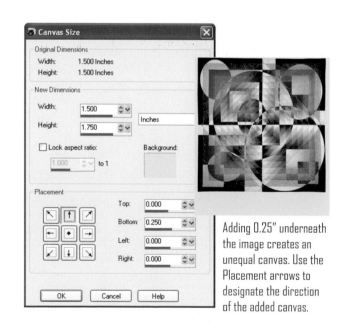

Adding 0.25" underneath the image creates an unequal canvas. Use the Placement arrows to designate the direction of the added canvas.

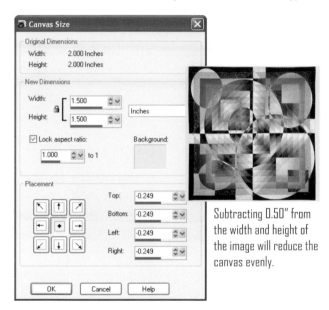

The current canvas size is 600 x 600 pixels or 2.0" x 2.0" at 300 ppi.

Subtracting 0.50" from the width and height of the image will reduce the canvas evenly.

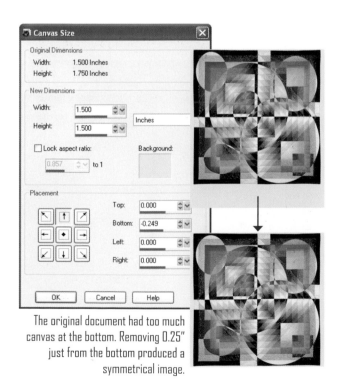

The original document had too much canvas at the bottom. Removing 0.25" just from the bottom produced a symmetrical image.

Decreasing Equal Canvas Dimension

To decrease the canvas size equally around the image so that the resulting image is 450 x 450 pixels, or a 1.5" x 1.5" at 300 ppi document, do the following:

1   Go to **Image > Canvas Size**.
2   Check the **Lock aspect ratio** box. Add the new dimensions of **1.5** inches in the width and the height will automatically adjust to 1.5 inches. Note that the placement values are −0.249 in all fields.*
3   Click **OK**. The canvas size is now decreased equally by 0.50" around the image.

Decreasing Unequal Canvas Dimension

An unequal amount of canvas can also be removed from your document. In this case, I am starting with the document in which canvas size was added. To remove 0.25" from the bottom of the image, do the following:

1   Go to **Image > Canvas Size**.
2   Uncheck the **Lock aspect ratio** box.
3   The current size of the document is 1.5 by 1.75 inches. To remove 0.25" from the canvas, keep the width at 1.5 inches and change the height to **1.5**.
4   To remove it from the bottom of the canvas, click the **Placement** arrow to indicate the direction to remove the extra canvas space. Note that the bottom placement field indicates −0.249.*
5   Click **OK**. The canvas size is now decreased by 0.25" under the image.

*If you open the Resize dialog box (Image > Resize), you'll see that the bottom dimension of −0.249 was rounded to 0.25 and the Resize dialog box shows the size as 450 x 450 pixels or 1.5" x 1.5" at 300 ppi.

(8) - - - - - *chapter* - - - - - - - - - - - - - - - - - - -

getting it down to size—the crop tool

Like the Canvas Size command, you can use the Crop tool to decrease your canvas size. But the Crop tool has one big advantage: it lets you see how much you're cropping. The cropping marquee that appears around your image as you use the Crop tool shows just how much and where you are cropping.

The Crop tool can be used for quick crops—simply cropping to what looks good. Or you can crop more precisely—decreasing your canvas to a specific size. For example, imagine cropping an image to a perfect 5 x 5 inch square to print onto fabric for use in a quilt. Or cropping to a standard photo size (6 x 4) to print on your inkjet.

This chapter shows you how to use the Crop tool to increase or decrease canvas size or to simply cut a section out of a larger image.

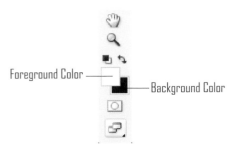

Foreground Color ——— ——— Background Color

Click and drag the cursor down to the bottom-right corner of the image. Notice there are 8 handles on the corners and sides of the image.

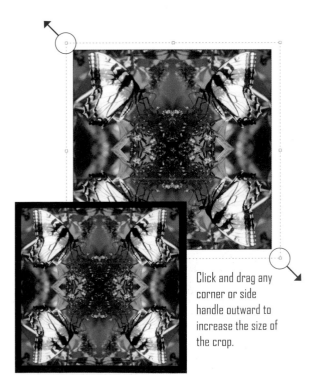

Click and drag any corner or side handle outward to increase the size of the crop.

Notice how the background color, black, fills the new space of the increased crop.

Using the Crop Tool in Photoshop and Photoshop Elements

In Photoshop and Photoshop Elements, you can use the Crop tool to quickly increase or decrease your canvas.

Increasing the Canvas Size

1   Confirm your background color. In this case, it is black.

2   Select the **Crop** tool from the toolbar. (In Photoshop Elements, you can also select the Crop tool from **Image > Crop**).

3   Starting at the upper-left corner of your image, click and drag your cursor diagonally (or to the right and down), until you surround your entire image. A bounding box with handles will appear.

4   To increase your canvas size, grab one of the handles and drag it outward, beyond the image. Continue to drag handles outward until you are satisfied.

5   To commit to the crop, press your keyboard **Enter** key (Win) or **Return** key (Mac).

Note: For more control, turn on the rulers. Go to **View > Rulers**. To change the ruler's unit of measurement, **right-click** (Win) or **Ctrl+click** (Mac) on the ruler to bring up a unit of measurement palette.

To more easily expand the canvas size using the Crop tool, select the magnifying glass from the toolbar. Hold down your keyboard **Alt** key (Win) or **Option** key (Mac) and the tool will reverse its magnification (putting you in zoom-out mode). Continue holding the **Alt** key (Win) or **Option** key (Mac) and clicking the tool within the document until you have enough background space to expand your document.

To cancel out of crop mode, you have several options:

- Click the **Move** tool. A dialog box will come up asking if you want to crop or not. Select **Don't Crop**.
- **Right-click** (Win) or **Ctrl+click** (Mac) inside the crop marks for a Crop or Cancel box. Select **Cancel**.
- Select the **Cancel current crop operation** icon on the right of the Crop tool options bar at the top.

Decreasing your Canvas Size

1 Select the **Crop** tool from the toolbar. (In Photoshop Elements, you can also select the Crop tool from **Image > Crop**).

2 Starting at the upper-left corner of your image, click and drag your cursor diagonally (or to the right and down), until you surround the area you wish to crop. A bounding box with handles will appear.

> **Note:** To constrain to a perfect square, hold down your keyboard **Shift** key while dragging diagonally to create the bounding box. The **Shift** key will also constrain proportions of an already drawn bounding box while moving a corner handle in or out.

3 Drag one of the handles inward. The darker gray color (the default color) around your image shows what area will be cropped away. Seeing this, you can drag the handles in or out until you are satisfied.

4 Once you are happy with your decreased size, press your **Enter** key (Win) or **Return** key (Mac) and your canvas will be cropped.

OR: Click the **Commit current crop selection** icon on the right side of the Crop tool options bar at the top of the screen. (In Elements, click the green checkmark at the bottom of the bounding box.)

> **Note:** If you find the handles "snapping" to an unwanted area while you are dragging, go to **View > Snap** and uncheck **Snap**.

Click and drag the cursor down to the bottom-right corner of the image. Notice there are 8 handles on the corners and sides of the image.

Click and drag any corner or side handle inward to decrease the size of the crop.

Using the Trim Tool

If you are trying to crop as close to your image edge as possible, for best results, use the Trim tool in Photoshop.

1 Select **Image > Trim**.

2 In the dialog box, select the **Top Left** or **Bottom Right pixel color** (unless you are removing transparent pixels), and select the areas you want trimmed away.

3 Click **OK**. The resulting image is trimmed as closely as possible based on the background color and the first color of your image.

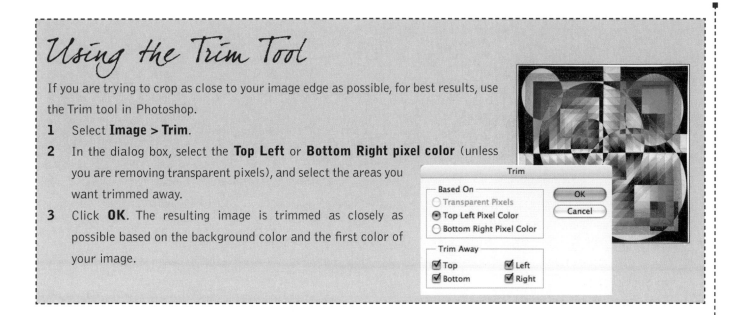

Decreasing to a Specific Size

Select the **Crop** tool from the toolbar. (In Photoshop Elements, you can also select the Crop tool from **Image > Crop**).

The **Crop tool options bar** will appear under the main toolbar.

This is where you can enter specific dimensions. For example, to crop a piece of this image to a 5 x 3 inch document:

1 Type **5** in the Width box. Type **3** in the Height box. To easily swap dimensions, click the arrow between the two fields. If you want to maintain the ppi of your image, type the ppi in the resolution box. This will resample the image to the stated ppi.

2 Click and drag diagonally in the image to start your crop. Notice how the crop box constrains to the size you typed in step 1. The area that will be cropped-out is darkened. You can move this area around, changing its position, by dragging the cursor inside the border of the crop.

3 To accept the crop, press the **Enter** (Win) or **Return** key (Mac). The cropped image will be a perfect 5 x 3 inch size.

Note: As you enter the crop dimensions in the Crop tool options bar, you may notice the program adding a "px" (pixels), "pt" (points), or any other unit of measurement. To set the crop to inches, you must change your rulers to inches to see "**in**" (inches) in the options bar. To do this, **right-click** (Win) or **Ctrl+click** (Mac) on the ruler in the document and choose **Inches**. Then re-enter the numbers in the options bar.

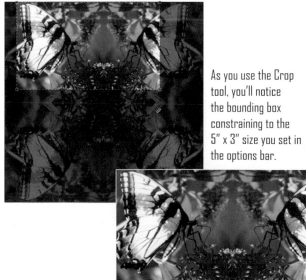

As you use the Crop tool, you'll notice the bounding box constraining to the 5" x 3" size you set in the options bar.

After finishing your crop, be sure to click the **Clear** button on the Crop tool options bar in Photoshop. Otherwise, the next time you try to crop, those preset sizes will remain. In Elements, simply delete the width and height entries.

After you establish your crop, but before accepting it, the Crop tool options bar in Photoshop changes its options. This is where you can, among other things, change the opacity and color of the "shield" (the darkened area indicating the crop). You can also toggle the shield on and off.

USE CAUTION WHEN CROPPING TO SPECIFIC SIZES

Cropping is one good reason to consider buying a high megapixel camera. Depending on the desired print size, the more resolution that your image has to start with, the smaller your crop can go without degrading the print quality.

For example, open an image from your digital camera and select the Crop tool. Set your Crop tool options bar to 2 inches by 2 inches and leave the Resolution blank (remember, this is the amount of resolution the document will print, not the pixel resolution of the image). Now, crop a **small area** of your image (can be very tiny). Go to **Image > Image Size** (or **Image > Resize > Image Size** in Elements), and notice the resolution of your image. The Pixel Dimensions width and height are very small which will make for a very pixelated image. Also, the Document Size resolution is very small as well. So although your image will still print at 2″ x 2″, the print quality will not be as good as you expect.

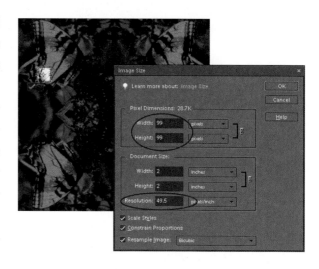

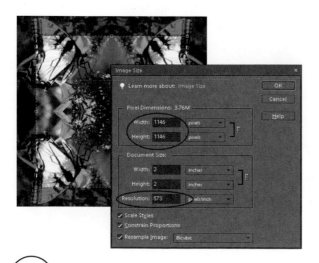

Now, undo the crop (**Ctrl+Z** in Windows, **Command+Z** on a Mac) and try cropping a **very large area** of your image. In the Image Size dialog, notice that the Pixel Dimensions are much larger and the Document Size resolution is very large as well. This means you still have enough pixel information to produce a high-quality printout. However, if you are going to print this image (still at 2″ x 2″), you will want to change the print resolution to something more reasonable (150-360 pixels/inch) with Resample checked so you don't waste too much ink. To learn more, see Chapter 4 "Resolution —It's the Pixels" on page 21.

Using the Crop Tool in Paint Shop Pro

In Paint Shop Pro, you can also use the Crop tool to quickly decrease or increase the size of your canvas.

Decreasing the Canvas Size

1   Select the **Crop** tool from the toolbar.

2   A default bounding box with handles will appear, but let's create our own. Right-click and choose **Clear** to remove the default bounding box.

3   Now, starting at the upper-left corner of your image, click and drag your cursor diagonally (or to the right and down), until you surround the area you wish to crop.

4   Drag one of the handles inward. Continue dragging the handles in and out until you are satisfied with the crop. In the Crop tool options bar, information about the document size will being displayed as the crop handles are dragged.

> **Note:** To constrain to a perfect square, first drag a bounding box on your image. Enter any number in the width and height of the Crop tool options bar making them both equal (example: width 5 and height 5). Now click **Maintain aspect ratio** on the options bar. Your bounding box will now constrain to a perfect square as you adjust the handles.

5   To reposition the crop box, click and drag within the interior of the crop.

6   Once you are happy with the crop, click the green **Apply** button on the Crop tool options bar or on the floating toolbar at the bottom of the bounding box.

7   The canvas is cropped.

If you are unhappy with the crop, press **Ctrl+Z** to undo. Then start again. To cancel the crop, right-click within the image and choose Clear, then try again.

Right-click and choose Clear to remove the default bounding box.

Click and drag the cursor down to the bottom-right corner of the image. Notice there are 8 handles on the corners and sides of the image.

Click and drag any corner or side handle inward to decrease the size of the crop. Click Apply to finish the crop.

Crop to Selection

Another way to quickly crop an image is "cropping to a selection."

1 Click the **Selection** tool.

2 Drag a select box to mark the area to be cropped.

3 Go to **Image > Crop to Selection**. Your image will be cropped to that selection.

To delete your selection before you crop, right-click on your mouse and start again.

To move the selection before you crop, select the **Move** tool from the toolbar, hold the **right mouse button** down, and drag the selection to reposition it.

Cropping to a Specific Size

Imagine your goal is to crop a 5″ x 5″ square of the image so you can later print it onto fabric.

1 Select the **Crop** tool from the toolbar. A default bounding box with handles will appear.

2 Click the **Specify Print Size** box on the Crop tool options bar. If this option is checked, it changes the resolution of the document based on the values in width and height. If it is unchecked, the resolution remains the same. Select **Inches** from the Unit drop-down menu and add the **5″ x 5″** dimensions to the width and height fields.

3 As you drag your handles in and out, the 5″ x 5″ dimension stays consistent as the resolution changes. After you've established where you want the crop, move the crop box exactly where you want it by clicking and dragging inside the bounding box. Once satisfied, click the green **Apply** button in the options bar.

4 The image is now cropped to a perfect 5″ x 5″ square.

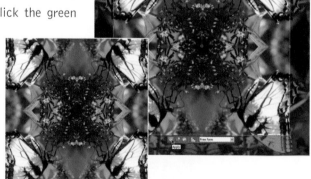

Note: If you select another tool by accident, clicking the **Crop** tool again will put you exactly where you left off. In other words, if you no longer want to crop your image, you need to cancel the crop. Do this by right-clicking in the image and selecting **Clear**.

Using Crop Tool Presets

A **tool preset** is a specific set of instructions associated with a particular tool. The easiest place to access a preset is in its palette, located on the left side of the options toolbar. In addition to using presets that come loaded with a program, it's easy to create your own. The beauty of doing this is that once you create a custom preset for one tool, you'll have the ability to create it for any tool. Photoshop Elements has built-in presets, but does not allow for custom presets.

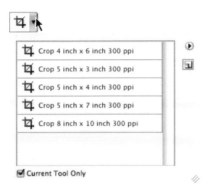

The Crop tool presets.

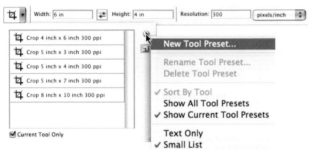

Enter the size in the Crop tool options bar. Then click the presets button to display the presets. Click the black arrow on the right and choose New Tool Preset. Or click the New Tool Preset icon below it.

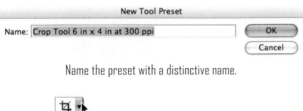

Name the preset with a distinctive name.

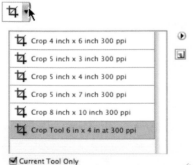

The new preset will now display in the palette with the other presets.

Crop Presets in Photoshop

Photoshop comes with several Crop tool presets. Access them by selecting the **Crop** tool, then clicking on the **Crop Tool Presets** button on the top-left on the Crop tool options bar. By selecting any of these presets, the instructions automatically fill the options bar for the selected tool.

CREATING A CUSTOM CROP TOOL PRESET

Remember, you can create a preset using whatever options you want. Let's create a Crop tool preset for a 6″ x 4″ 300 ppi image.

1   Click the **Crop** tool on the toolbar.

2   Type **6** into the Width box and **4** into the Height box. Type **300** into the Resolution box.

3   In the Crop tool presets palette, click the small upper-right arrow for the fly-out menu. Select **New Tool Preset**. Or, you can select the **New Tool Preset** icon. Depending on which version of Photoshop you are using, this can appear along the right or bottom-right of the palette.

Note that the "current tool only" button is checked on the bottom of the tool preset palette. This means the preset will only be stored with the Crop tool options.

5   Name the preset—I called it **Crop Tool 6″ x 4″ 300 ppi**—and click **OK**.

6   The next time you want to crop to a 6″ x 4″ 300 ppi document, simply select the **Crop** tool, click on the Crop tool icon on the left of the Crop tool options bar, and you'll see the new preset in the pop-up menu.

To change the name of your crop preset:

1 Select the **Crop** tool. Open the Crop tool presets palette. Select the preset that you want to rename.

2 Click the black arrow and select the **Rename Tool Preset** from the fly-out menu.

3 Rename the preset and click **OK**.

To change the order of your presets:

1 Select the **Crop** tool. Open the Crop tool presets palette.

2 Click the black arrow and select the **Presets Manager** from the fly-out menu.

3 In the Presets Manager dialog box, be sure **Tools** is selected in the Preset Type drop-down menu. Then scroll to locate the item you want to move. Click and drag it to its new location. Continue until your Crop tools are in the order you want. When finished, click **Done**.

Crop Presets in Paint Shop Pro

The crop presets are located on the left of the Crop tool options bar. Clicking on the preset button displays a palette of saved crop instructions. By selecting any of these presets, the instructions automatically fill the options bar for the selected tool.

CREATING A CUSTOM CROP TOOL PRESET

When selecting the Crop tool, you'll notice that it saves the last dimensions you entered in the options bar.

1 To create a custom preset based on those dimensions, in this case 5″ x 5″, be sure your menu is set to **Last Applied**.

2 Select the **Save Preset** icon.

3 Name the preset in the Set Preset Dialog box. (Note that you cannot include the inch mark.) Click the **OK** button.

The next time you want a 5 x 5 crop, you can select it from the crop preset palette. It will automatically be added in numerical order.

Note: Use the **Resource Manager** (third icon down on the right of the Crop tool preset palette) to change the name of a preset or to delete a preset.

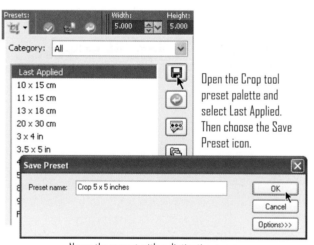

Open the Crop tool preset palette and select Last Applied. Then choose the Save Preset icon.

Name the preset with a distinctive name.

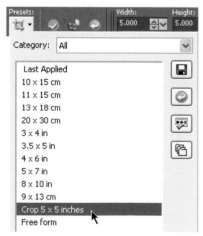

The new preset will now display in the palette with the other presets.

Quick Q & A

answers to common image size woes

I confess, when I need a certain size image, I insert the numbers I need into Photoshop's Image Size box, use the Crop tool, and let Photoshop do the math!

Don't be impressed by the following. It's for your benefit.

Q: **How come when I resize an image, it does not conform to a standard 4" x 6" or 5" x 7" print size?**

A: The proportions you are able to get from your digital camera will depend on its aspect ratio. A 35mm full frame image (24 x 36mm on film) has an aspect ratio of 1.5:1—the same as a 6" x 4" image. However, most consumer digital cameras use a traditional TV display aspect ratio of 4:3 (or 1.33:1—the same as an 8" x 6" print). While some digital cameras can produce 1.5:1 aspect ratio images (check your manual), this does not solve all resizing issues, since different print sizes have different aspect ratios.

> For example:
> 5 x 7 inch print = 1.4:1 ratio
> 10 x 8 inch print = 1.25:1 ratio
> 11 x 17 inch print = 1.55:1 ratio
> 20 x 30 inch print = 3:2 ratio

Q: **What is an aspect ratio? And how do I calculate it?**

A: An aspect ratio is the relationship between the vertical and horizontal dimensions of any two-dimensional rectangular object. Two objects of different sizes can have the same aspect ratio.

For example: A 5" x 4" photograph has the same aspect ratio as an 10" x 8" photograph.

To calculate an aspect ratio, divide the small number into the large number.

> For example:
> 10" x 8" photograph = 10 divided by 8 = 1.25:1 aspect ratio. (Pronounced 1 point two five to one).

To calculate other sizes with the same 1.25:1 aspect ratio:

- Look at the fractional number. In our example it is 0.25.
- See how many you need to get a whole number. If 0.25 x 4 = 1, then 4 is our answer.
- Next, multiply that number by the number prior to and after the colon (:).

  $$4 \times 1.25 = 5$$
  $$4 \times 1 = 4$$

- Thus, 1.25:1 is the same as 5:4 (five to four), and a 5 inch by 4 inch print has a 1.25:1 aspect ratio.

To calculate larger sizes with a 1.25:1 aspect ratio, double each number. For example, sizes with a 1.25:1 aspect ratio include:

5 x 4

10 x 8

20 x 16

40 x 32 (and so on)

Q: How do I change the dimensions of an image so that it conforms to a particular size?

A: This is discussed in detailed steps in Chapter 12 "Preparing Images for Digital Show Entry" on page 134. But, in short, there are three ways to do this: (1) oversize the image and crop it; (2) add a colored background around your image; or (3) distort your image. Note: These instructions are specific to Photoshop. For instructions using Photoshop Elements and Paint Shop Pro, see pages 134-137.

Oversize the image and crop it:

Imagine you have an image you want to have made into a 35mm slide. A 35mm slide has an aspect ratio of 1.5:1 or 3:2. (In other words, a 6" x 4" document.) Suppose your digital image opens to 35.556" x 26.667" at 72 dpi.

1. Uncheck the **Resample Image** box.
2. Type **300** (ppi or pixels/inch) next to Resolution. The image will resize to 8.533 by 6.4. Since this image is larger than 6 x 4, it can be cropped.
3. Select the **Crop** tool from the toolbar, and type 6 inches width by 4 inches height by 300 dpi in the options menu. The Crop tool will then stay to that ratio and you can to crop to taste. (When finished, be sure to click the Clear button in the options bar. Otherwise the next time you crop, you'll be cropping to 6 x 4.)
4. After you crop, check the Image Size dialog box to confirm the final image size.

Add a color background:

Suppose you cannot crop your image, or prefer to add a color around the image. In this case, you can make the image smaller than needed, then increase the canvas size.

1   Go to **Image > Image Size**.
2   Check the **Constrain Proportions** box.
3   Check the **Resample Image** box.
4   Change one dimension in the Document Size box to something smaller than the size you need. For example, change the width to 5 inches. The program proportions the image and changes the height to 3.75 inches.
5   Double-click the Background color box. Select an appropriate color (slides with a neutral gray to black background often project better than a white background).
6   Go to **Image > Canvas Size** and insert the 6 x 4 dimensions. The image canvas will automatically enlarge and fill the area around the image with the selected color.

Distort your image:

You can also distort an image to force it to the desired dimensions.

1   Go to **Image > Image Size**.
2   Uncheck the **Constrain Proportions** box.
3   Check the **Resample Image** box.
4   Type in the desired width and height measurements. The program will resize, distorting your image to the desired size. However, unless the amount is very small, I don't recommend it.

working in layers

Digital layers remind me of tracing paper layers. When I started designing quilts, I went through rolls of the stuff. I'd sketch my idea on white paper, then layer tracing paper onto my original, try out lots of variations, and let new ideas develop.

Today you can use digital layers. Whether you start a new document or open an image (for example, a digital photo), that document or image sits on the background layer. Think of this background layer as your original drawing on white paper. New layers (think tracing paper) can be added to the background layer, providing you with all types of options.

Working in layers, you can:

- Change the stacking order of the layers.
- Link layers so they work together as a single unit.
- Merge certain layers into one.
- Vary the opacity of layers
- Turn off the visibility of a layer (like removing a piece of tracing paper but not throwing it away).
- And more—read on...

The Benefits of Layers

Working with layers is intuitive. The more you learn about layers and use them, the more powerful your options become. Plus, like filing away an original drawing with tracing paper overlays, layers are saved with your digital document. They are "non-destructive," meaning they do not permanently alter the image. This means that as long as you save the original image as one of the layers in your document, you can easily return to that original by simply turning off all other layers.

I'll show you layer basics—what you need to start working with layers. Get in the habit of leaving the layers palette open. It's like having a roll of tracing paper nearby.

IN PHOTOSHOP
Go to **Windows > Layers**.

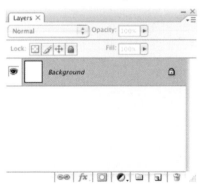

The Photoshop default layers palette.

IN ELEMENTS
Go to **Windows > Layers**.

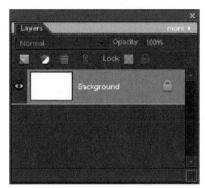

The Elements default layers palette.

IN PAINT SHOP PRO
Go to **View > Palettes > Layers**.

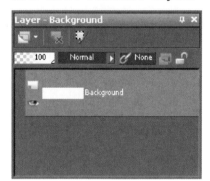

The Paint Shop Pro default layers palette.

Special Properties of Background Layers

Whenever you open a new document, or open a digital image, most image-editing programs automatically create that document on a layer called "Background." The background layer has some unique properties:

- A background layer cannot be deleted
- A background layer cannot be moved.
- A background layer must always remain on the bottom of the stack.
- Doing anything to the background layer permanently alters it.
- A background layer can be converted to a normal layer, and in Photoshop and Elements a normal layer can be converted to a background layer.

Layer Basics

Adding, naming, visibility, opacity/transparency, moving, linking, duplicating, merging, grouping, deleting, and converting the background layer.

In Photoshop and Photoshop Elements

ADDING

There are several ways of adding a new layer in Photoshop.

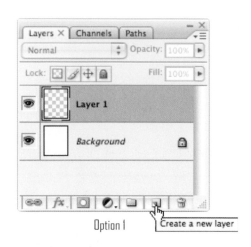

Option 1

Create a new layer

Option 1: With the Layers palette open, and the **Move** tool selected, click the **Create a new layer** icon on the bottom-right of the palette (at the top-left of the palette in Elements).

Option 2: Click **Layer > New > Layer**.

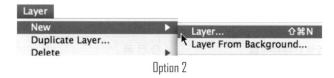

Option 2

Option 3: With the **Move** tool selected, select **New Layer** from the fly-out menu on the layers palette.

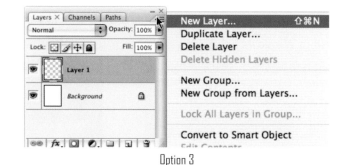

Option 3

Option 4: The keyboard shortcut is:

- **Ctrl+Alt+Shift+N** (Win)
- **Command+Option+Shift+N** (Mac)

Adding a Layer Underneath the Selected Layer

When a new layer is created, the default is for it to appear **above** the selected layer. **Ctrl+click** on the New Layer icon (**Command+click** on a Mac) to create a new layer **under** the selected layer.

NAMING

The easiest way to name a layer is to click the layer in the palette to select it. Then double-click directly on the layer name and rename it.

By **Alt+clicking** on the **New Layer** icon (**Option+click** on a Mac), you can name your layer before creating it.

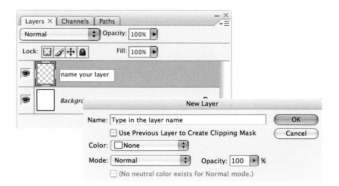

VISIBILITY

Next to each layer you'll see an eye. An eye indicates that whatever is on that layer is visible on your document.

This document has two layers, one with a red circle and another with a blue square. Each layer has an eye, and the contents of both layers are showing on the document.

With the **Move** tool selected, click on the eye and it disappears. When there is no eye showing, the contents of that layer are not displayed on the document. With the eye off on the blue square layer, the blue square is no longer showing on the image although the square is still part of the document.

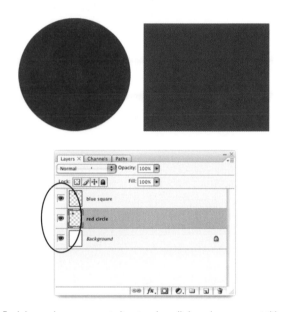

Each layer shows an eye, indicating that all three layers are visible.

The blue square layer no longer shows an eye since it is now hidden.

Change the opacity or transparency of your image by adjusting the Opacity slider or by entering an new value in the box.

OPACITY/TRANSPARENCY

Each time a new layer is created, it defaults to 100% opacity. But the opacity of each layer can be adjusted.

To change the opacity, so that one layer has some transparency:

1   Select the layer in the Layers palette.
2   Drag the opacity slider to the left to decrease the opacity. Dragging to the right increases opacity again.

For example, with a 100% opacity setting on a layer (the default), that layer would be totally opaque, completely covering any layer below it.

With a 50% opacity, that layer would be half opaque —meaning that the layer beneath it would show through. The lower the opacity, the more the layer underneath will show through.

The opacity value can also be typed in. (Additionally, a new feature in Photoshop allows you to click and drag directly on the word "opacity" to increase and decrease it. This is known as a "scrubby slider.")

LINKING

Linking layers allows you to keep the elements of one layer in tandem with the elements of another layer. (Think of paper-clipping your tracing paper sheets to your background sheet, to keep them all connected.)

To link two or more contiguous layers, hold the **Shift** key and select the first and last layer to highlight. Then click the **Chain Link** icon on the bottom of the Layers palette (on the top in Elements). To link two or more non-contiguous layers, **Ctrl+click** (**Command+click** on a Mac) on each layer that you want to link. Then click the **Chain Link** icon on the bottom of the Layers palette (on the top in Elements). Or right-click or use the fly-out menu on the Layers palette to select **Link Layers**. A chain link icon will appear on the right of each linked layer.

After selecting one layer in the linked set, you can use the **Move** tool or **Transform** tool to adjust all of the linked layers at once. The Transform tool (located under **Edit > Transform** in Photoshop and **Image > Transform** in Elements) allows you to scale, rotate, skew, distort, etc.

To unlink the layers, click one layer of the set, right-click or use the fly-out menu on the Layers palette to select Unlink Layers. To unlink only one layer from the set, click on the layer in the palette, then click the Chain Link icon. This will release that layer from the set.

50% Opacity

100% Opacity

Background layer

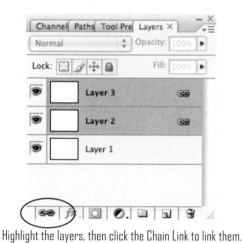

Highlight the layers, then click the Chain Link to link them.

Link layers using the fly-out menu on the Layers palette.

Unlink layers using the fly-out menu on the Layers palette.

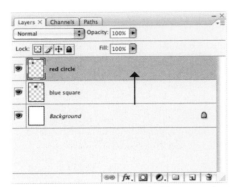

The red circle layer is now above the blue square layer.

Before move.   After move.

MOVING

With the **Move** tool selected, click and hold on the layer you want to move and drag it to a new location. The red circle is now above the blue square.

The keyboard shortcut to move a layer up or down is:

*   **Alt+right Bracket** key or **Alt+]** (or **Command+right Bracket** key on a Mac) to move the selected layer up in the palette.
*   **Alt+left Bracket** key or **Alt+[** (or **Command+left Bracket** key on a Mac) to move the selected layer down in the palette.

Moving from one document into another:

Both files need to be opened and their document windows reduced in size so both fit on your screen. It may be easiest to go to **Windows > Arrange > Tile Horizontally** (In Elements, it's **Window > Images > Tile**).

Select one document to make it active. From the active document, click onto the layer, drag from that document into the second document, and release the mouse button. The layer also remains in the original document. This can be very handy when you want to repeat effects that you created in one document to apply to another.

DUPLICATING

There are two ways to duplicate a layer:

Option 1: With the **Move** tool selected, drag the layer you want to duplicate to the **New Layer** icon on the bottom of the palette. A copy of the layer will appear above the selected layer. (This is when double-clicking on the layer name and renaming it comes in handy.)

Option 2: You can also use the fly-out menu from the Layers palette and select **Duplicate Layer.**

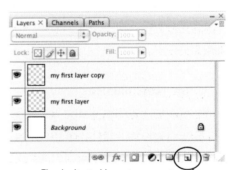

The duplicated layer is now on top of the original layer.

GROUPING (Photoshop only)

With the **Move** tool selected, click the **New folder** icon on the bottom to create a new group. A folder appears with the default Group 1 (Group 2, etc.).

Name the folder. Move whatever layers you'd like into the folder by dragging the layers on top of the folder layer. The layers will indent to indicate they are in the folder.

By clicking on the arrow to the left of the folder, you can collapse the folder so that the layers within it are not visible. The name of the folder tells me what is inside.

Clicking on the arrow again re-opens the folder and displays the layers inside of it.

MERGING

Each time you add a layer to your document, you increase the document's size. But if there are layers you can combine, or merge together, this will reduce the file size. However, merge with caution. **Once layers are merged, they cannot be unmerged** (unless you use the Undo command). The merging options are available from the fly-out menu on the Layers palette.

To merge one layer with the layer beneath it:
Select the top layer, and from the fly-out menu select **Merge Down**.

To merge more than one layer, but not all layers:
Turn off the visibility of the layers you want to save. Click on a visible layer. Select **Merge Visible** from the fly-out menu.

To merge all layers:
Click on a visible layer. Right-click (or from the main menu select Layer) and select **Merge > Flatten Image.** (This is also called "flattening" your document.)

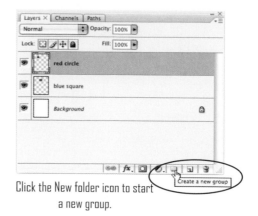

Click the New folder icon to start a new group.

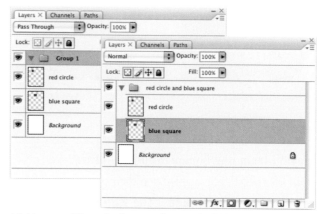

A folder named Group I will appear. Rename the folder by double-clicking on the folder name. Click, hold and drag the layers into this folder by dropping them onto the folder layer. Click the arrow next to the folder to open and collapse the group.

Merging layers helps reduce the file size of the document.

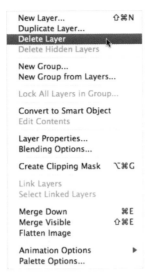

Select Delete Layer from the fly-out menu.

DELETING

There are two ways to delete a layer:

Option 1: With the **Move** tool selected, drag a layer to the **Trash** icon in the Layers palette. You can also delete a group folder by moving it to the trash (Photoshop only).

Option 2: With the **Move** tool selected, select **Delete Layer** from the fly-out menu on the Layers palette.

> **Remember:** Use **Ctrl+Z** (**Command+Z** on a Mac) if you make a mistake. Use **Ctrl+Alt+Z** to revert more than one step (**Command+Option+Z** on a Mac).

CONVERTING A BACKGROUND LAYER TO A NORMAL LAYER

Double-clicking the name **Background**, brings up a dialog box and automatically names your layer "Layer 0." You'll also see various options you can experiment with. You can rename your layer or simply click **OK** to change the background layer to a normal layer.

The background layer is now a normal layer, called **Layer 0** unless you gave it a new name.

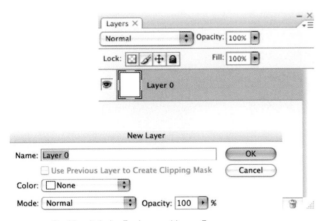

Double-click the Background layer. Type a new name in the New Layer dialog then click OK.

CONVERTING A NORMAL LAYER TO A BACKGROUND LAYER

Select the layer in the palette that you want to convert. Click **Layer > New > Background from Layer**. (There cannot be a Background Layer currently in the document, otherwise this will not be available.)

The layer is now a background layer.

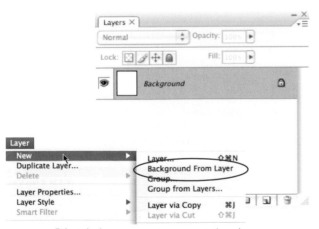

Select the layer you want to convert, then choose
Layer > New > Background from Layer.

In Paint Shop Pro

When a new layer is created in Paint Shop Pro, the default is a "Raster 1" layer. For learning the basics, we'll stick with the default raster layer.

ADDING

There are three ways to add a new layer:

Option 1: Click the **New layer** icon on the upper-left corner of the Layer palette once to bring up the New Raster Layer dialog box. Give your layer a name and click **OK**.

Option 2: Click and hold on the arrow to the right of the New layer icon and select **New Raster Layer**. Give your layer a name and click **OK**.

Option 3: Right-click on the layers palette (or from the main menu select Layers) and select **New Raster Layer**.

Option 1

Option 2

Option 3

NAMING

Click onto the name directly in the layer and rename. Or, double-click on the layer name to open the Layer Properties dialog box and rename your layer.

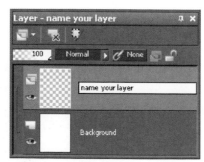

Click on the layer name to rename it.

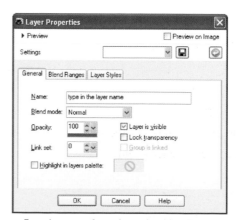

Type the name of your layer then click OK.

VISIBILITY

Next to each layer you'll see an eye. An eye indicates that whatever is on that layer is visible on your document.

This document has two layers, one with a red circle and another with a blue square. Each layer has an eye, and the contents of both layers are showing on the document.

Click on the **eye**. A small red circle with a diagonal red line goes over the eye, and the contents of that layer are not displayed in the document. With the eye off on the blue square layer, the blue square is no longer showing on the image although the square is still part of the document.

The visibility of layers can also be edited through the Layers menu. Go to **Layers > View** and select from the choices. **Invert** reverses the current choice. If, for example, you have one layer visible, selecting Invert will change the one visible layer to no visibility and turn the visibility on the other layers off.

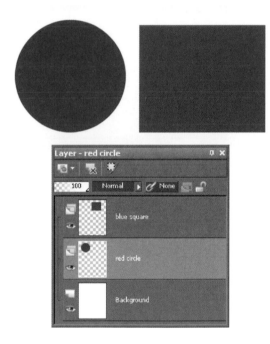

OPACITY/TRANSPARENCY

Each time a new layer is created, it defaults to 100% opacity. You can adjust the opacity of any layer.

*   Select the layer.
*   Drag the opacity slider to the left to decrease the opacity. Dragging to the right increases opacity again.

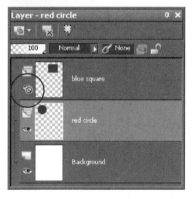

You can also double-click the layer to bring up the Layers Properties dialog box and type in an opacity value.

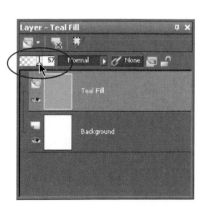

For example, with a 100% opacity setting on a layer (the default), that layer would be totally opaque, completely covering any layer below it.

With a 50% opacity, that layer would be half-opaque meaning that the layer below it would show through. The lower the opacity, the more the layer underneath will show through.

50% Opacity →

100% Opacity →

Background layer →

MOVING

There are two ways to move a layer:

Option 1: Click the layer in the palette and drag it up or down into a new position.

Option 2: Right-click (or from the main menu select Layers) and select **Arrange**. Then select where you'd like to move your layer.

Moving from one document into another:

Both files need to be opened and the document windows reduced in size so that both are showing on your screen. It may be easiest to go to **Window > Tile Horizontally**. Select one document to make it active. From the active document, click onto the layer <u>in the Layers palette</u>, drag from the palette into the second document, and release the mouse button. The layer also remains in the original document. This can be very handy when you want to repeat effects that you created in one document to apply to another.

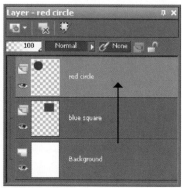

The red circle layer is now above the blue square layer.

Before move.

After move.

DUPLICATING

Click the layer you want to duplicate. Right-click (or from the main menu select Layers) and select **Duplicate** from the pop-up menu. Remember to name the layer so you can better identify it when working with your document.

The duplicated layer displays above the original layer.

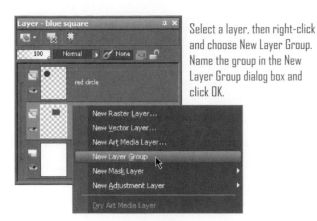

Select a layer, then right-click and choose New Layer Group. Name the group in the New Layer Group dialog box and click OK.

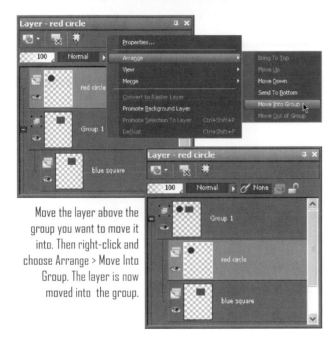

Move the layer above the group you want to move it into. Then right-click and choose Arrange > Move Into Group. The layer is now moved into the group.

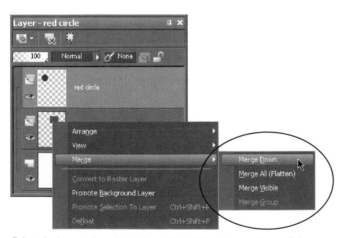

Select the layer in the palette, then right-click and choose Merge. Select from the different merging options here.

GROUPING

A group must contain at least one layer.

To create a group:

Click a layer to select it. Right-click (or from the main menu select Layers) and select **New Layer Group**. The selected layer will be placed into a group.

To move a layer into a group:

Select the layer you want to move. Right-click (or from the main menu select Layers) and select **Arrange**. Then choose from the options to move the layer up or down <u>so that it is on top of the group you want to place the layer into</u>. Then right-click (or from the main menu select Layers) and select **Arrange > Move Into Group**.

To move a layer out of a group:

Select the layer you want to move. Right-click (or from the main menu select Layers) and select **Arrange > Move Out of Group**.

MERGING

Each time you add a layer to your document, you increase the document's file size. Combining, or merging layers together will reduce the file size. However, merge with caution. Once layers are merged, they cannot be unmerged (unless you use Undo).

To merge one layer with the layer beneath it:

Select the top layer. Right-click (or from the main menu, select Layers) and select **Merge > Merge Down**.

To merge all layers:

Click on a visible layer. Right-click (or from the main menu select Layers) and select **Merge > Merge All**. (This is also called "flattening" your document.)

To merge more than one layer, but not all layers:
Turn off the visibility of the layers that you want to save. Click onto a visible layer. Right-click (or from the main menu select Layers). Select **Merge > Merge Visible**.

To merge all of the layers within a group:
Select the group or a layer within it. Right-click (or from the main menu select Layers). Select **Merge > Merge Group**.

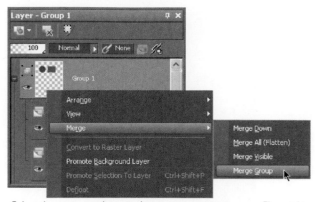

Select the group or a layer in the group you want to merge. Then right-click and choose Merge Group.

DELETING

There are a couple ways to delete a layer:

Option 1: Select the layer and click on the **Delete Layer** icon on the top of the Layer palette.

Option 2: Right-click (or from the main menu select Layers) and select **Delete**.

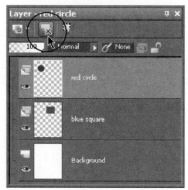

Click the Delete Layer icon on the top of the Layers palette.

CONVERTING A BACKGROUND LAYER TO A NORMAL LAYER

Special effects cannot be applied to a Background layer.

Option 1: By double-clicking on the name **Background** in the Layers palette, a dialog box comes up and automatically names your layer "Raster 1." Rename your layer and click **OK**.

Option 2: With the background layer selected, right-click (or from the main menu select Layers) and select **Promote Background Layer**. Your layer is now named "Raster 1."

The background layer is now a normal layer, called Raster 1 unless you gave it a new name.

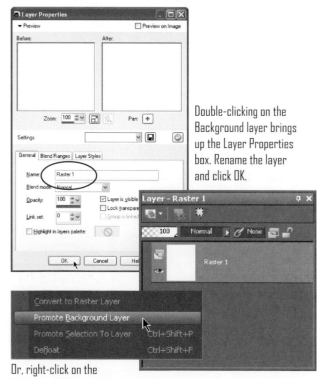

Double-clicking on the Background layer brings up the Layer Properties box. Rename the layer and click OK.

Or, right-click on the Background layer and choose Promote Background Layer.

The Power of Adjustment Layers

Adding an adjustment layer to your document lets you alter the image without actually changing the pixels of the original image. You can brighten, darken, adjust the colors, and more. You can add multiple adjustments.

Adding an adjustment layer is easy. The basic steps are:

1 **Select the layer** you want to add the adjustment layer to.

2 **Select the adjustment layer** that you want from the palette of adjustment layers. A dialog box for that adjustment layer will appear.

3 After making your selections to it, click **OK**.

The new adjustment layer will appear in the Layers palette. When your document is saved, the adjustments are saved with it. In the future, should you decide to return to the unaltered original, simply turn off that adjustment layer's visibility.

To modify the settings of an adjustment layer, double-click on it in the Layers palette. The settings dialog box that you first worked with will reappear. Make whatever changes you need, click **OK**, and your image is further modified. **Adjustment layers can be named, moved, organized, and deleted as a normal layer**.

In most image-editing programs, under the Layer menu, you'll see a variety of options for adjusting your image.

> **To access the adjustment layer options in Photoshop** either use the drop-down menu on the top-left of the Layers palette or select **Layer > New Adjustment Layer** from the main menu.

> **To access the adjustment layer options in Photoshop Elements** either use the drop-down menu on the top-left of the Layers palette or select **Layer > New Adjustment Layer** from the main menu.

> **To access the adjustment layer palette in Paint Shop Pro**, use the layer drop-down menu on the top-left of the layers palette or right-click on the selected layer and select New Adjustment Layer and select an adjustment.

Improving the quality of an image with adjustment layers is discussed in more detail in Chapter 10 "Easy Photo Fixes and Beyond" (page 94). Other layering topics, including blending modes and masks, are beyond the scope of this book. I encourage you to visit the help section of each topic in your software and explore them further.

easy photo fixes and beyond

When it comes to photography and editing, many questions will come to mind. For example, imagine you need quilt images for a show:

- Should you have your quilt professionally photographed?
- Or should you photograph your own quilt?
- And if you do the photography, is it okay to edit the photo?
- And if so, how much editing is okay, and how do you do it?

This chapter will help if you decide to take and edit your own photos. It's a long chapter, and may seem daunting. But it's full of easy editing tips that can make a real difference to the final look of your image.

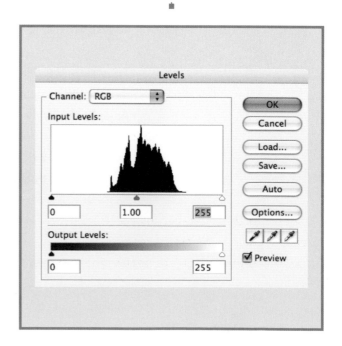

Photographing Your Quilts

In many instances you can get good results photographing your quilt yourself. **It is very important to do whatever you can to get the best picture quality possible at the point of capture**. In other words, don't rely on Photoshop (or other software) to fix a mediocre photo. Photo editing can help improve the quality of your image, but don't rely on it to be the fix-all for a bad image.

In some cases, you'll want to consider using a professional photographer:

- If image quality is imperative. For example, if it's for an intensely competitive show. Or you need high-end images for a book or catalog.
- If you're not comfortable with your picture-taking skills.

Professional photographs usually don't need any photo editing, so don't try to adjust a professional photo unless it really needs it (in that case, your photographer probably wasn't as professional as you thought). It's the photographer's job to capture the photo at its best to avoid a lot of editing. However, if the photographer feels it necessary, he or she will most likely adjust the images for you.

Digital Photo Concerns

Is it really okay to edit a quilt photo you'll submit for a show? Usually digital image corrections are acceptable, and even desirable. The big concern is just how far you go when improving the photo. Take fashion magazines for example. A model's skin is made to look perfect. Eyes are widened, noses reshaped, teeth whitened, and pounds are shaved off. It's no wonder some quilt makers feel that a digital image gives an unfair advantage!

You may remember the brouhaha over an image taken in Iraq by a photojournalist that was digitally-forged. The image was published by Reuters—a highly respected news organization. The published photograph looked very grim, with thick clouds of smoke and other ravages of war. When it was later learned that the original photo was far less threatening and that the photo was doctored, it made news worldwide. Reuters took a lot of heat. As a result, it published very specific guidelines as to what photojournalists can and cannot do when using Photoshop.

At the top of the rules is **"No additions or deletions to the subject matter of the original image."** Allowed are lighting adjustments, color corrections, cropping, removal of dust, and other items that do not materially affect the subject of the image.

These are exactly the types of photo adjustments—straightening a crooked subject, adjusting the lighting, making minor color corrections—that are the focus of this chapter. These are not cheats, but rather adjustments you can make to your images if they are needed. **The goal is always for your quilt to look like your quilt—nothing more**.

Straightening a Crooked Image

If your quilt is crooked in your photo it can make your image look anything from somewhat off to downright amateurish. So straightening the quilt would be the first thing to do.

PHOTOSHOP

With the image open:

1   Select the **Ruler** tool from the tool palette. If you don't immediately see it, look for it under the Eyedropper tool.

2   Find a horizontal line (or a vertical line) in the image that should be straight. In this case, I am using the top edge of the quilt. Drag the **Ruler** tool across the part of the image that should be horizontal (or vertical).

3   Go to **Image > Rotate Canvas > Arbitrary**.

4   In the Rotate Canvas box, the value of the angle you described with the measure tool will appear in the Angle box. Whatever it is, click **OK**.

5   The image will rotate by that angle, in this case straightening the quilt.

If you are unhappy with the rotation, use the **Undo** command and start again. If you need just a bit more tweaking, try it again.

To finish the image, select the **Crop** tool to square it up.

PHOTOSHOP ELEMENTS

With the image open:

1   Select the **Straighten** tool from the tool palette.

2   Drag the **Straighten** tool across the part of the image that should be horizontal (or vertical).

3   When you lift the mouse button, the image automatically straightens and crops.

To finish the image, select the **Crop** tool to square it up.

Original image

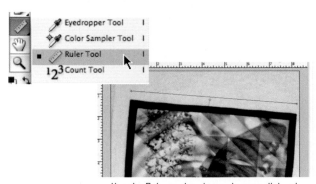

Use the Ruler tool to draw a line parallel with either the horizontal or vertical line of your quilt.

The angle of the line you drew with the Ruler tool will display in the Rotate Canvas box. Simply click OK.

Your quilt will be straightened. Use the Crop tool to finish the image.

Click the Straighten tool. A bar will display in the center of the image.

Adjust the angle of the bar by moving its ends up and down so they are parallel with the quilt's edge. Click Apply to straighten.

Your quilt will be straightened. Use the Crop tool to finish the image.

PAINT SHOP PRO

With the image open:

1   Select the **Straighten** tool from the tool palette.

2   A bar appears in the center of the image. In this case, I moved the bar above the image so I can see it better. Then click each end of the bar and move it so it follows the angle of the line that should be horizontal (or vertical).

3   Click the **Apply** button in the tool options palette (or double-click directly on the image).

4   The image will rotate.

To finish, select the **Crop** tool to square it up.

The Auto Fix Tools—One Stop Image Correction

Many image-editing programs, such as Elements and Paint Shop Pro, offer **auto fix** tools specifically designed to make image adjustment easy. These programs analyze different aspects of your image—such as lightness, darkness, and color—and can adjust the image accordingly. In many cases they also offer an added bonus: slider controls that let you further tweak the adjustments to best suit your eye.

These auto fix tools that include variable adjustments are a welcome addition to image-editing programs. They provide a happy compromise between allowing the program to control all the adjustments and doing all the adjusting yourself. If you're a bit intimidated about altering your image, using the auto fix tools is a great place to start. Even if you're not intimidated, give them a try. These tools may be all you need to satisfactorily improve the quality of your image.

Before applying an auto fix to your image, you may first want to save the original image. Or duplicate the background layer of your image and apply the auto fix to it. Either way, if you need to return to your original, you can.

PHOTOSHOP ELEMENTS—THE QUICK FIX MODE

Photoshop Elements has three editing modes: **Full Edit**, **Quick Fix**, and **Guided Edit**.

To access Quick Fix, click the **Quick** tab under the main menu bar on the right. The image opens in the default "After Only" view. While there are four different ways you can view your image, I prefer the before and after so that I can see how the changes affect my image. Therefore, I selected **Before & After-Horizontal**, as that matches the orientation of my image. This option displays a before and after view of the image.

In the Quick Fix mode, several menus (on the right) provide quick fixes. You can have Elements automatically adjust the levels (more on that later), the contrast, the color, and apply sharpening. One easy way to fix your image is to click the various Auto options and see how they affect your image.

View the image at different magnifications, including 100%, so you can better see what is happening to your image. If you're not happy with the results or want to experiment with a different setting, click the **Reset** button on the top. When you are satisfied with the adjustments, click the **Full Edit** mode tab under the main menu. The image now appears with the corrections.

In addition to the Auto buttons in the Quick **Fix** mode, you can use the sliders to vary the amount your image is adjusted. This lets you fine tune the adjustments.

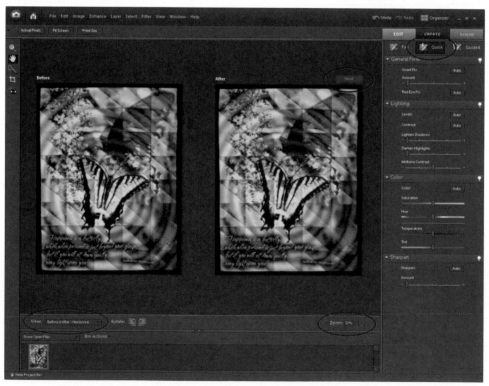

The Photoshop Elements Quick Fix window.

Q: What if, after going to the Full Edit mode, I decide I want to return to the original?

A: You could close the document, not save it, and reopen the original. However, you can also use Undo History.

    1 Go to **Window > Undo History**. The Undo History palette opens.

    2 To return to the original image, click the layer with your original image. The previous adjustments—in this case Auto Levels, Auto Contrast, and Auto Color—are no longer applied and you are back to the original image.

Undo History palette

Click the Image layer to return to the original image.

Q: In Quick Fix, how is Levels different from Contrast?

A: **Levels** adjusts the overall tonal range and can fix a colorcast. (In Quick Fix mode, there is no control over levels.)

Contrast adjusts the contrast of the image without affecting the color. (In the Quick Fix mode, you have the ability to adjust the shadows, highlights, and mid-tones, which is a good thing. When using the Quick Fix mode, your image may require both fixes.)

PAINT SHOP PRO—THE SMART PHOTO FIX

With your image open, go to **Adjust > Smart Photo Fix**. The Smart Photo Fix dialog box opens (see images on next page). It displays a before and after of your image, as well as controls for brightness, saturation, and focus.

To start, click the **Suggest Settings** button. Zoom into the image so you can better see how the adjustments affect your photo as they are applied. To tweak the suggested setting, click a slider in the desired area and move the slider bar. When you release the mouse, you'll then see the adjustment. So make your adjustments in small steps.

Click **Advanced Options** to bring up additional options. **Color Balance** is very useful. It lets you place points on the original image. These points help the program calculate which adjustments should work best to improve your image. When you hover your mouse over the "before" image, the pointer will turn into an eyedropper tool. As you move the eyedropper tool around the image, the RGB value of the pixel beneath the eyedropper will display. The key is selecting the best white (or light), black (or dark), and neutral gray area of your image. When you locate each, click the mouse and a small mark will appear on the "before" image. Placing the mark to indicate a grey helps to remove a color cast.

This area is essentially giving you a "levels" control (More about levels later in the chapter). The "after" image is adjusted according to the points you select. While adjusting, if you dislike the results, click the **Suggest Selections** button to return to where you started.

The **Black and White** sliders let you further adjust the darker and lighter areas of your image. The graph beneath the sliders, called a "histogram," shows how the adjustments are affecting the original image. (You will learn more about histograms later in the chapter also.) When you are satisfied with the changes in your image, click **OK**. Your image will update with the changes.

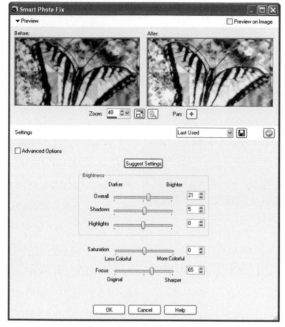

Smart Photo Fix dialog box.

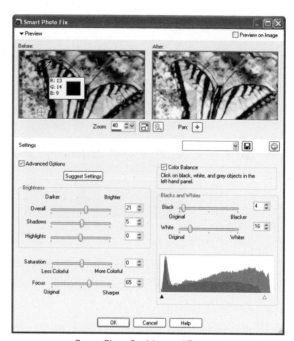

Smart Photo Fix Advanced Options.

PHOTOSHOP—AUTO-LEVELS, AUTO-CONTRAST, AND AUTO-COLOR

Photoshop provides some automatic image adjustment tools, but doesn't let you vary the adjustment. (Therefore you'll have more control over the adjustment by using the Quick Fix and Smart Photo Fix tools, described previously). Even so, Photoshop's automatic tools are still worth a try, since some images respond very well to auto-commands.

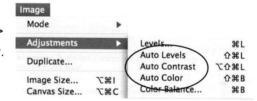

To access the auto adjustment commands in Photoshop, go to **Image > Adjustments**, then select **Auto Levels**, **Auto Contrast**, or **Auto Color**. If you want to use them all, use them in that order.

Also, if you like the adjustment but it's a bit too much, you can tone it down. Photoshop (and Elements) have a feature that allows you to "fade" the last command made. This applies to auto-corrections. For example, if you apply an Auto Levels command, the very next thing you can do is fade the adjustment. To do so (immediately after the Auto Levels), go to **Edit > Fade Auto Levels**. This brings up an opacity box which affects the last command you gave (in this case Auto Levels). Decreasing the opacity lessens the Auto Levels adjustment. Click to check and uncheck the **Preview** box, to toggle it on and off, and you'll see how your fade is adjusting the image. For those who use blending modes, notice you can also apply a particular blending mode to the fade.

If you apply an **Auto Contrast** (or **Auto Color**) command, and want to lessen the effect, immediately go to **Edit > Fade**. This time you'll see **Fade Auto Contrast** (or **Auto Fade Color**).

Beyond One-Stop Fixes—An Introduction to Levels, Other Adjustment Layers, and Creative Color Changes

Remember adjustment layers from the "Working in Layers" chapter? (Adjustment layers are the oh-so-fabulous layers that allow you change your image without harming a single pixel.) A **Levels adjustment layer** lets you improve the tonality of your image and do basic color correction—keeping those improvements with your image for as long as you'd like. When you save your image with the adjustments, you can return to the image whenever you want, and even change your settings again repeatedly—all without hurting a single pixel in your image. If you later decide you don't like the adjustment, you can toss it into the Layers palette's trash and be back to the original image you started with.

Levels adjustment layers offer an excellent way to improve tone (brightness/contrast) and basic color issues. (I'll touch on some other adjustment layers later in this section.) But we'll just scratch the surface. Tone and color adjustments can get quite complex. Color correction alone fills entire books, is the subject of classes, and can take years to master. But don't be scared off. Really! I'll show you some adjustments I routinely use to quickly improve my images. Often just a few small adjustments make all the difference.

As a bonus, understanding some key concepts will give you a jump start if you later start working with RAW images— the very large digital camera file that captures everything and processes nothing, meaning you do all the work—should you enter that arena.

This section (pages 101-112) does not give specifics for working in Paint Shop Pro. But these same techniques will apply in that program. Visit the Chapter 9 "Working in Layers" (page 80) for information on accessing adjustment layers. I realize this information may look daunting to you. But it's really exciting stuff—especially if you enjoy incorporating imagery into your work.

Levels

The **Levels** command lets you adjust your image's overall tones in three specific areas: **Shadows**, **Mid-tones**, and **Highlights**. It can also help correct a color cast.

To open the Levels adjustment layer, go to **Layer > New Adjustment Layer > Levels**. (The Levels adjustment layer is also accessible from the Adjustment Layer drop-down menu in the Layers palette. In Photoshop this is located on the bottom of the palette; in Elements it's located on the top.)

Beneath the graph (called a "**histogram**") there are three "input level" slider arrows—white on the right, grey in the middle, and black on the left. By moving the sliders, you can lighten or darken your image.
- **White slider** = controls highlights
- **Black slider** = controls shadows
- **Grey slider** = controls "gamma value," meaning you can adjust the mid-tones—simply brightening or darkening the middle values of your image—while leaving the very lights and very darks untouched

There are three eyedropper tools—white, gray, and black—on the right side of the dialog box. Using the corresponding eyedropper enables you to set a **white point**, a **black point**, and a **neutral gray point**. When you select these points, Photoshop redistributes the tonal information based on those points. When you set these points, Levels redistributes the tonal information.

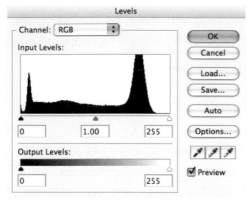

The Photoshop Levels dialog box may look a bit intimidating, but you only need to use a few areas to get good results.

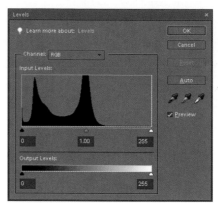

In Elements, the Levels dialog box has fewer options than its older sibling Photoshop, but it has what counts.

Question for the expert

Q: What is a histogram?

A: In short, it's a bar graph that shows how your photo's tones are distributed. The histogram lets you evaluate what's going on in your image. Many digital cameras offer the ability to display a histogram with your image on the camera's LCD preview screen. Looking at the histogram can indicate if there are any exposure issues. If necessary, you can then adjust your settings and reshoot your image.

If the graph does not extend all the way to the left, then there are no fully black areas.

If the graph does not extend all the way to the right, then there are no fully white areas.

If the graph "climbs the wall" on the left, then your image is underexposed.

If the graph "climbs the wall" on the right, then your image is overexposed.

Generally full ranges of tones are desirable in an image—meaning a histogram that stretches from the left to the right but does not "climb the wall." However, there may be times when you do not want a full range. (For example, imagine you take a picture of a snow scene with no dark darks.) The changes you make to your image will reflect your tastes and what looks good to your eye. The histogram simply shows how the distribution of the tones changes based on your adjustments.

By using Photoshop's fly-out menu on the histogram, there are several options for viewing the information, including looking at each individual color channel to see its distribution of tones (this is not currently available in Elements).

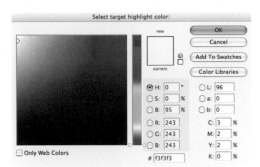

Select target **highlight** color dialog box.

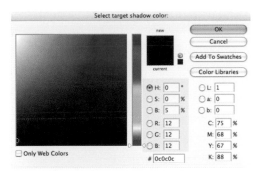

Select target **shadow** color dialog box.

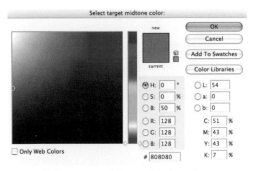

Select target **midtone** color dialog box.

Click Yes to save the target colors as default.

Setting the White, Black, and Neutral Gray Target Values

Tip! Before beginning to work with the Levels dialog box, let me pass along a great tip I learned from a wise instructor long ago: **First set the white and black target values**. You'll see what a positive difference this makes in the adjustment of your image.

With the Level adjustment dialog box open, double-click on the **white eyedropper**. The Select target highlight color box appears. Rather than keeping the brightness (B) at 100% (white) change it to **95%** and add the valuels of **243** in the R, G, and B boxes. With the numbers evenly balanced, this will help to keep too much of one color out of your highlights, which is what introduces a color cast. Click **OK**.

Double-click on the **black eyedropper** tool. The Select target shadow color box appears. Instead of brightness (B) at 0% (black), change it to **5%** and add the value of **12** into the R, G, and B boxes. Click **OK**.

Double-click on the **gray eyedropper** tool. The Select target midtone color box appears. With the above settings, the brightness (B) value in the midtone color box should be **50%** and the R, G, and B values should be **128**. If it is not, change it. Click **OK**.

Click **OK** in the Levels box. A dialog box will appear, asking to save the target colors as defaults. Click **Yes**. Then the next time you use the Levels command, those values will remain.

Why did I have you change white to slightly less than white, and black to slightly less than black? It's to keep some tone info in the whitest white and shadow info in the darkest dark. This improve the quality of the image, and helps avoid printing highlights without any tone—meaning a white so white that no color will print on the paper—or a shadow so dark that detail is lost.

Improving Brightness with Levels

METHOD 1:

Here is one easy way to improve image tonality. **Move the white slider to the left** until it is <u>just inside the beginning</u> of the black graph above it. **Move the black slider to the right** until it is <u>just inside the end of the black graph</u> above it.

With your image open:

1 Go to **Window > Layers** to open the Layers palette.

2 Go to **Layer > New Adjustment Layer > Levels**. When the New Layer dialog box comes up, click **OK**. (The Levels adjustment layer is also accessible from the Adjustment Layer drop-down menu on the bottom of the Layers palette. In Elements the drop-down menu is located on the top-left of the Layers palette.)

Two things will happen: A Levels dialog box will open, and a Levels Adjustment Layer will appear above your image layer. In this example, the histogram in the Levels dialog box indicates an <u>underexposure</u>—the information in the graph is too left-heavy.

3 **Drag the right input slider to the left** until the pointer is just inside the black graph above it. If you want to lighten up the mid-tones, move the mid-tone slider to the left. Click **OK**.

There is an Auto button which works the same as using Auto > Levels Adjustment. You can certainly give it a try. But often you'll get better results adjusting manually.

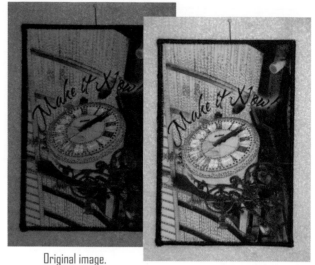

Original image.

Image after levels adjustment.

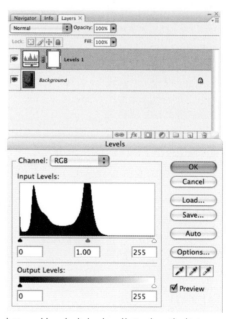

Layers palette and Levels dialog box. Notice how the histogram does not extend to the right, indicating an underexposed image.

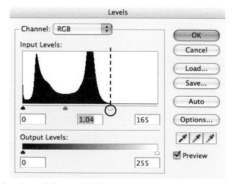

Move the white slider to the left until it reaches the starting point of the histogram. Adjust the midtone slider if necessary.

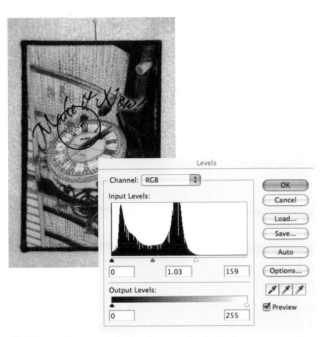

Click the eyedroppers in the Levels box and individually set target points in your image. You'll notice a change in your image after each click.

Above you see the same image. The first with an Auto Level adjustment (in other words, I had no control over the adjustment) and the second with manual Level adjustments.

METHOD 2:

Another method is to first **establish a black point and a white point, then move the sliders accordingly**. When looking for the black and white points, do not use elements outside of the image. For example, if there is a black border around the image, or if you scanned an image and it has bits of white in the border, ignore them. You want to work with the pixels within the image.

With your image open:

1 Repeat steps 1-2 on the previous page.

2 In the Levels box, click the **black eyedropper**. Move it around your image and search for what looks like the darkest area of your photo. **Click to establish a black point** (although avoid a pure black).

3 Next, select the **white eyedropper**. Move it around the image and search for what looks like the lightest area of your photo and look at the feedback in the info palette. **Click to establish the white point** (although avoid selecting a pure white).

4 Now drag the **right input slider to the left**.

5 Next click the **gray eyedropper**. Finding a neutral gray is often the hardest to locate. If you click and your photo is knocked out of whack, just click another area that you think is a neutral gray. Or, if your image looks good after locating a white and black point, stop there.

Try simply adjusting the sliders, or only using the eyedroppers. Then try using the eyedroppers first and then tweaking the sliders. See which method works best for your image.

Tip: To return to the starting point of your adjustment, hold down the **Alt** key (**Option** on Mac). The Cancel button turns into a Reset button. Then click Reset.

LEVELS ADJUSTMENT COMPARISON:

Here's a side-by-side comparison of each image (from left to right).

1 The original image.

2 The image with input slider adjustments.

3 The image with a black and white point set and input slider adjustments.

4 The image with an auto level adjustment.

Which is best? The image that looks best to you.

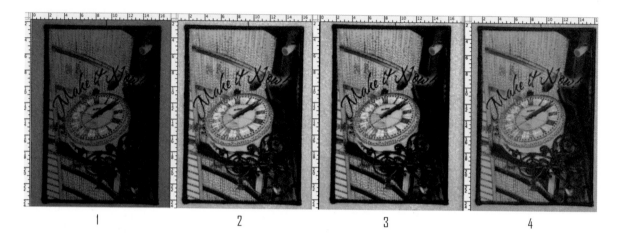

1   2   3   4

Question for the expert

Q: Why can't I just use the brightness and contrast command?

A: You can. But it's not recommended because using it can help one area of your image while hurting another. Generally, adjusting the brightness and contrast ends up reducing the detail in your image, by removing some of the lightest lights and darkest darks from the image. This isn't an absolute, however, and what looks good to your eye is what matters. Also, the brightness and contrast command in Photoshop CS3 is greatly improved. If you're working in CS3, give it a try.

A tip for better contrast when printing on fabric.

Did you ever try to increase the saturation on your image using the Brightness and Contrast control and end up with lights that lost detail and darks that became muddy? Instead, try a mid-tone Levels adjustment. The lights and darks will not change, but you can tweak the mid-tones for a better print.

Improving Brightness and Removing a Color Cast

What is a color cast? A **color cast** is a tinge or tint of unwanted color that negatively affects the quality of an image. For example, have you ever photographed a quilt indoors with flash and the image looked too warm, maybe yellow or orangey? Or maybe outside on a cloudy day and the colors looked too cool, maybe green or bluish? These are color casts, and they will negatively affect the accuracy of your colors.

In film photography, color casts were avoided by either using a specific filter for certain lighting situations or a specific type of film. In digital photography, using the correct "white balance" is key. Simply put, a correct **white balance** setting creates an image where white areas are white rather than having a tinge of another color. If the setting is left on Auto, as most people do, the camera averages the lighting situation. In many cases this can be fine. Most digital cameras now come with a range of white balance presets for different lighting situations such as tungsten, fluorescent, daylight, flash, cloudy, and so forth. Consider experimenting with the different settings to see how they affect your image. As your skills and desire grows, you may also want to experiment with creating a **custom white balance**. This is done by photographing a neutral gray reference (such as a gray card made for this purpose) in the lighting you are using. The camera then analyzes the color of the light hitting the sensor and creates a setting based on how warm or cool the color is.

Even with the best of settings, color casts still happen. Luckily, image-editing software contains tools that will help you correct your image. Additionally, if your have the option, experiment with shooting in the RAW file format. (Your camera's manual can tell you if your camera can shoot RAW files, and how to set your camera to do it). RAW uses no compression and contains all of the untouched (or raw) pixel information straight from the camera's sensor. The beauty of shooting RAW is that you can adjust the exposure and temperature (the warmth or coolness) of your image after the fact—a sort of do-over that is quite powerful. When I shoot RAW, I sometimes am lazy and leave the white balance on Auto, knowing I can adjust the exposure afterwards, if needed.

This image is totally out of whack. It is extremely dull and has a bluish color cast. I do have well-exposed photos of this quilt, and I'll compare the two on the next page.

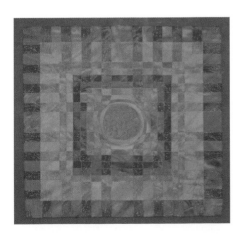

1 Go to **Window > Layers** to open the Layers palette.

2 Go to **Layer > New Adjustment Layer > Levels**. When the New Layer dialog box comes up, click **OK**. OR, select Levels from the Layer Adjustment drop-down menu in the Layers palette.

3 This histogram has no lights or darks. All the tones are concentrated in the middle.

4 For the first attempt, move the sliders until they are just inside of the corresponding black graph above it. Click **OK**. The resulting image still doesn't look too good.

5 This time establish white, black, and gray points like we did in Method 2 on page 105. While I can locate a good light and a good dark, I'm having trouble with the neutral gray. Some results are downright awful and others are better but still kind of flat and with an overcast.

6 While I can continue clicking around and may or may not find something else that works, I am instead going to adjust the individual color channels.

The top of the Levels dialog box displays the channel I am working in. I am working in RGB, and my Channel mode shows I am working in a composite RGB (in other words, all three channels, **R**ed, **G**reen, and **B**lue, at once). Click and hold to show the three individual color channels.

7 Select the **Red** channel and **move the sliders** accordingly. Do not click OK yet. The image looks awful, but carry on.

8 Select the **Green** channel and **move the sliders** accordingly. Do not click OK yet. The image still looks bad, but carry on.

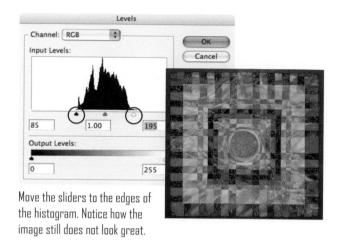

Move the sliders to the edges of the histogram. Notice how the image still does not look great.

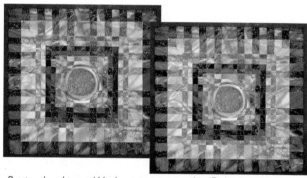

Setting the white and black points is easier than finding a neutral gray. Notice how the quilts still don't look quite right.

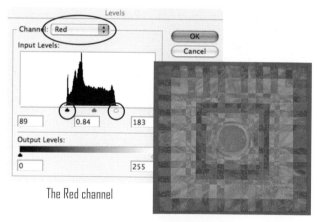

The Red channel

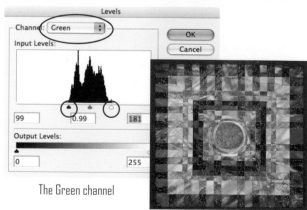

The Green channel

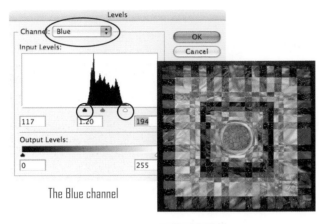

The Blue channel

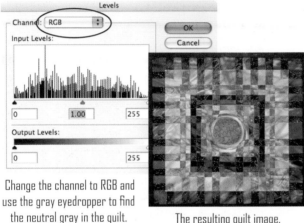

Change the channel to RGB and use the gray eyedropper to find the neutral gray in the quilt.

The resulting quilt image.

9 Select the **Blue** channel and **move the sliders** accordingly. Do not click OK yet. This time the image is much Improved, although I still see a very slight blue tinge.

10 Return to the **RGB** composite channel. Use the **gray eyedropper** to locate a neutral gray. This time it is much easier, and the resulting image now appears to have no color cast. Before you click OK, notice the spaces (empty columns) showing in the histogram. This shows how the program stretched the values based on the input slider settings used in each individual channel. The spaces appear because while the tonal range was expanded, there isn't enough data in the image to fill the full range of values. While you cannot avoid this when making corrections, you need to be careful not to overdo it. The more tones that are eliminated, the rougher the image will look.

11 Click **OK**.

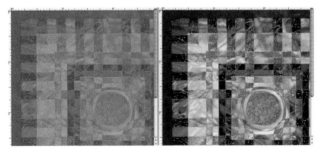

A before and after shows the huge improvement in the image. Although this image was corrected in Photoshop, there is still no excuse for taking such a bad image to begin with!

Finding the Best Black or White Point in your Image

There will be times when it will be hard to locate a very dark or very light area of your image. This is often the case when scanning older images. (Remember, don't use the white frame of the image to set the white point. Use the pixels inside of the image.)

I used this particular method (explained in the next few pages) to help rescue an image taken from a poorly scanned slide. The image was greatly improved just by establishing the white and black points of the image.

For illustration purposes, I'm starting with the poorly-exposed image with the blue overcast. (The following directions are for Photoshop only.)

1   Go to **Window > Layers** to open the Layers palette.

2   Go to **Layer > New Adjustment Layer > Threshold**. OR, select **Threshold** from the Layer Adjustment drop-down menu in the Layers palette. When the New Layer dialog box comes up, click **OK**.

3   The Threshold dialog box will open, and a Threshold Adjustment Layer will appear above your image layer. Your image will also turn black and white.

4   To find a black point, first drag the slider all the way to the left so that the image is completely white. Then very slowly start dragging the slider towards the right. Keep going until the very beginning of black appears. Click **OK**.

5   Select the **Color Sample** tool from the toolbar.

6   Place the very tip of the tool directly into the black area and click. (Zoom in if necessary.) A small reference circle will appear with the number 1. You have established the black point of your image.

If you don't like where you placed your reference point, or want to get rid of them after you correct your image, here's how: With the **Color Sampler** tool selected, hover over the reference point until the tool turns into a pointer (becomes the Move tool). Then click and drag the point directly off your image.

7   Open the Threshold dialog box by double-clicking directly on the thumbnail adjustment layer in the Layers palette. It's the box to the right of the eye-visible icon. (If you accidently click on the mask icon and the Layer Mask Display Options palette opens, just click Cancel.)

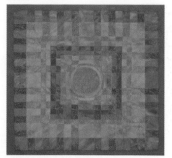

The original quilt image.

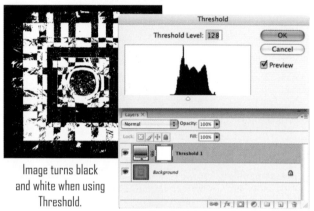

Image turns black and white when using Threshold.

The Threshold dialog and the Threshold Adjustment Layer.

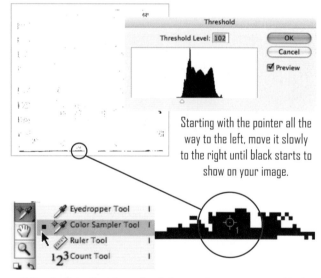

Starting with the pointer all the way to the left, move it slowly to the right until black starts to show on your image.

Select the Color Sampler tool and place a reference point on a black area of the quilt. Zoom in if necessary.

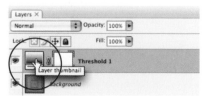

Double-click on the adjustment layer thumbnail to open the Threshold dialog box.

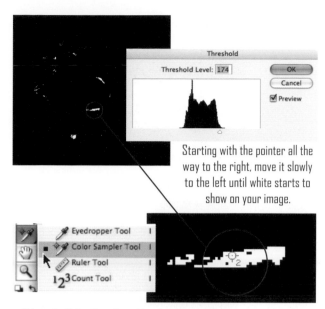

Starting with the pointer all the way to the right, move it slowly to the left until white starts to show on your image.

Select the Color Sampler tool and place a reference point on a white area of the quilt. Zoom in if necessary.

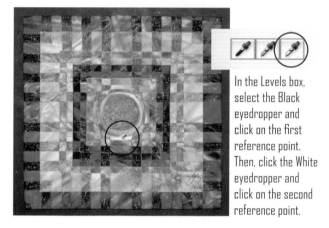

In the Levels box, select the Black eyedropper and click on the first reference point. Then, click the White eyedropper and click on the second reference point.

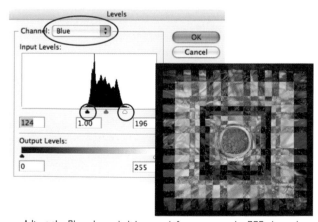

Adjust the Blue channel sliders, and if necessary, the RGB channel midtones to finish your adjustment.

8 With the Threshold dialog box open, drag the slider all the way to the right so that the image is entirely black. Then slowly start to drag the slider towards the left. Keep going until a bit of white starts to appear. Click **OK**.

9 Select the **Color Sampler** tool from the toolbar.

10 Place the very tip of the tool directly into a white area and click. (Zoom in if necessary.) A second small reference circle will appear with the number two. You have just established your white point.

11 In the Layers palette, grab the **Threshold Adjustment layer** and drag it to the trash. You read correctly. **Delete it**. You now have your original image with the two reference points still in place. Pretty nifty! (If you don't see your reference points on the image, click the Color Sampler tool again. The two points will display on your image.)

12 Go to **Layer > New Adjustment Layer > Levels**. When the New Layer dialog box comes up, click **OK**. OR, select **Levels** from the Layer Adjustment drop-down menu in the Layers palette.

13 In the Levels box, select the **black eyedropper**. Click directly into the first reference circle. Then select the **white eyedropper** tool and click directly into the second reference circle. The resulting image is better than what I originally came up with when I eyeballed the values, but the image is still too blue.

14 Because the problem seems only to be too much blue, go directly to the **Blue channel** and adjust the sliders. That alone adjusted the problem. So I didn't need to visit the other two channels.

15 Return to the **RGB channel**. I nudged the mid-tones just a tad darker, and the resulting image is much improved.

> **Elements users:** While you cannot set a reference point, you can see where the darkest and lightest area of your image is. Follow steps 1-4 on page 110 to find the darkest area. Reverse the directions to see where the lightest area of the image is.

When to Leave Levels Alone

The human eye responds well to luminance or brightness, which is why images with more contrast are generally more appealing. However, that is not to say that all images must have high contrast. There are many instances where different moods—romantic, mysterious, soft, etc.—are set in images with low or minimal contrast.

Important: Just because a histogram shows an uneven distribution of value doesn't mean the image needs to be adjusted.

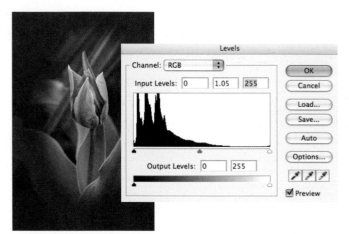 

I photographed this image while a diffused ray of light was on the tulip head. To my eye it's attractive as is. The histogram in the Levels dialog box shows me the concentration of darker tones.

After I adjust the levels to stretch the tones, my eye is no longer attracted to the image. I not only removed the mood of the image, I introduced some problems. This is an example of an image that lends itself nicely to other types of adjustments.

Other Adjustment Layers

As you can see in the Layers > Adjustment Layers option, there are several different types of adjustment layers. In this section, I'll give a brief overview of two adjustment layers found in Photoshop and Paint Shop Pro (but not in Elements). The examples are shown in Photoshop, but they work the same way in Paint Shop Pro.

Curves

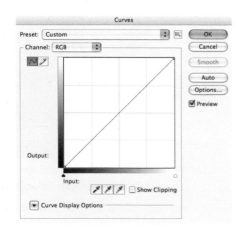

Like Levels, **Curves** is a type of tonality/contrast and color correcting tool. Unlike Levels, Curves does not limit you to adjusting three fixed tonal ranges. Instead, **Curves can adjust any point along the 0-255 range**. Now that's a lot of correcting ability! And it explains why **Curves is considered the most powerful image correction tool**. It may seem a bit daunting, but once you start working with it, you'll wonder how you did without.

Here's a quick overview:

To open the Curves adjustment layer, go to **Layer > New Adjustment Layer > Curves**. The **diagonal line** represents the "curve" of your image because each input value is equal to the corresponding output value. The **default grid** represents quarter-tones, mid-tones, and three-quarter tones. **Ctrl+click** (**Option+click** on Mac) on the grid and the default grid switches to a 10 x 10 grid for even more control. A curve can have up to 16 anchor points. When a curve is set to the composite channel (all three channels), the entire brightness of the image is adjusted. When a single color channel is selected, only that color is being adjusted. Whew! Don't worry if it doesn't yet make sense. This is another tool you learn best simply by using.

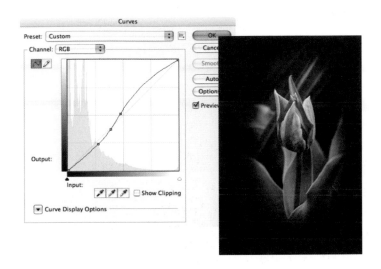

With the Curves dialog box open, as you click anywhere in your image, a small circle appears over the diagonal line which indicates the tonal value of the selected pixel. You can control specific areas of your image, because you can first define that area and then gently reshape the curve to adjust the tonality of those pixels. Taking another look at the tulip (the picture I liked as it was shot), I can make a few small adjustments between the three-quarter tones and mid-tones, pushing some pixels slightly lighter and some slightly darker. Do the small adjustments make that much of a difference? It's all in the eye of the beholder.

Hue/Saturation

In addition to adjusting hue and saturation, the **Hue/Saturation adjustment layer** also works with lightness. **This adjustment is helpful when you notice one particular color looking too loud and you want to tone it (and only it) down**. You can also have a lot of fun with this adjustment layer. You can recolor areas of your image, create the look of a Duotone image, and create rich black and white images.

To open the Hue/Saturation adjustment layer, go to **Layer > New Adjustment Layer > Hue/Saturation**. There are three sliders in the Hue/Saturation dialog box:

- **Hue slider**—acts as a color changer. When the Edit mode is in Master, you can change the entire color of the image or a selection of it.

- **Saturation slider**—increases or decreases saturation. It increases the saturation of the primary color when dragged to the right. It decreases it when dragged to the left. It works in absolutes, meaning from -100 which is completely desaturated to +100 which is completed saturated.

- **Lightness slider**—increases or decreases the lightness of the image. It also works in absolutes, meaning from −100 which turns every pixel black to +100 which turns every pixel white.

REDUCING SATURATION IN ONE RANGE OF COLORS

1 This image has red areas that are jumping out and looking too saturated. To adjust, go to **Window > Layers** to open the Layers palette.

2 Go to **Layer > New Adjustment Layer > Hue/Saturation**. When the New Layer dialog box comes up, click **OK**. OR, use the Hue/Saturation from the Layer Adjustment drop-down menu in the Layers palette.

3 In Hue/Saturation, select **Red** from the Edit drop-down menu, and adjust the **Saturation** and **Lightness** sliders to the left to taste. Click **OK**.

4 The reds in the resulting image are far less jumpy.

Original image

Image after Saturation adjustment

SOME CREATIVE COLOR FUN

Hue/Saturation can change the predominant color from one hue to another.

1 Go to **Layer > New Adjustment Layer > Hue/Saturation**. When the New Layer dialog box comes up, click **OK**. OR, use the Hue/Saturation from the Layer Adjustment drop-down menu in the Layers palette.

2 Move the **Hue** slider a bit to the right and the **Saturation** slider a bit to the left.

3 The resulting image has the new hue affecting the entire image.

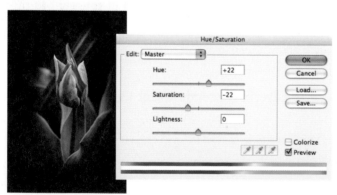

Original image

Image after adjustment

For some more creative fun, try combining different adjustment layers to make dramatic changes to your images.

COLORIZING THE OVERALL IMAGE

1 Go to **Layer > New Adjustment Layer > Hue/Saturation**. When the New Layer dialog box comes up, click **OK**. OR, use the Hue/Saturation from the Layer Adjustment drop-down menu in the Layers palette.

2 Check the **Colorize** box. Then experiment with moving the sliders until you have a coloration that you like.

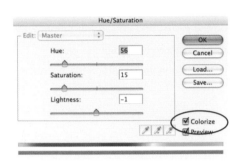

Click the Colorize box, then adjust the sliders a new beautiful image.

Image after adjustment

CREATIVE BLACK AND WHITE IMAGES

Instead of creating your black and white image in the Grayscale Mode, do it in RGB. You'll have far more creative control. Then, when you're finished, convert it to Grayscale (only if it's necessary for output, such as offset printing in monochrome) or leave it in RGB.

1 Go to **Layer > New Adjustment Layer > Hue/ Saturation**. When the New Layer dialog box comes up, click **OK**. OR, use the Hue/Saturation from the Layer Adjustment drop-down menu in the Layers palette.

2 Move the **Saturation** slider completely to the left.

3 The image becomes totally desaturated and turns into a black and white image. The advantage of creating a black and white image this way (rather than changing your image to grayscale) is that it retains all the RGB channel information, giving you far greater control over the image tonality.

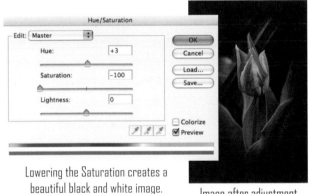

Lowering the Saturation creates a beautiful black and white image.

Image after adjustment

Once you have the black and white image, try changing the lightness of different color areas within the image.

4 Select a color from the Edit pop-up menu.

5 Move the **Lightness** adjustment slider.

6 By changing the lightness of individual colors, you can make very appealing variations of your black and white image.

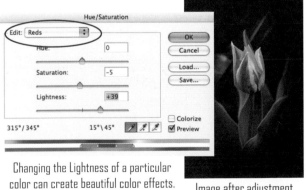

Changing the Lightness of a particular color can create beautiful color effects.

Image after adjustment

The Black and White Adjustment Layer in Photoshop CS3

In Photoshop CS3, there is a powerful adjustment layer called Black and White. Select it from the list of adjustment layers on the bottom of the Layers palette. Or go to **Layer > Adjustment Layer > Black & White**. This will bring up a New Layer dialog box. Simply click **OK**.

Immediately your image changes to black and white, and the Black and White dialog box appears. This palette gives you control over the luminance of six different regions of color. By moving the sliders, you can effect the luminance of each selected color and create very beautiful grayscale images based on your taste. Also, because this is an adjustment layer, you can always return at a later date and re-adjust it.

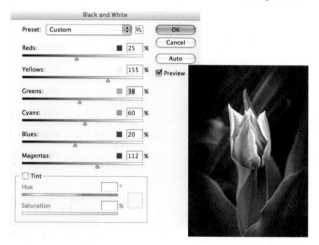

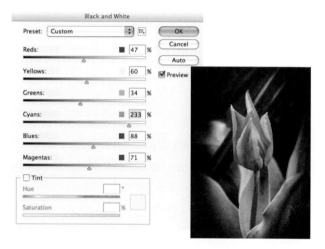

Click the **Tint** button on the lower-left of the Black and White dialog box. By selecting it and adjusting the sliders you can create more special effects, such as a sepia tone. Notice that you can control the hue and saturation of the tint.

There are more ways of creating black and white images, but the above methods will give you plenty of options for creating many beautiful images. **The biggest key is not to convert your image to grayscale.** Otherwise you will lose the color data of your image and in the process lose creative control.

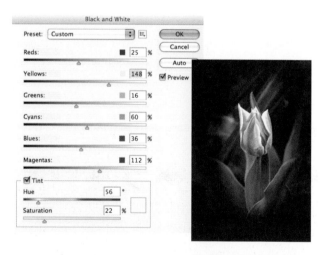

Tip: Here's a cool tip that I learned from an extraordinary teacher, Scott Kelby. With the Black and White dialog box open, move your cursor outside of the dialog box so it's over your image. The cursor turns into an eyedropper. When you click and hold the mouse over a particular gray color, the eyedropper turns into a two-way arrow. By dragging the arrow to the right, the color under the mouse-click will lighten. By dragging it to the left, the tones will darken.

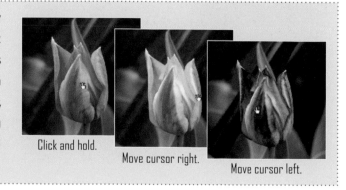

Click and hold.

Move cursor right.

Move cursor left.

chapter · ⑪

removing a quilt from its background

"Images must be in good focus and against a solid color background."

Does the sentence above look familiar? Juried show entry forms have contained guidelines like this for years. In your entry photo, your quilt will look best if there is good contrast between the quilt and the background surrounding it. Today's digital tools make it possible for you to "cut out" the quilt and put it on a new background. But the crucial factor is maintaining a good quilt edge.

This bears repeating: The biggest factor in success, when removing a quilt from its background and placing it on a new background, is the quality of the quilt's edge.

It's All About the Edges

If the quilt edges are cut out accurately, the resulting image will work. But if the edges look chopped or ragged, the image will look badly altered. (Nor should the quilt edges look straighter than they really are. This is not fashion photography. This is showing your quilt to its best, but being true to your quilt in doing so.) I'll show you how to cut your quilt from its background, using selection tools.

Quilt image with bad edges.

Quilt image with good edges.

Image-editing programs offer a wide variety of selection tools; some more sophisticated than others. Selection tools let you isolate pixels, to give them special attention. Once selected, the pixels can be re-colored, enlarged, made smaller, and so on. They can also be removed. The removal method depends on how complex the edges are, and the contrast between those edges and the surrounding pixels (the pixels of the background).

Removing a quilt from its background is generally much easier than removing a person with flyaway hair, or a tree with lots of branches and leaves. But you still need to pay attention to ensure that the quilt's edges retain their natural variations in straightness and bumpiness.

An Overview of Selections

All image-editing programs have tools that select an area of pixels, so these pixels can be adjusted. A selection is indicated by an animated series of dashes appearing around the selected area. These dashes are known as "**marching ants**."

Selection tools typically fall into four groups (with some programs having more selection options than others):
*   **Geometric** — Rectangular Marquee, Elliptical Marquee, and in some programs a Single Row Marquee, and a Single Column Marquee.
*   **Drawing** — Lasso, Polygonal Lasso, and Pen.
*   **Tone and color-based** — Magic Wand, Quick Selection, Color Range, Magnetic Lasso. There are also variations depending on the program you're working with, such as the Magic Eraser, Background Eraser, Selection Brush, Magic Selection Brush, Freehand Selection, Object Remover.
*   **Mask-based** — Quick Mask, Luminosity and Channel masks.

Hiding the marching ants: To better see the edge, press **Ctrl+H** (Win) or **Command+H** (Mac) to hide the marching ants indicating the selection. Even though you cannot see the selection, it is still selected. When you're finished with the selection, remember to press **Ctrl+H** (Win) or **Command+H** (Mac) again to turn off the hide mode.

Some programs also include an **Extract filter**, which is designed to remove an object from its background. Photoshop CS3 and Photoshop Elements 6 includes a very useful feature called **Refine Edges**. After making a selection, it offers five options to refine the edge with a live preview.

There are other options that can be used with your selection to modify it. Some examples:

- Selections can be contracted or expanded.
- A hard edge can be smoothed or softened by anti-aliasing or feathering.
  - **Anti-aliasing** softens the color transition between the edges of the selection and its background, while retaining detail. This feature must be selected while using a tool. It cannot be applied afterwards.
  - **Feathering** blurs the edges by adding a transition between the selection and surrounding pixels. This can cause some loss of detail along the selection's edge.
- Before releasing the mouse when making a selection, you can also hold down your keyboard Spacebar to move (or pan) the selection to a different position on your image (two hands are required, one for making the selection, the other for moving).
- A selection can be saved with an image, allowing it to be selected again at a future time when the image is opened (see page 125).

As you can see, there are a lot of options for isolating a quilt and removing it from its background! The good news is you only need to use a couple to get excellent results.

Selection Tips

- Zoom into the edges to see them clearly.
- Don't rush the selection.
- To return to a prior point in your selection, click the **Backspace** (Win) or **Delete** (Mac) key.
- To deselect a selection, click **Ctrl+D** (Win) or **Command+D** (Mac).
- If you accidentally click away from the selection and it disappears, immediately go to **Select > Reselect** to return your selection. **Ctrl+Shift+D** (Win) or **Command+Shift+D** (Mac) to Reselect.
- To add to a selection, hold the **Shift** key with the selection tool.
- To subtract from a selection, hold the **Alt** key with the selection tool.
- To nudge a selection by a pixel, press your **keyboard up, down, left, or right arrow** keys to nudge in that direction. Hold the **Shift key with an arrow key** to move the outline in 10 pixel increments.
- Make sure the **anti-alias box is ON** in the options bar.
- When changing the size of a brush (this works for a selection brush or any brush), use the **left bracket** key to make the brush size smaller and the **right bracket** key to make it larger.

Rules for Quilt Removal from Background: Keep the Original Image Safe and the Selection Easy

RULE ONE: KEEP A COPY OF THE ORIGINAL IMAGE

Whenever you alter an image, get into the habit of working on a copy of the original rather than working directly on the original. This way, should you ever need to return to your original for whatever reason, you have it. Here are two methods of making a copy:

- Open your original image. Immediately resave it with a new name, prior to starting any edits.
- OR, duplicate the background layer of the image. Edit directly on that copy. This method's advantage is that your original and edits are in one document.

RULE TWO: KEEP THE BACKGROUND COLOR ON ITS OWN LAYER

When a background is removed from an image, it's tempting to fill the removed area with a new background color. Instead, create a new layer beneath your edited layer, and fill it with a new background color. This way you can change the background color with a couple mouse clicks. You can also create and save a couple of layers, each with a different color, under the edited layer. Then you can toggle background colors on and off to see which color you prefer.

RULE THREE: ZOOM IN CLOSE WHILE MAKING SELECTIONS AND USE THE HAND TOOL TO PAN AROUND THE IMAGE

It's far easier to select the quilt edge when you can clearly see it. Zoom into a corner of the quilt to begin your work. Whenever you need to re-adjust the image within the window, hold down your keyboard Spacebar. With the Spacebar held down, whatever tool you are working with will turn into the Hand tool. While still holding the Spacebar down, use the Hand to drag (pan) the image around the document window. When the Spacebar is released, the Hand tool immediately turns into the tool you were previously working with, and you can continue on with your selection. The dance between using the Hand tool to move your document and using the selection tool to define your edge works very well.

RULE FOUR: REMAIN FLEXIBLE

The selection tools offer so many different ways to accomplish the same goal. (So do most tools, for that matter.) So don't worry about learning the right way, or get nervous when someone tells you they create a selection differently. As your skills advance, you'll discover different combinations of selections that you prefer. There are many "right ways" to create selections, and you'll know it's right by the final result.

The Selection Tools

The Marquee Tool and Selection Tool

The Marquee tool (Photoshop and Elements) or Selection tool (Paint Shop Pro) are designed to select a geometric shape. All work in a similar manner. After selecting the tool, click and drag the mouse to create the shape. Let go of the mouse when the size of your selection is complete. The resulting "marching ants" define the selected area.

PHOTOSHOP AND ELEMENTS

The **Marquee selection** tool offers two basic geometric shapes: The Rectangular Marquee and the Elliptical Marquee. Select the tool from the toolbar or press the keyboard shortcut: **M**. For our purposes, we will not be using the two Single Marquee tools (not available in Photoshop Elements).

After the selection is complete, the Marquee options bar includes a small palette for additional options.

- Click the first icon to create a New selection.
- Click the second icon to Add to the selection.
- Click the third icon to Subtract from a selection.
- Click the fourth icon to Intersect with a selection.
- Be sure the Anti-alias option is checked. For now, keep the Feather at 0. (When using the Rectangular marquee, the Anti-alias option is disabled. However, you can adjust the edge by going to Select > Refine Edge and adjust the Feather.)

The two geometric selections can be changed by holding a modifier key while making the selection:

- **Shift:** The Rectangular Marquee becomes a square, and the Elliptical Marquee (oval) becomes a circle.
- **Alt** (Win) or **Option** (Mac): Creates the selection from the center out.
- **Shift+Alt** (Win) or **Shift+Option** (Mac): Both constrains the shape to either a square or circle and creates it from the center out.

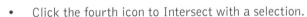

PAINT SHOP PRO

The **Selection** tool includes a marquee for geometric shapes. Select the tool from the toolbar or press the keyboard shortcut: **S**. Once the tool is selected, a Selection type drop-down menu and a Mode drop-down menu is available in the options bar. The Selection type drop-down menu includes a range of geometric shapes.

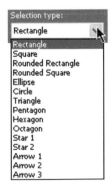

The Mode drop-down menu includes:

- Select Replace to create a New selection.
- Select Add (Shift) to Add to the selection.
- Select Remove (Ctrl) to Subtract from a selection.
- Be sure the Anti-alias option is checked. For now, keep the Feather at 0.

The Polygonal and Magnetic Lasso Tools in Photoshop and Photoshop Elements

THE POLYGONAL LASSO

The Polygonal Lasso tool (with a couple modifications) is often a very successful combination for removing a quilt from its background. The Polygonal Lasso allows you to draw along a polygonal shape however desired. I find it excellent to use for removing a quilt from its background. Here's how to use it:

1   Select the **Polygonal Lasso** tool from the toolbar.

2   Click along an edge to begin the selection. <u>Do not hold the mouse button down</u> to continue the selection. Instead, just move the mouse. As you move the mouse along the edge, click to set points along the edge. Avoid long areas between points, and add whatever points may be necessary around the corners to keep the selection of the edge accurate. If adjustment is needed along the way, use the **Backspace** (Win) or **Delete** key (Mac) to return to the last point on the line.

3   When finished, click on the first point to complete the selection. (A double-click will also complete the selection.)

THE MAGNETIC LASSO

The Magnetic Lasso is a cousin to the Polygonal Lasso tool. It is not considered a drawing selection tool, because it creates a selection based on the tonal changes in the area you drag the tool over. As a result, the one value in the options bar to be aware of is the Width value. While the default can be fine, the lower the contrast in the tonal values between the edge of the quilt and the background, the lower the Width value should be. To use it:

1   Select the **Magnetic Lasso** tool from the toolbar.

2   Click along an edge to begin the selection. Do not hold the mouse button down to continue the selection. Instead, just move the mouse along the edge of the image. As you move the mouse around the edge, the selection snaps (hence magnetic) to the edge adding points along the way.

Sometimes the tool goes a bit nutty when detecting certain tonal issues, going off the edge and adding unwanted points. When this happens, press the **Backspace** (Win) or **Delete** key (Mac) to return to the prior point. Continue in this manner as many times as needed, until you return to the point along the line you are happy with (you may need to move your cursor backwards along the selection as you delete points). Then continue. When you near the place where you started, a small circle will appear. Click into it to compete the selection. (A double-click will also complete the section.)

Which tool is better to use? I like the Polygonal Lasso better. I get far better control with it. However, others turn to the Magnetic Lasso. I included both so you can discover which works best for you.

DIGITAL ESSENTIALS: A Quilt Maker's Must-Have Guide to Images, Files, and More!

Freehand Selection Tools in Paint Shop Pro

A quick glance at the Selection tools in the Paint Shop Pro palette appears to offer three tools: a Selection, Freehand Selection, and Magic Wand. However, clicking on the Selection tool then the Freehand Selection tool brings up an options bar with additional selections. The Freehand Selection tool has two selection types that are particularly useful for quilt selection: The **Edge Seeker** and **Smart Edge**. Both are designed to hug the edge of a shape.

EDGE SEEKER

1 After selecting the Freehand Selection tool from the toolbar (under Selection tool), select **Edge Seeker** from the Selection type drop-down box in the options bar.

2 When you move your cursor into the document window, a lasso icon appears. More important is the double-cross that appears with it. It is the center horizontal portion of the cross that needs to move along the edge of the quilt. Click along an edge to begin the selection. Do not hold the mouse button down to continue the selection. Instead, just move the mouse. Move it along the edge of the shape, slowly, lining up the horizontal line of the cross along the edge of the quilt. Click to establish points that hold the selection to the shape. As you move the mouse, continue clicking to establish points. If adjustment is needed along the way, use the **Delete** key to return to the last point on the line.

3 Double-click to complete the selection.

SMART EDGE

1 After selecting the Freehand Selection tool from the toolbar (under Selection tool), select **Smart Edge** from the Selection type drop-down box in the options bar.

2 When you move you cursor into the image window, a lasso icon appears. More important is the double-cross that appears with it. It is the center horizontal portion of the cross that needs to move along the edge of the quilt. Click along an edge to begin the selection. Immediately you'll see that Smart Edges uses a selection to create a selection. The key of using this tool is that half of the selection should be on the background and half in the foreground. In other words, like the Edge Seeker, the horizontal area of the cross should be along the quilt edge. Do not hold the mouse button down to continue the selection. Instead, just move the mouse to establish the next click. Fewer clicks rather than more using this tool is often more efficient. If there is more contrast between your quilt edge and the background, try a click in each corner (as the tool does a good job at detecting the edge). Continue around the shape.

3 Double-click to complete the selection.

Other Selection Tools in Photoshop and Elements

There are other selection tools included in Photoshop and Elements that also work well for removing a quilt from its background. In Paint Shop Pro there are other methods of selection that work, but I found that Edge Seeker or Smart Edge work best for me (that's not to say you won't discover something that works best for you).

QUICK SELECTION

This tool is similar to a Magic Wand, but far more useful. To use the **Quick Selection Brush**, first select it. Then click once into the object that you want to select. Immediately it begins to make a selection based on the color and texture you click on. The more you click (or click and drag), the more the selection expands. If you select more than you intend, either select the **Subtract from Selection** brush tool from the options bar or hold the **Alt** key (Win) or **Option** key (Mac) to remove part of the selection. After the section is made, the easiest thing to do to fine tune the edges is to select the **Refine Edges** command in the toolbar options menu and use the sliders to refine.

THE REFINE EDGES COMMAND

This is not a selection tool per se, but it's a powerful tool to use after a selection. While the selection is active, a Refine Edges button appears in your options bar. (Note that the Refine Edges command is not available in the options bar when the selection was made with a Marquee tool.) However, to refine those edges, go to **Select > Refine Edges** and you'll have the same dialog box. While making the adjustments, there are buttons for viewing the image against different backgrounds. Photoshop offers a few more viewing options but both offer standard viewing—meaning you can see the marching ants—and a color overlay mode (also known as a Quick Mask mode in Photoshop). Under this viewing option, the selected area is filled with color. This shows exactly how soft or hard the selection edge is. Then, by moving the sliders, you can refine that edge.

Often the Magic Wand isn't very magical...

The Magic Wand tool works by selecting pixels whose tonal value is within a particular range. The range of tones it selects is defined by the tolerance number inserted in the options. For example, if 30 is inserted, the tool will select 30 levels of lightness and 30 levels of darkness from the click point. Shift+clicking adds 30 more levels of lightness and 30 levels of darkness from that click point. The problem is that the tool is often imprecise and therefore difficult to control, especially for novices, who can find it frustrating. Hence its nickname: The Tragic Wand. That being said, if there is a solid block of color, this tool can create a quick selection. It's also useful when making small refinements to another selection. For the most part, avoid it for isolating a quilt from its background (or a background from a quilt).

Before Final Polishing, Save your Selection

While saving the selection is certainly not necessary for a basic selection, I find it very helpful when I'm extracting a quilt. After examining the selection edges to confirm it is tightly around the edges, save the selection. Do the save before the final polishing. The selection should be of the quilt without any contracting, feathering, or being inverted. Later, if you discover there is something amiss with the edge, you can return to the original selection, load the selection, and fix it. Photoshop, Elements, and Paint Shop Pro all offer the option to save the selection. Saving works the same in all three. Here's how:

1 After your selection is complete (before final polishing) go to **Select > Save Selection**.

2 Name the selection. In this case, I named it **selection**. Because this is the first selection, "New Channel" is the default operation.

3 Click **OK**.

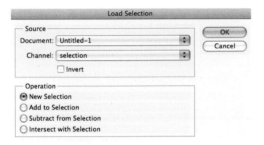

RELOADING THE SAVED SELECTION

To reload the saved selection. Simply go to **Selection > Load Selection** and the selection will return. You can also save multiple selections within one document. In that case, you would save each selection with its own name. Note that the Load Selection option is only visible if you have a selection saved with the document. Then, to return to a particular selection, go to **Selection > Load Selection**, select the named selection from the drop-down menu, and click **OK**.

Recipe for Selection Success

Examine and Refine the Edge

Refining the edge of your selection is imperative to create a polished finish to your extracted quilt. If using Photoshop or Elements, use the Polygonal Lasso tool. If using Paint Shop Pro, use the Edge Seeker tool. Here's how to refine the edge.

STEP ONE:

After you make your initial selection or load a saved selection, zoom in on your quilt edges and inspecting your selection. Use the **Hand** tool (hold down the **Spacebar**) to look for any areas of the selection that are not hugging the edge. Learn the keyboard shortcuts to add and subtract pixels. It will make things far easier.

• Hold the **Alt** key (Win) or **Command** key (Mac) with the Polygonal Lasso tool to subtract from the selection.

• Hold the **Shift** key with the Polygonal Lasso tool to add to the selection.

STEP TWO:

Examine the edges to determine where you need to add or subtract pixels from your edge. The best way I've found to do this is to first move the selection tool outside of the quilt's edge (this is just so you know where the tool is at when starting). Then hold down the appropriate modifier key (**Shift** if adding pixels, **Alt** (Win) or **Option** (Mac) if subtracting) and click directly onto the selection. Once you see the plus or minus symbol, you no longer need to hold the modifier key. Then correct the problem and double-click near the starting point to complete the selection. If you knock the selection out by mistake, remember to undo using **Ctrl+Z** (Win) or **Command+Z** (Mac). Keep the corrections small. Don't stretch the marquee into a lengthy line. Remember, the selection will not be perfectly straight. The selection should hug the edge of your quilt.

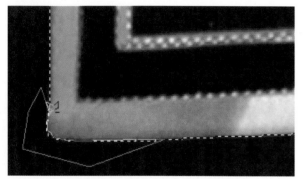

When adding to a selection, make the adjustments on the outside and double-click to complete.

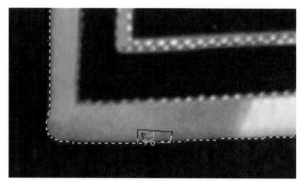

When subtracting from a selection, make the adjustments on the inside and double-click to complete.

- Be sure your snap-to functions are off. Otherwise, you may not be able to make the fine-tuned selections you desire.
- If you click into the image without first holding the modifier (Shift or Alt) key, your selection will disappear. Don't panic. I do this all the time! Immediately undo, **Ctrl+Z** (Win) or **Command+Z** (Mac).
- Do your rectangular selections have an unwanted rounded edge? Take a look at the options bar. The feather should be set to zero (0). The higher the number in this field, the more rounded the edge will be.

STEP THREE: FINAL POLISHING

After your selection is complete, the defining difference between a jagged edge selection and an edge that smoothly conforms to the edge of your quilt is to make small modifications to the edge. By contracting one pixel, the selection is very slightly pulled in. By feathering by one half of that amount, a very slight softness is added to the edge. In Paint Shop Pro, a similar softness is added by contracting one pixel and then applying a modifier to very slightly smooth. Using these modifiers brings back a very slight realistic roundness to the edge, which makes all the difference in your success.

Making Selections

Unless otherwise stated, the following tutorials for making selections will each start with the these steps:

1 Open your image.

2 Duplicate the Background layer. (In Photoshop/Elements, drag the background layer to the New Layer icon in the Layers palette. In Paint Shop Pro, right-click and select Duplicate.) Rename the copy of the background layer **Extracted Quilt**.

3 Create a new layer under Extracted Quilt and name it **White Background**. Fill it with white.

4 Turn off the visibility of the Background layer (the layer with your original quilt image) by clicking off the **Eyeball** icon.

Tip: When creating the selection, remember to zoom into the quilt to better see the edges. Hold the **Spacebar** to change the tool into the **Hand** tool and move the image within the window as needed.

Basic Selection and Background Removal of a Mounted or Framed Quilt

Some images are very easy to remove from their backgrounds. The quilt on the right is mounted on Plexiglas and photographed against a wall. Removing the background takes only a few steps because the Plexiglas has a straight flat edge that if chopped into will not create a visual problem. The same holds true of a framed quilt. If you have never selected and removed anything from a background, a great place to start is using a Geometric Shape Selection tool.

1 After completing the "Making Selections" steps above, click on the **Extracted Quilt** layer to select it.

2 Select the **Marquee** tool from the toolbar and use the Rectangle marquee.

3 Starting at the top-left corner, **click and drag to the bottom-right corner**. Release the mouse to create the selection.

4 Go to **Select > Inverse**. This inverts the selection so that rather than the foreground (in this case the quilt) being selected, the reverse (or background) is selected.

5 Click the **Backspace** (Win) or **Delete** (Mac) key. The quilt on Plexiglas now appears on a white background.

Removing a Quilt from its Background in Photoshop and Photoshop Elements

The following is one formula that works very well to create a clean, accurate edge.

1 After completing the "Making Selections" steps on page 127, select the **Polygonal Lasso** tool from the toolbar. The option toolbar settings are **Feather 0**; **Anti-alias checked**.

2 While on the **Extracted Quilt** layer, and while zoomed in, click to set a beginning point on the edge of the quilt. Move the mouse and continue on the edge, clicking points as needed. More points are generally best for accuracy, but don't go overboard. The selection line will not, and should not, be perfectly straight. Keep to the actual edge. Click at the start to complete the selection.

3 Pan around the selection to ensure it is the way it should be. If there are any sections that look off, hold the **Shift** key to add to the selection or **Alt** (Win) or **Option** (Mac) to delete from the selection. You'll know you have the right tool when a + or – symbol appears with the tools.

4 With the selection complete and active, make the following modifications that will subtly, yet very effectively, smooth the edge:

   a Go to **Select > Modify > Contract**. In the Contract Selection box insert **Contract by 1 pixel**. Click **OK**. This nudges in the selection by one single pixel.

   b Go to **Select > Feather**. In the Feather Selection box insert **Feather Radius 0.5**. Click **OK**. This nudges in the edge by one pixel, and we feathered that selection by one half of the amount.

5 Currently the selection is around the quilt. To remove the background rather than the quilt, the selection must be inverted. Go to **Select > Inverse**.

6 Click the **Backspace** (Win) or **Delete** (Mac) key to remove the background. The quilt now appears on a white background. Zooming into the quilt and inspecting the edges shows they are very clean and very true to the quilt.

Use the Polygonal Lasso tool to click around the edge of the quilt.

Smooth the selection by using the Shift and Alt keys (or Option on a Mac) to add to or subtract from the selection.

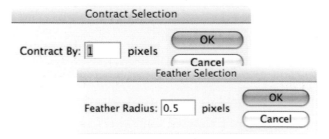

Contract the selection by 1 pixel and feather it by 0.5 pixels.

Click Select > Inverse to change the selection from the quilt, to the area surrounding the quilt. Click Delete to remove.

Click the Freehand Selection tool to display the options bar. Select either Edge Seeker or Smart Edge with the corresponding values.

In this example, I'm using Edge Seeker to make my selection. Notice how with each click the selection line hugs the edge of the quilt.

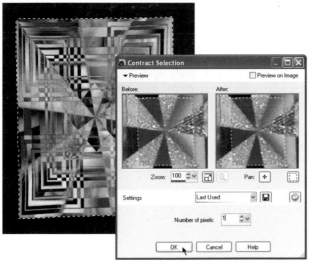

Contract Selection dialog box.

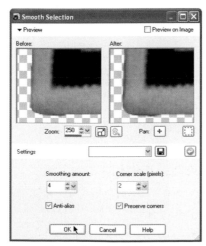

Smooth Selection dialog box.

Removing a Quilt from its Background in Paint Shop Pro

The following is one formula that works very well to create a clean, accurate edge.

1 After completing the "Making Selections" steps on page 127, select the **Freehand Selection** tool, then choose either of the **Edge Seeker** or **Smart Edge** options. The settings in the option bar are **Feather 0**; **Range 10**; **Smoothing 0**; **Anti-Alias checked**; **Use all layers unchecked**.

2 While on the **Extracted Quilt** layer, and while zoomed in, click to set a beginning point on the edge of the quilt. Move the mouse, keeping the center horizontal portion of the cross along the edge, clicking points as needed. (More points are generally best for accuracy when using the Edge Seeker, fewer when using Smart Edge.) The selection line will not, and should not, be perfectly straight. Keep to the actual edge. Double-click at the start to complete the selection.

3 Pan around the selection to ensure it is the way it should be. If there are any sections that look off, hold the **Shift** key to add to the selection or the **Alt** to delete from the selection.

4 With the selection complete and active, make the following modifications to subtly yet effectively smooth the edge:

a Go to **Selections > Modify > Contract**. In the Contract Selection box insert **1** for **Number of pixels**. Click **OK**. This nudges in the selection by one single pixel.

b Go to **Selections > Modify > Smooth**. In the Smooth Selection box use the Zoom tool to enlarge the quilt to **250%**. Put your cursor inside the After window to display the Hand tool, and move the quilt to expose a quilt edge. Check **Anti-alias** and **Preserve Corners**. Set the **Corner scale to 2**. The smoother amount may vary, but keep the number low. (Generally a 4 works well.) Use the **Hand** tool to pan the quilt around in the After window to better inspect the edges. Click **OK**.

5 Currently the selection is around the quilt. To remove the background rather than the quilt, the selection must be inverted. Go to **Selections > Invert**.

6 Click the **Delete** key to remove the background. The quilt now appears on a white background. Zooming into the quilt and inspecting the edges show they are very clean and very true to the quilt.

Click Selections > Invert to change the selection from the quilt, to the area surrounding the quilt. Click Delete to remove.

Removing a Quilt from its Background using Quick Selection and Refine Edges in Photoshop and Photoshop Elements

1 Select the **Quick Selection** tool from the toolbar.

2 One click on the quilt creates a selection based on the color and texture immediately under the click point. Click again for the selection to expand. It generally only takes a few clicks to select the entire quilt.

3 From the option bar, you can modify the selection by using the **Subtract** tool (or use **Alt** (Win) or **Option** (Mac)) to subtract from the selection or the **Add** tool (Shift) to add to it. Zoom into the document, select a small brush size, and use the modifier keys as necessary.

4 Click the **Refine Edge** button in the toolbar. The Refine Edge dialog box is also available under the Select menu.

5 In Photoshop, my Refine Edges box for quilt removal uses the same modifications of **Contract -1 percent** and **Feather 0.50 pixel**, which is used with the Polygonal and Magnetic Lasso tools.

In Elements, my Refine Edges box uses **Contract -1 percent** and **Feather 1 pixel**. Elements does not permit feathering under one pixel.

Modify the selection using the Add to Selection tool or the Subtract from Selection tool in the options bar. Click Refine Edge to clean up your selection.

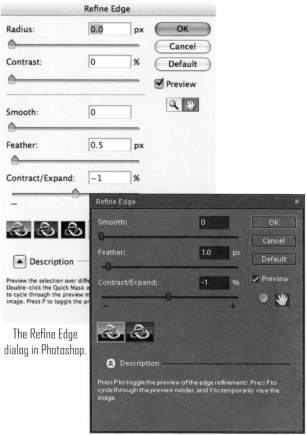

The Refine Edge dialog in Photoshop.

The Refine Edge dialog in Photoshop Elements.

Closing Words on Selections

While these techniques will successfully remove a quilt from its background, the selection methods used are only the beginning of what is possible with selections. Consider making selections to collage together various elements from different photos. For example, if you have flowers from various images that you'd like to combine, you can select a flower from one image, copy it, and paste it into another. Each item pasted into a document goes onto its own layer. That means you can use the Move tool to arrange the flower wherever it looks bests, layer order can be rearranged to overlap your flowers in a different manner, and you have all of the options that layers offer!

To experiment more with selections, Photoshop and Elements include an **Extract** tool designed for removing more complex elements than simple geometric shapes from the background. Extract in Photoshop is located at **Filter > Extract**. Extract in Elements is located under **Image > Magic Extractor**.

Photoshop, Elements, and Paint Shop Pro all have a **Background Eraser** tool that's also fun to try out. Additionally, with each new version of software, selection and extraction tools will continue to evolve, allowing you to become extremely precise. When experimenting with these tools, keep in mind that you are removing pixels from the image. Thus, work on a copy of your image rather than the original.

As you can see, there are many methods for selecting and extracting elements from an image, with some methods working better than others depending on what it is you are selecting. If at some point you find yourself wanting to make more complex selections, do an Internet search on **quick mask**, the **Pen tool**, **masks**, and **channels**. This is yet another example of how there is more than one way to do things in image-editing programs with no one way being the only way.

chapter

preparing images for digital show entry

"Digital submissions accepted." When you read this in a quilt show entry form does it make you smile with relief, or groan in despair? If it's the latter, read through this chapter to understand the concepts. Then give it a try. Submitting digital images of your quilts is easier than you may think.

The Quick and Easy Way to Resize Images for Digital Show Entry

For this method, **you must start with an image that is larger than the size requested by the show**. Otherwise, if your image is smaller and you resample it to make it larger, you run the risk of degrading it.

Example Show #1

Quilt Show #1 is asking for a standard (or "baseline") JPEG image that measures 1800 pixels (which at 300 dpi would print at 6 inches) on the long side **OR** 1200 pixels (which at 300 dpi would print at 4) on the short side.

*Please note: Some show organizers will ask for a digital image that will be used for multiple output; for example, to first view on a monitor and to later use for print. In that case, the image should simply be requested in a pixel dimension; however, it's still common that the image is requested in dpi and print dimension. The reasons are defined in Chapter 4 "Resolution—It's the Pixels" (page 21). For purposes of this chapter, I'm including both the pixel measurement and a 300 dpi equivalent for print.

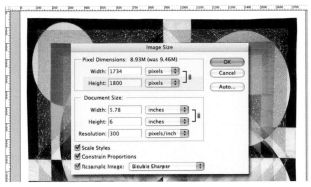

Change the larger pixel dimension, in this case the Height, to 1800 with Constrain Proportions checked. Notice the Height in the Document Size. This proves that 1800 pixels at 300 dpi is 6 inches when printed.

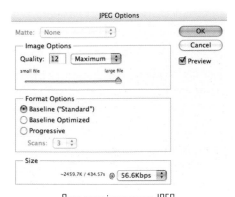

Save your image as a JPEG.

PHOTOSHOP AND PHOTOSHOP ELEMENTS

1   Open your quilt image (**File > Open**).

2   Go to **Image > Image Size** (In Elements go to Image > Resize > Image Size) to open the Image Size dialog box. Look for the larger of the two pixel dimensions.

3   Change the larger pixel dimension to **1800**. Notice how the height of the document size (the print size) is 6 inches at 300 dpi. Check **Constrain Proportions** so that the image correctly resizes in proportion. Click **OK**.

4   To save the image, go to **File > Save As**. Select **JPEG**, give your document a new name (based on whatever naming convention is asked for). Select the **Maximum Quality**, and check **Baseline**. Click **OK**.

> **Note:** In the Format Options, there are three choices: Baseline ("Standard"), Baseline Optimized, and Progressive. Selecting Baseline as this setting gives the most reliable results. Baseline Optimized produces a smaller file but possibly at the cost of not working on older browsers, and Progressive first displays a blurry image then builds up the picture as the image downloads. In other words, you see so much of the image on the first pass, more of the image on the second pass, and so on.

PAINT SHOP PRO

1 Open your quilt image (**File > Open**).

2 Go to **Image > Resize** to open the Image Resize dialog box. Select **Pixels** from the drop-down menu in the Pixel Dimensions box. Change the pixel Height to **1800** pixels. Check the **Lock Aspect Ratio** box. Click **OK**. Note: You can use **Smart Size** or **Bilinear** as your resampling option. Click **OK**

3 **File > Export > JPEG Optimizer**.

4 Under Quality, insert a value of **one (1)**. This gives you the maximum quality.

5 Under Format, select **Standard**.

6 Click **OK**, and give your document a new name (based on whatever naming convention is asked for).

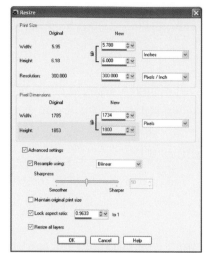

Change the larger pixel dimension, in this case the Height, to 1800 with Lock Aspect Ratio checked. Notice the Height in the Print Size. This proves that 1800 pixels at 300 dpi is 6 inches when printed.

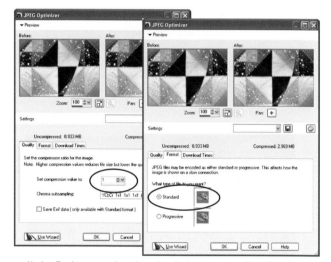

Under Quality, enter 1 as the value. Under Format, select Standard.

Resizing an Image to Fit Within a Requested Document Size

Some shows ask for an image of a particular size. While you may be able to resize to one dimension, resizing to the second dimension may not work as smoothly as you'd like—depending on the shape of your quilt. In that case, another way to create your document is to start with a document in the requested size and then scale your image to fit inside of it. As with the quick and easy way, **you must start with an image larger than the requested document size**.

Example Show #2

Quilt Show #2 is asking for a standard (or "baseline") JPEG that is 1800 x 1200 pixels (at 300 dpi, this would print at 6 x 4 inches).

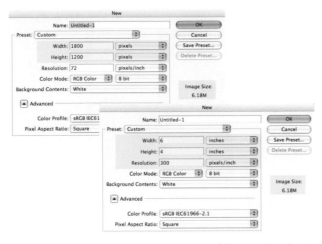

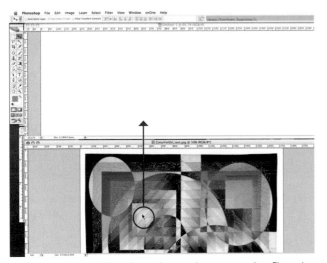

Enter either 1800 x 1200 pixels or 6 x 4 inches at 300 pixels/inch for the dimensions of your new document.

Click, hold and drag the quilt into the new document window. The quilt will look very large in this window.

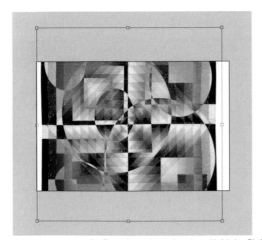

Zoom out so you can see the Transform bounding box. Hold the Shift key down while dragging one of the corner handles in towards the center of the quilt. The Shift key constrains the proportions of your image.

PHOTOSHOP AND PHOTOSHOP ELEMENTS

1 Open a new document by going to **File > New** (in Elements go to File > New > Blank File).

2 In the dialog box, you can either set it up as **1800 x 1200 pixels**. OR, you can select **Inches** from the drop-down menu, and insert **6** inches by **4** inches at a resolution of **300 pixels/inch**. Note that both options are exactly the same 6.18M file size. Click **OK**.

3 A new document will open in the exact dimensions Quilt Show #2 specified.

4 Open your quilt image (**File > Open**).

5 To see both documents and work with them more easily, go to **Window > Arrange > Tile Horizontally**. (You can also arrange them vertically if you prefer.) Both documents are now open horizontally next to each other. (In Photoshop Elements, select Window > Images > Tile. This tiles the images horizontally.)

6 Using the **Move** tool, click into your quilt image, <u>drag it into your new blank document</u>, and release the mouse. Close your original quilt image to focus on your new image. You'll notice that your image is too large to fit into the requested document size.

7 Select the **Zoom** tool. By holding down the **Alt** key (Win) or **Option** key (Mac) the Zoom tool will zoom out rather than in. Click to zoom out until you can see the edges of your document.

8 Go to **Edit > Transform > Scale**. In Elements go to **Image > Transform > Free Transform**. A bounding box will appear around your document, showing you the edges of the image.

9 Grab a corner handle, <u>hold down your keyboard **Shift** key</u>, and drag towards the center of the document until the image fits within the document. If you need to move the document to place it, just release the **Shift** key and move off of a corner handle to the interior of the image, then move the image into the center area.

If you made the image too small, you can also hold down the **Shift** key and drag a corner handle away from the center to better fill the space. When you are satisfied with the placement, press the **Enter** key (Win) or **Return** key (Mac).

10 The image will resize to fit the document. If you are unhappy with what you did, go to **Edit > Undo** and try again.

A quick look at the Image Size dialog box (Image > Image Size in Photoshop or Image > Resize > Image Size in Elements) shows that your image now fits exactly within the requested image size specification. Follow the previous instructions to save your image as a JPEG.

If your image has a large background, first crop the image as close to the edges as possible without clipping the image itself. Then drag that image into your new document.

PAINT SHOP PRO

1 Open a new document by going to **File > New**.

2 In the New Image dialog box, you can either set it up as **1800 x 1200 pixels**. Or, select **Inches** from the drop-down menu and insert **6** inches by **4** inches at a resolution of **300 pixels/inch**. Click **OK**.

3 A new document will open in the exact dimensions Quilt Show #2 specified.

4 Open your quilt image (**File > Open**).

5 To see both documents and work with them more easily, go to **Window > Tile Horizontally**. (You can also arrange them vertically if you prefer.) Both documents are now open horizontally next to each other.

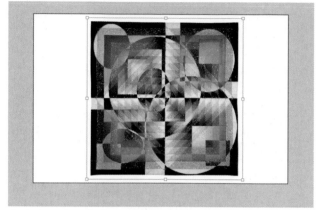

Scale the quilt until it fits inside the new document window. Press Enter (Win) or Return (Mac) when finished.

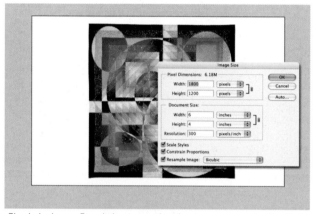

Check the Image Size dialog to see that the sizes are exactly what Quilt Show #2 requested.

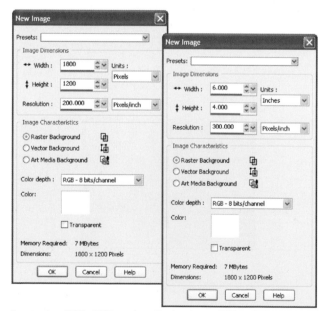

Enter either 1800 x 1200 pixels or 6 x 4 inches at 300 pixels/inch for the dimensions of your new document.

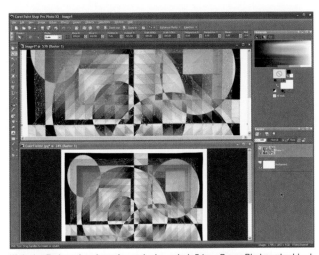

With the Pick tool, select the quilt then click Edit > Copy. Click in the blank new window, then choose Edit > Paste as New Layer. Your quilt is now in the new document. The quilt will look very large in this window.

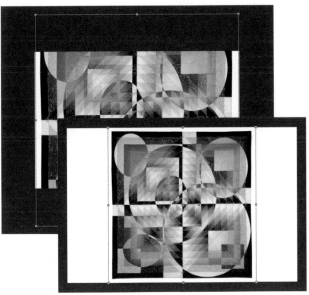

Use the Pick tool to scale the quilt to fit inside the new window.

6 Click the **Pick** tool, then select the document with your quilt image. Go to **Edit > Copy** to make a copy of your quilt image.

7 Click into your new document to make it the active window. Go to **Edit > Paste as New Layer**.

8 Close your original quilt image to focus on your new image. You'll notice that your image is too large to fit into the requested size.

9 In the toolbar select the **Zoom** tool. (If the Zoom tool is not visible, click the arrow next to the Pan tool to display the fly-out. Then click to select the Zoom tool.) Right-click on the image to zoom out until you can see the edges of your document.

10 In the toolbar, select the **Pick** tool. Grab a corner handle and drag towards the center to proportionally decrease the size of the image.

11 You may need to nudge the image to center it. To do so, move from the corner handle to the interior of the image. The icon will turn into a four-way arrow. Then drag the image into place. When you are satisfied with the placement, click on another tool to release the transformation. If you are unhappy with what you did, you can undo by going to **Edit > Undo** and try again.

A quick look at the Resize dialog box (Image > Resize) shows that your image now fits exactly within the requested image size specification. Follow the previous instructions to save your image as a JPEG.

Question for the expert

Q: How can I make sure that my Web image, the image I submit to a jury, looks like what I see on my monitor?

A: You can't control the monitor setup they'll use to view your image. What you can control is the color space. Using the **sRGB space** will lessen the number of colors available, but allow a wider audience to see the image as you intend.

In Photoshop, to use the sRGB color space, go to **Edit > Convert to Profile** and select **sRGB**. Then check what Proof Setup view you're in: **View > Proof Setup > and select Monitor RGB**. (Go to **Image > Convert Color Profile** in Elements. Go to **File > Color Management** in Paint Shop Pro.) That will give you a close approximation of what your image will look like on the average monitor and for projection purposes. You can then make your adjustments as needed. Do a **Save for Web** to optimize the image and embed the sRGB profile with the image. **Very important:** Use Adobe RGB for your own print purposes. If you are submitting an image for print, ask what color space you should use.

and, in the end...keep the focus and sharpen

Almost all images can benefit from a bit of sharpening. Sharpening an image helps emphasize detail and texture that often gets blurred when a digital image is captured and adjusted.

Sharpening is all about increasing the contrast of a pixel's edge. When done right, sharpening an image makes it look better. But over-sharpening can ruin an image—making awful-looking halos and nasty sharpening artifacts. A "halo" is created when the contrast of a pixel's edge is sharpened so much that an inverse of the pixel color is created along its edge.

Sharpening Using Unsharp Mask

Image without any sharpening.
This looks okay, but the individual quilting stitches could be better.

Image with sharpening.
Now I can see each stitch clearly.

Image with over-sharpening.
Too much! Now I can see white "halos" all over my image.

Important:
- If your image is out of focus, sharpening will not fix it.
- Sharpening your image should be the **last step** before the final save.

As with all digital options, many methods and tools can get the job done—everything from Auto-Sharpen (which I'm not keen on because of its lack of control), to Smart Sharpen (which is excellent). I'm going to focus here only on the currently most common method of sharpening—the **"Unsharp" Mask**. You'll find this tool in Photoshop, Elements and Paint Shop Pro. In all three it gives a good range of options and excellent results.

Question for the expert

Q: Why is it called an "Unsharp" Mask if the image is getting sharpened?

A: The name sure does seem counter-intuitive. Its origins come from the conventional photo darkroom method, which the digital method mirrors: First the image is blurred a bit. Then that blur is subtracted from the original to detect the presence of edges. The controls within an Unsharp Mask then allow you to selectively increase those edges, or "sharpen" them. Easier answer: It comes from a conventional darkroom technique.

After Unsharp Mask is selected, its dialog box opens with three slider controls. These define how much sharpening an image will receive. But the control names are not helpful clues in determining how much these sliders should be moved.

Understanding the Unsharp Mask Dialog Box

PHOTOSHOP AND PHOTOSHOP ELEMENTS

- **Amount:** This changes the amount of sharpening.
  The setting is like a volume control; the higher the number, the brighter the edges of the pixel will become, and the more pronounced the effect.

  > Too low = no change
  > Too high = produces unwanted halos
  > 50%-150% is generally a good range

- **Radius:** Once the edge is defined, radius sets the strength or thickness of the sharpened edge.

  > Lower numbers = keep edges crisp
  > Higher numbers = mean thicker edges, adding more contrast (and halos)
  > 0.05 – 2.0 is generally a good range

- **Threshold:** This sets how far apart the tonal value of a pixel and its neighbor must be in order to get any sharpening.

  > The lower the number = the higher the sharpening
  > If the number is too high = nothing happens
  > Most images start very low, like 1 or even 0

PAINT SHOP PRO

- **Radius** = "Amount" in Photoshop/Elements
- **Strength** = "Radius" in Photoshop/Elements
- **Clipping** = "Threshold" in Photoshop/Elements

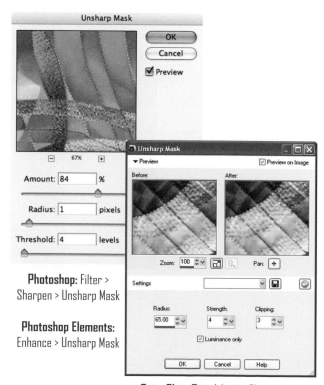

Photoshop: Filter > Sharpen > Unsharp Mask

Photoshop Elements: Enhance > Unsharp Mask

Paint Shop Pro: Adjust > Sharpness > Unsharp Mask

Sharpening Guidelines

Now that you understand how those sliders can sharpen, I'll give you guidelines for using them.

- **Sharpen last**. Sharpening should only be applied after the photo has been straightened, the image resized for its final destination, and any minor tonal value or color corrections are made.

- When sharpening, **always view your image at 100%**. It's hard to see if you've gone too far if you are zoomed out from your image.

- Duplicate your image layer. Name it: **Sharpened layer**. Not only can you return to the original if there is a problem (over-sharpening does rear its ugly head), but you can change the opacity level on the duplicated layer, meaning you can soften the sharpening effect, and you can change the blend mode, if desired.

- A general formula that works nicely for a broad range of images is:

Photoshop/Elements:	**Paint Shop Pro:**
Amount: 85	Radius: 85
Radius: 1	Strength: 1
Threshold: 4	Clipping: 4

  If more sharpening is needed, repeat the same formula a second time. If necessary, repeat it a third time. Don't be tempted to double the numbers, thinking you can get the same effect in one pass. It's much better to do the sharpening in small increments. Also, if one pass isn't enough, and two passes are too much, change the opacity of the layer.

- **To avoid color halos, apply your sharpening using the Luminance mode**. Photoshop and Elements users, follow the directions on the next page. Paint Shop Pro users, check the Luminance only box in the Unsharp Mask dialog box. But watch your 100% Preview box. Avoiding color halos doesn't prevent other uglies that come from over-sharpening.

Sharpen Like a Pro

A Formula for Sharpening Quilt Images Using the Luminance Blend Mode

Anything done on the "Luminance" blend mode only affects the luminosity, or the lightness/darkness, in underlying layers. Some pros only sharpen in this blend mode (others use LAB, and you know who you are) because it's a great way to prevent those nasty color halos while nicely sharpening your image.

To sharpen in the Luminance mode, Paint Shop Pro users only need to check the **Luminance only** box in the Unsharp Mask dialog box.

Photoshop and Photoshop Elements users need to change the blend mode. Here's how:

1 Open your image, duplicate the layer, and display the image at 100%. One way of doing this is go to **View > Actual Pixels** (Elements users should be in the Full Edit mode).

2 (Paint Shop Pro Users: skip this step) In the duplicated layer, change the blend mode from Normal to Luminosity. The blend modes are located in the top-left of the Layers palette. The default is set to Normal. Click the drop-down menu, scroll to the bottom, and select **Luminosity**.

3 Select Unsharp Mask:

- In Photoshop, go to **Filter > Sharpen > Unsharp Mask**.
- In Photoshop Elements, go to **Enhance > Unsharp Mask**.
- In Paint Shop Pro, go to **Adjust > Sharpness > Unsharp Mask**.

4a In **Photoshop** and **Elements**, use these settings:

Amount: **85**

Radius: **1**

Threshold: **4**

Click **OK**.

Be sure to look at the image in the preview box at 100%. To apply more sharpening, repeat steps 3 and 4a. For even more sharpening, repeat a third time. Adjust the opacity of the layer if necessary. **Save** your image.

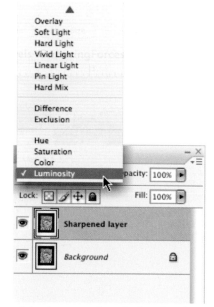

Select Luminosity from the drop-down list.

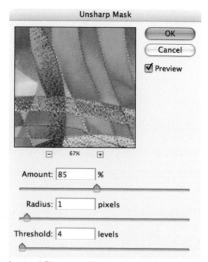

Photoshop and Elements: Change the settings then click OK.

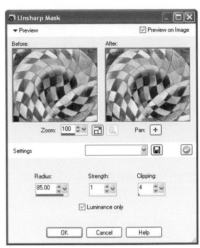

Paint Shop Pro: Change the settings then click OK.

4b In **Paint Shop Pro**, use these settings:

Radius: **85**

Strength: **1**

Clipping: **4**

Check the **Luminance only** box.

Check the **Preview on Image** box, and keep an eye on the After preview.

Click **OK**.

To apply more sharpening, repeat steps 3 and 4b. For even more sharpening, repeat a third time if necessary. Adjust the opacity of the layer as necessary. **Save** your image.

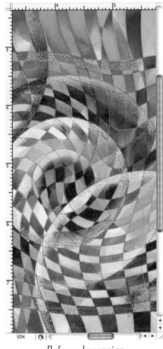

Before sharpening

After sharpening

Alternate Values for Sharpening Slightly Out of Focus Quilts

This set of values is helpful if your quilt is a bit out of focus. It gives more sharpening. It also can look good with any quilt image, but the opacity generally needs to be lowered.

In Photoshop/Elements

Amount: 65

Radius: 4

Threshold: 3

In Paint Shop Pro

Radius: 65

Strength: 4

Clipping: 3

Discovering Your Unique Balance of Sharpness

Now that you understand how the sliders affect image sharpness, and have experimented with the settings, you may want to try some settings for different types of images. We'll start by totally overdoing it. Then move sliders to discover what works. Here's how:

1 Start by opening your image, duplicating the layer, and displaying the image at 100%.

2 (Paint Shop Pro users, skip this step.) Change the blend mode to **Luminosity**.

3 Select Unsharp Mask:

   • In Photoshop, go to **Filter > Sharpen > Unsharp Mask**.

   • In Photoshop Elements, go to **Enhance > Unsharp Mask**.

   • In Paint Shop Pro, go to **Adjust > Sharpness > Unsharp Mask**.

4 Select the first slider and set it high—in the **250%-350%** range.

5 Gradually move the middle slider **from a low setting of 0.5 to a higher value**. Keep your eye on the 100% preview. Chances are you won't get higher than 5.

6 When the first and second sliders are in balance, move to the third slider. **Start at 0 and very slowly increase its value**.

7 Once you come up with your unique balance of sharpness, note the numbers and click **OK**.

8 **Save** the file.

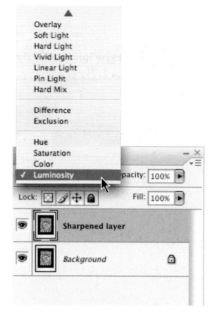

Select Luminosity from the drop-down list.

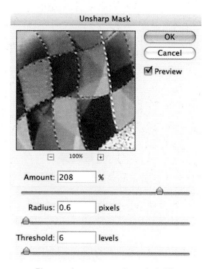

Change the settings then click OK.

Sharpen in Action

Soon you'll find yourself in the habit of sharpening your images on a regular basis. To save time, consider making an action for this task. Visit Chapter 16 "Batch Processing Images for the Web" on page 167, and follow the directions for creating an action. If you're feeling adventurous, you can create a sharpening action in IrfanView for the PC and GraphicConverter for the Mac.

Saving for the Web

saving photographs for the web

When it comes to viewing images on the Web, two things matter most to your viewers: image quality and download speed. Although you may have a high-speed connection, you cannot assume that everyone else does. While the number of high-speed connections is certainly growing, there remains a large group of Internet users that are still on dial-up.

While all image-editing programs allow you to resize/resample your image as described in Chapter 6, some programs optimize your image specifically for a Web site. This gives you more control over balancing image quality with file size.

It is common to start with a high-resolution image to create a lower-resolution image for a Web site. To fit an average monitor resolution, a large image should be downsampled in the range of 425 pixels to 500 pixels in width depending on the design of the site. (This pixel width dimension is sure to grow in the future, as higher resolution monitors become the norm.)

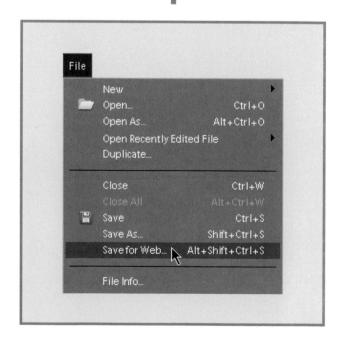

Using the Save for Web Feature in Photoshop and Photoshop Elements

With your image open, go to **File > Save for Web** (or File > Save for Web & Devices, depending on which version of Photoshop/Elements you are using).

In the Save for Web (or Save for Web & Devices) window, the image will display at 100%. In our example, immediately it's clear that the image is far too large for a Web site. The bottom-left corner indicates that the JPEG is 911.4k in size and could take as long as 325 seconds to load on a slow speed connection. However, this is easy to correct.

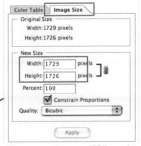

The original size is 1729 pixels wide which is way too large to display on the average monitor.

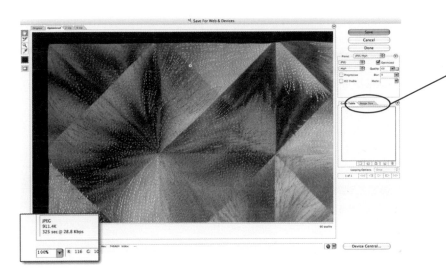

Click the **Image Size** tab on the right side of the Preview box. The Image Size box contains only the information needed for a Web image—that is, the resolution size of the document in pixels. This document shows the image is 1729 pixels in width.

Change the size to 450 pixels using Bicubic Sharper.

To change the size of the image, enter a number for the width (I used 450 pixels). With the **Constrain Proportions** box checked, the program will calculate the correct height. (You can also do this by entering a number for the height, and the program will calculate the correct width.) Since the image is going from larger to smaller, in Photoshop you can select the **Bicubic Sharper** option in the Quality window. Then click the **Apply** button, and the image will adjust in size.

> **Note:** In Elements the Bicubic Sharper option is not available here. However, you can first resize the image to 450 pixels using the Bicubic Sharper option by going to **Image > Resize > Image Size** and then select the **Save for Web** option to optimize the image.

The resized image displays in the Preview window.

1 The Image Size box displays the original size of the document and the new size underneath. The new pixel size is now appropriate for a Web browser, and the file size is 76.8k, meaning it will load far faster.

2 The file format and quality settings are set in the area above the Image Size box. **Generally, use the JPEG setting for photographs**. There are various quality settings in the presets drop-down menu that range from maximum to low. The highest quality JPEG will look the best. However, it also produces the largest file size meaning it will take the longest time to download. The lowest quality JPEG will create the smallest file size and will be the fastest to download. **The trick is finding the right balance between quality and file size**.

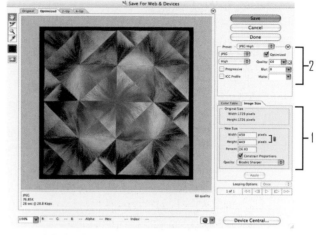

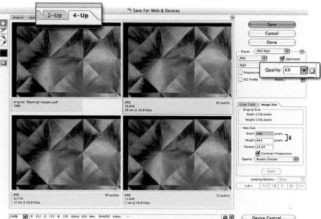

In Photoshop, using the **2-Up** tab or **4-Up** tab, you can visually compare one quality against another and see the physical file size. In this case, the original file size is displayed in the upper-left. Three additional versions of the document are displayed with differing quality settings. Besides the quality settings, you also have the option of typing a value into the quality box located on the right of the document window. In Elements, the original image displays in the left and a preview of the optimized image displays on the right.

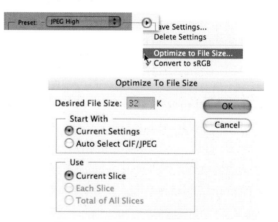

The preview shows the original file in the upper-left corner, as well as three other quality options to choose from.

Usually you'll be making the final file size decision. But sometimes you are asked to provide an image of a specific size. In that case, click the arrow to the right of the Presets menu to bring up the **Optimize** menu. Select **Optimize to File Size**. Type in the file size. The image will automatically resize.

Set a specific file size using the Optimize menu.

Question for the expert

Q: What are presets?

A: Presets are a group of choices made for you. There are several JPEG presets included in the Save for Web dialog box (there are presets for other Web formats too, such as GIF images). You can access them on the top-right drop-down menu. Each provides a defined set of options that can work as a good starting point.

File > Export > JPEG Optimizer

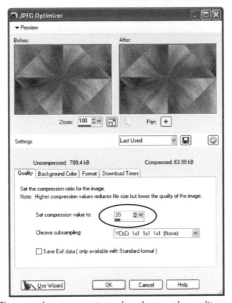

View > Toolbars > Web. Click the JPEG button.

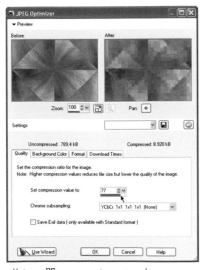

Changing the compression value changes the quality and download time of the image.

Using Paint Shop Pro JPEG Optimizer

With your image open, go to **File > Export > JPEG Optimizer**. Or open the Web toolbar by clicking **View > Toolbars > Web**. This will bring up a small palette with options for JPEG, GIF, and PNG optimizers. Click the **JPEG** option on the left.

In the JPEG Optimizer dialog box, you can visually compare one quality against another.

You can use the up or down arrows (or click directly into the slider bar under value window) to change the **Set Compression Value**. The more compression, the lower the quality of the image and the faster the download time.

Since the pixel dimensions of your image are not displayed in the JPEG Optimizer box, be sure to first check the dimensions of your image before optimizing. To do so, go to **Image > Resize**. If the pixel dimension is over 500 pixels in width, downsample the image. See Chapter 6 "Resizing and Resampling Images" (page 52) for more information.

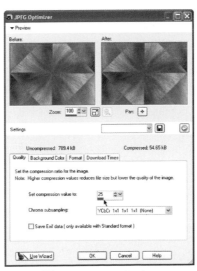

Using a 77 compression rate value creates an unacceptable image quality.

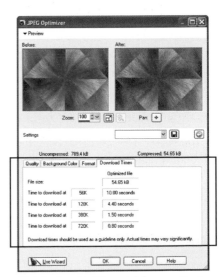

Using a 25 compression rate value creates an acceptable image quality.

Click the Download Times tab for an estimate of how long the file will take to display.

Another way to optimize your JPEG is by clicking the **Use Wizard** button on the lower-left of the dialog box.

By moving the slider up or down, you can balance the quality of the image against its size.

Moving the slider all the way down to the smallest image will give the lowest quality. To see the results of this setting, click the **Next** button two times (leave the Chroma subsampling set as is to None). The result of the selected setting will appear. In this case, it's far too pixelated. Click the **Back** button two times to return to the slide setting.

Sliding the scale to about **75%** of best quality, click **Next** two times, and view the results. In this case, the quality looks good and the file size is small.

> **Note:** You can use the up or down arrows to zoom in and out on your image. Or use the slider bar below the zoom value box. However, it's important to view at 100% so you can see exactly how it will appear.

Click the **Finish** button. You may now save your image.

Note that a "Save Copy As" dialog box comes up rather than a Save As box. Paint Shop Pro is saving a copy of the original file. It also defaults to the JPEG file type. Select a location for your file, a name, and click Save.

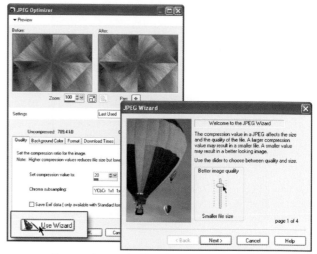

You can also use the Wizard to optimize your JPEG.

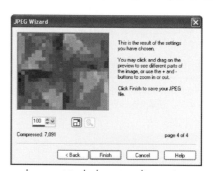

Image set to the lowest quality setting.

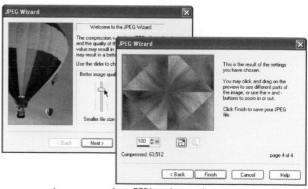

Image set to about 75% quality produces a good quality image with a small file size.

chapter ---- ⑮

working with the gif format

Not all Web images are JPEG files. In creating Web graphics, the GIF file format is also popular. Preference for one format rather than another depends on the image (just like preferring a rotary cutter over scissors depends on what you're cutting out.)

JPEG: If the image contains continuous tones, such as a photograph, JPEG wins. It supports millions of colors.

GIF: If it's line art such as a logo, or a quilt block colored in solids, then GIF is the best choice. It supports 8-bit or 256 colors—enough for lines and solids.

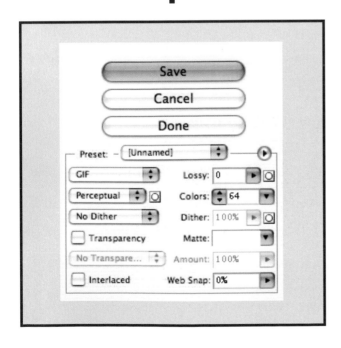

Saving and Optimizing Color Designs for the Web

Simply changing the JPEG format to the GIF format, without using any other optimization, dramatically decreases the file size. In the image below, the block on the left is a JPEG with a file size of 218k. The block on the right is the same block, in the GIF format, at 26.56k in size. By making a few more choices to optimize the GIF, the file size can be even smaller.

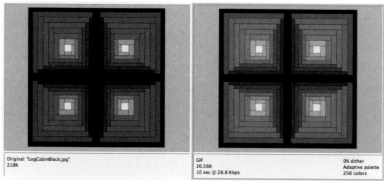

JPEG format at 218k.   GIF format at 26.56k.

Questions for the expert

Q: Since a JPEG supports millions of colors, then why not simply create all images as JPEGs?

A: The answer is download speed. If you save the same image twice (once as a GIF and once as a JPEG), the GIF file will often be far smaller, and therefore faster to appear on a site. So using JPEGs when you should be using GIFs will slow your site down—often considerably so. And nothing annoys a viewer more than waiting for a site page to appear (and this is despite today's high speed connections).

Q: Are there any other advantages to GIF?

A: A GIF can also support transparency and animation, something a JPEG cannot do.

If the image is being used several times on a Web page—for example, as a navigation button—the page's download time can be substantially affected by the image's file format.

So while you can save the image as a JPEG, and the color fidelity in some instances can be better, it comes at the price of a much higher file size. It all comes back to finding the right balance between image quality and file size to meet your needs.

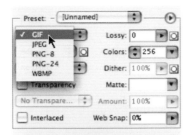

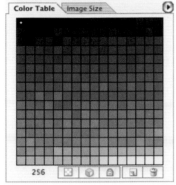

Select GIF from the presets and choose 256 colors. In Photoshop, the Color Table will display all 256 possible colors in the image. In Elements, while there is no Color Table, you can reduce the number of colors in the GIF image from 256 down.

Lower the number of colors to reduce the file size of your image.

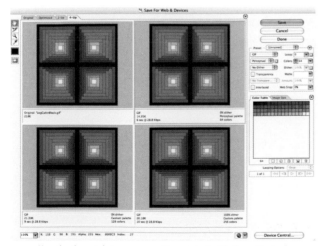

Use the 4-up tab to compare the original with the optimized versions of your image.

Saving and Optimizing in Photoshop and Photoshop Elements

Saving Your Artwork as a GIF—Quick and Easy

Open the file you want to save as a GIF. Then:

1 Go to **File > Save for Web**.

2 Select **GIF** from the drop-down menu located under the Preset menu. Select **256 colors**, which is the maximum number of colors that a GIF can display.

3 Click the **Save** button and name your file.

Optimizing a GIF

Open the file you want to optimize. Then:

1 Go to **File > Save for Web**.

2 Currently the colors are set to 256. The color table displays the full range of the 256 colors that make up the image.

3 Lowering the number of colors will remove unused colors from the 256 and decrease the file size. To change the number of colors, select a number from the drop-down menu, use the up/down arrows to increase or decrease the number of colors, or simply type in a new number.

> **Note:** The trick is continuing to lower the number of colors until there is an unacceptable quality difference.

4 When using the **4-up** tab in Photoshop, you can compare the original quality GIF with other optimized versions to see the difference between them. In Elements you can compare the original to the optimized image. Reducing the colors the file to 128 creates a 21.39k file, and to 64 colors reduces it further to 14.35k.

5 Under the GIF selection, you'll see a drop-down menu offering various color choices. The only ones primarily used are **Perceptual**, **Selective**, and **Adaptive**. Some images look better with one setting over another. If you don't see any difference, just stick with Perceptual. Once you are satisfied with your image, click **Save**.

Questions for the expert

Q: Do I need to work in the Index color mode when creating a GIF?

A: No. Stick with RGB. The Index color mode can only display 256 colors—216 of which can be displayed on an 8-bit monitor. The term "Web safe" comes from this palette of 216 colors, because anyone with an 8-bit monitor is able to see them. Today's monitors are 24-bit, meaning they can display 16.8 million colors. With that in mind, work in RGB. Then let the Save for Web dialog box handle the color management. (It will look at all the RGB colors, and choose the best ones to match to the 216 in the Web palette, and handle the conversion for you.)

Q: What is dither?

A: Dithering is a method of combining the pixels of two colors to give the illusion of a third color. Photoshop/Elements offers different types of dithering and a sliding scale to indicate the amount of dithering you can apply to the image. The best thing is to experiment with the settings to see how they affect your image. Remember to view the image at 100%.

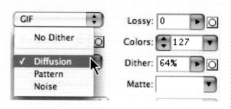

Q: What is lossy?

A: Lossy means that you will lose some information in the file compression process. JPEGs use lossy compression. GIFs use a "lossless" compression, meaning no information is lost in the compression process. However, you can apply some lossy compression to further reduce a GIF file size. Unless you want to experiment further, you can leave the lossy setting in the preset section to the default setting of zero.

Locking Colors When Optimizing in Photoshop

If your image has certain colors that you want to remain no matter how many other colors are removed, you can "lock" those colors. For example, perhaps your logo uses four very distinct colors. If you are using Photoshop (the feature is not currently in Elements or Paint Shop Pro), such colors can be "locked" in your color palette so that they can't be removed. To lock a color:

1 Select the **Eyedropper** tool on the left side of the Save for Web & Devices dialog box.

2 Click on the color in your image that you want to lock. In this case, I selected the yellow interior box. Once you click, a square will surround the color within the color table.

3 Click the **Lock** icon on the bottom-center of the color table.

4 This will put a small lock on the bottom-right of that color indicating that it cannot be removed when further reducing colors.

Now, no matter how many colors I remove, the yellow color that was locked remains.

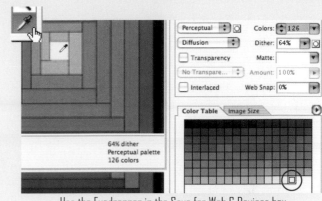

Use the Eyedropper in the Save for Web & Devices box to select the color you want to lock.

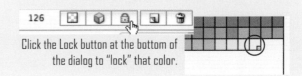

Click the Lock button at the bottom of the dialog to "lock" that color.

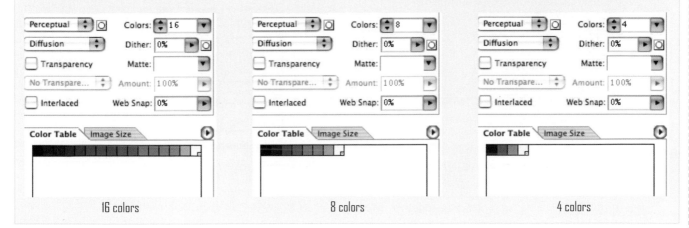

16 colors   8 colors   4 colors

Saving and Optimizing in Paint Shop Pro

Saving Your Artwork as a GIF—Quick and Easy

Open the file you want to save as a GIF. Then:

1   Go to **File > Export > GIF Optimizer**. (Or open the Web toolbar by clicking **View > Toolbars > Web**.) This will bring up a small palette with options for JPEG, GIF, and PNG optimizers. Click the **GIF** option on the left.

2   Click the **Colors** tab on the GIF Optimizer dialog. The palette defaults to 256 colors. Ignore the Standard/Web Safe option and take a look at both the **Optimized Median Cut** and **Optimized Octree**. Some images can show an improvement with one over the other, although for most images this will be small. Keep it at the default **Optimized Octree** unless the other setting looks better. Keep dithering to **0**. Comparing the before and after images, there is a file reduction from 223.3k to 23k.

3   Click **OK** and save your image.

Question for the expert

Q: Why ignore the Web Safe color option?

A: For the same reason that you don't generally need to work in the Index color mode. Start in RGB and let the software calculate your options. In this case, you can compare the Optimized Median Cut to the Optimized Octree. The software put together two different combinations of its 16.8 million colors to match those in the 216 color palette.

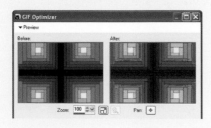

File > Export > GIF Optimizer

View > Toolbars > Web. Click the GIF button.

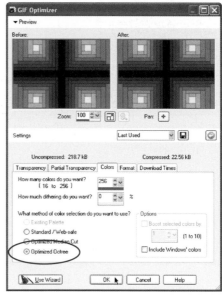

On the Colors tab, leave Optimized Octree selected.

File > Export > GIF Optimizer

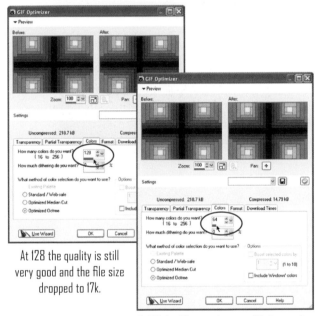

View > Toolbars > Web. Click the GIF button.

At 128 the quality is still very good and the file size dropped to 17k.

At 64 the file size drops to 15k, but quality begins to deteriorate.

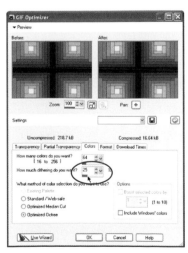

At 64 colors with 25% dithering, I get a better image but an increased file size of 16.8k.

Optimizing a GIF

Open the file you want to optimize. Then:

1. Go to **File > Export > GIF Optimizer**. (Or open the Web toolbar by clicking **View > Toolbars > Web**.) This will bring up a small palette with options for JPEG, GIF, and PNG optimizers. Click the **GIF** option on the left.

2. In the dialog, there are five tab options: Transparency, Partial Transparency, Colors, Format, and Download Times. In this image, there is no area that needs to be transparent or partially transparent, so we'll skip those. That brings us to the Colors tab.

3. Under "How many colors do you want?" either type in a number lower than 256 or use the slider to reduce (or increase) the colors. Currently the colors are set to 256. Continuing to half that number is a good place to start. In other words 128, 64, 32, 16, 8, 4, and 2.

   Continue comparing the quality of the before and after. And click back and forth between Optimized Median Cut and Optimized Octree to see if one looks better than the other. Be sure to view your image at 100%.

4. Dithering gives the illusion of more colors by combining neighboring colors. By increasing the dithering, you can improve the quality of the image. Depending on how much dithering you add, you'll also increase the file size.

   Again, it comes back to finding a balance between file size and image quality. In many instances, simply reducing the colors to 128 works fine.

5 The **Format** tab allows you to choose between interlaced and non-interlaced. **Interlaced** loads the entire image, from top to bottom, in one pass. **Non-interlaced** loads the image in lines from top to bottom, top to bottom, top to bottom, until the image has completely loaded.

Because of the small file size, I always select non-interlaced. There is also a Version 87a and 89a, with the first not supporting transparency and the second supporting it. My image has no transparent areas so I select Version 87a.

6 The **Download Times** tab tells you approximately how long the image will take to download.

7 Once you are satisfied with your image, click **OK** and save.

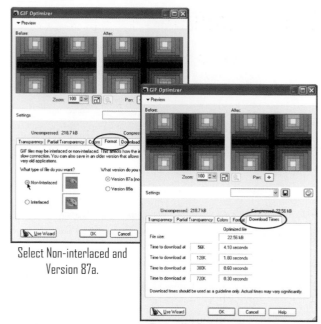

Select Non-interlaced and Version 87a.

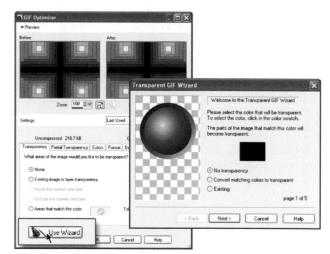

Review the Download Times tab to see how fast your image will download on screen.

Optimizing a GIF Using the GIF Wizard

Using the GIF Wizard walks you step-by-step through the optimization process. While it gives you some control over your optimization, you'll get the maximum control by not using it. To use:

1 Click the **Use Wizard** button on the bottom-left of the GIF Optimizer box.

2 This will bring up a series of five menus. Note that you cannot see the result of your selections until you reach the end of the process.
   - Transparent color
   - Background color
   - Number of colors
   - Set of colors. Always select "No, choose the best colors."
   - The results. This allows you to see the results of the settings you selected. When using the Wizard, remember to use the Back and Next buttons to change your settings and see the results of them.

3 Once you are happy with the image, click **Finish** and save your image.

Select Use Wizard, then use the Back and Next buttons to change and modify your settings on each of the five menus.

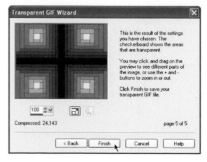

The final menu will display your results. You can use the up or down arrows to zoom in and out on your image. Or use the slider bar below the zoom value box. However, it's important to view at 100% so you can see exactly how it will appear.

Understanding a GIF with Transparency

How to Avoid the Dreaded White Halo and Jagged Edges

All images are saved in some kind of a rectangle. But perhaps you have a triangular logo, and don't want to see a rectangle around it. Or you want to add your signature to your site to give it a personal touch. For this you need to give the illusion that there is no rectangle surrounding your image—in other words, the image needs transparency. The GIF file format (unlike a JPEG) supports one layer of transparency. This layer can be on and totally transparent, or off and totally opaque.

Smooth-edged graphics that will be placed over a solid colored or patterned background are best for transparent GIFs. Graphics that contain fuzzy elements, such as drop shadows, do not look as good (although can look acceptable if on a white background).

A GIF image with a transparent background (or transparent area of the image) has three distinct areas:

1   The **non-transparent pixels** (the image itself).
2   The **matte color** which separates the edge of the non-transparent pixels from the transparent pixels.
3   The **transparent pixels**.

The matte color is important. Generally the default matte color is white. This white color won't be noticeable if your site has a white or very light background. But if your site's background is a darker color, or a pattern, the white matte color will give your GIF a detracting white halo. If your matte defaults to "none" rather than white, then the edges are "alias" (or not "anti-aliased"). This means your edge will have the dreaded jagged edge. Simply changing the matte color to match the site's background makes a huge difference. No more white halo. No more jagged edges.

In short: "no matte" means no blending of the edges, and "matte" blends the edges to match the site's background color.

Question for the expert

Q: What is anti-alias?

A: The "alias" refers to the edge of a graphic, such as a circle, that appears to have a jagged edge. Anti-aliasing is a technique used to blur the edges between a high contrast boundary and its background, resulting in a smooth gradation between the two. In other words, something like a circle or text would appear smooth, without the dreaded jagged edge.

The edge of the circle is smooth because it is anti-aliased.

Enlarging the edge shows the shades of color between the edge of the circle and the background.

The edge of the circle is ragged because it is not anti-aliased.

Enlarging the edge shows no shades of color between the edge of the circle and the background.

In this example, the GIF is a red circle with a transparent background. The "matte" color surrounding the red circle is white. On a white background, (1) the circle looks good. On a black background, (2) the default white matte appears as a distracting white halo. Changing the matte color to black (3) eliminates the problem.

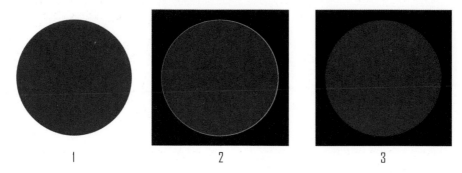

1	2	3

Sure you could create a JPEG of the above circle simply using a black background. But what if your red circle was sitting on a patterned background (4)? Now it doesn't look so good. Even changing the color of the background to an average color used in the background (5) doesn't look good. But using a GIF with a transparent background and using a matte color that matches the background (6) looks seamless. Additionally, the GIF is much smaller than the JPEG would be.

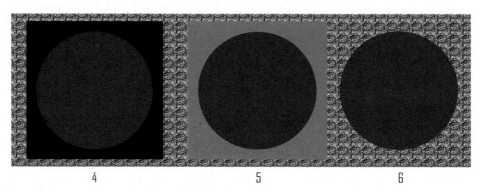

4	5	6

Most of today's image-editing programs use anti-alias as a default. In some situations, there is a level to toggle how much anti-aliasing is used or the ability to turn anti-aliasing on or off. If there is a choice between the type of edge (this is common with text), try out the various choices to see what looks best.

Paint Shop Pro's anti-alias options

Question for the expert

Q: A PNG file can support transparencies. Why not use it instead?

A: PNG files were developed as a royalty-free alternative to GIF and JPEG files. An 8-bit PNG has much the same functionality as a GIF file, including transparency. But, as it tends to produce larger files, it is not widely used. 24-bit PNGs allow you to have 254 levels of transparency allowing much greater freedom when designing visual effects. Unfortunately, Internet Explorer versions prior to version 7 do not support the transparency levels rendering the advantages basically useless for the majority of Web users. As Internet Explorer version 6 dies a natural death you'll see 24-bit PNGs being more widely used.

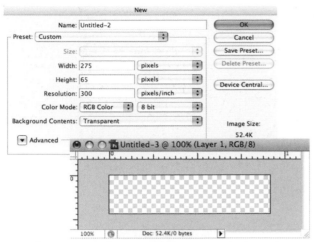

Set up your new document with a transparent background. The gray/white checkerboard indicates transparency.

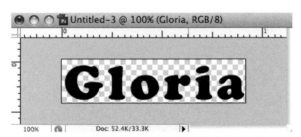

Type your name in your document. Adjust the font size if your name does not fit in the document.

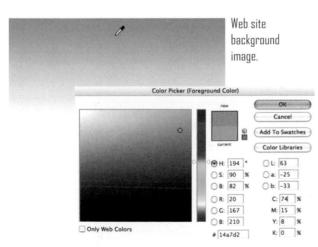

Web site background image.

Use the Eyedropper tool to pick up the color of your Web site background. This will be the color you matte your transparency to.

Saving an Image with Transparency and Matting it to the Web Site Background using Photoshop and Photoshop Elements

I am starting with a document that has transparency in it. Here is how I created it:

1   Go to **File > New**. (In Elements: File > New > Blank Document.)

2   The document is **275** pixels in width by **65** pixels in height. I ignore the 300 ppi because my image is for the Web and the only numbers that matter are the pixel dimensions. The color mode is **RGB**. In Background Contents, use the drop-down menu to select **Transparent**. Click **OK**.

3   A new document in that size with a transparent layer is created.

4   Using the Text tool, I selected **Cooper Black** as my font, **18** as my font size, and **Smooth** as my anti-alias selection, and I typed in my name.

5   Save this document as a Photoshop/Photoshop Elements file (.psd).

STEP 1: DETERMINE WHAT COLOR YOU WANT TO MATTE THE BACKGROUND TO

1   Open the background graphic for your Web site.

2   Select the **Eyedropper** tool. Move the Eyedropper around the document until you find a color that you think will work best. Once selected, that color will become your Foreground color. Double-click on the Foreground color at the bottom of the toolbar to bring up the Color Picker. Make a note of the RGB values shown on the bottom-left of the Color Picker box. In this case **20, 167, 210**. Click **Cancel**.

STEP 2: WORKING WITH A GIF IMAGE WITH TRANSPARENCY AND MATTING IT TO THE WEB SITE BACKGROUND

Open your name graphic with transparency.

1   Go to **File > Save for Web**.

2   Select **GIF** as the optimized file format. After experimenting with the number of colors, I reduced the colors to **8**. (Even though only black and a transparency are used here, I reduced the number to 8 rather than 2. That's because reducing it to 2 colors would cut off the "anti-aliasing" edge—the bits of grey that smooth out the edge of the letters.) Notice that the original file size is 69.8k and the new file size is 1.4k—quite a huge difference!

3   Click the **Matte** drop-down menu ("Defines colors to map transparent pixels onto") and select **Other**. In the Color Chooser box (or Color Picker box in Photoshop Elements) insert the RGB values **(20, 167, 210)** so that the color selected earlier to blend with the Web site background appears. Click **OK**.

4   The Matte color is now the selected color. If you are using Photoshop, you'll see the slight blue edge on your graphic and the additional colors in the Color Table box. If you are using Elements, you'll see the blue edge on your graphic. Click **Save** in Photoshop, click **OK** in Elements.

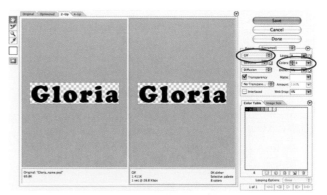

Choosing 8 colors rather than just two for this black and transparent image allows the anti-aliasing greys to smooth out the edges of the text.

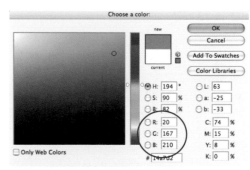

Click the Matte button then choose Other. The Color Chooser box will display. Enter the RGB values you noted from earlier in this lesson.

With the Matte color now the blue of your background, you can see a slight blue edge around the letters in your images. This will keep the white halo from showing up on your Web site background.

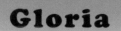

Browser Window

Gloria

The blue matte blends perfectly with the Web site background.

Gloria

If I did not matte the transition color to my Web background color, the resulting image would have a very distracting white ragged edge around the letters.

New Image

Presets:

Image Dimensions

Width: 275   Units: Pixels

Height: 65

Resolution: 300.000   Pixels/inch

Image Characteristics

- Raster Background
- Vector Background
- Art Media Background

Color depth: RGB - 8 bits/channel

Color:

☑ Transparent

Memory Required: 192 KBytes
Dimensions: 275 x 65 Pixels

OK   Cancel   Help

Set up your new document with a transparent background. The gray/white checkerboard indicates transparency.

Image1 @ 100% (Raster 1)

Image1* @ 100% (Vector 1)

Type your name in your document. Adjust the font size if your name does not fit in the document.

What a difference this simple step makes! Now the GIF image sits beautifully on the background with no harsh edges.

Question for the expert

Q: Why is the matte color not showing around my GIF?

A: Chances are you were not working in a native program file when you applied the matte color. In order to matte a color to a transparent GIF, you must be creating the document within the program in which you are working. In other words, if you start with a GIF and try to set a matte color using, for example, Photoshop's Save for Web, it will not work. I learned this the hard way! Instead, you need to copy/paste the image into a new document within the program in which you are working. Then optimize and matte the color.

Saving an Image with Transparency and Matting it to the Web site Background using Paint Shop Pro

I am starting with a document that has transparency in it. Here is how I created it:

1. Go to **File > New**.
2. In the Image Dimensions area, inches is changed to pixels. The document is **275** pixels in width by **65** pixels in height. I ignore the 300 ppi because my image is for the Web and the only numbers that matter are the pixel dimensions. The Image Characteristics is set to **Raster Background**, the Color depth to **RGB—8 bits/channel**. Under Color, the **Transparent** box is checked. Click **OK**.
3. A new document in that size with a transparent layer is created.
4. Using the **Text** tool, I selected **Arial Black**, **20** points, with my anti-alias set to **Smooth** and I typed my name.

STEP 1: DETERMINE WHAT COLOR YOU WANT TO MATTE THE BACKGROUND TO

1 Open the background graphic for your Web site.

2 Select the **Eyedropper** tool. Move the Eyedropper around the document until you find a color that you think will work best. A small RGB box will give you the values of that color. Make a note of them. In this case **51, 160, 201**. Close the document.

STEP 2: WORKING WITH A GIF IMAGE WITH TRANSPARENCY AND MATTING IT TO THE WEB SITE BACKGROUND

1 With your native Paint Shop Pro image open, go to **File > Export > GIF Optimizer**.

2 Under the Transparency tab, select **Existing image or layer transparency**.

3 Under the Partial Transparency, under **Would you like to blend the partially transparent pixels?** select **Yes, blend with background color**.

4 Click the **Blend Color** box to bring up the Color box. Type in the RGB values **(51, 160, 201)** so that the color selected earlier to blend with the Web site background appears. Click **OK**.

5 The Blend Color box now displays the selected color, and that color is visible along the edges of the text.

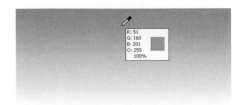

Use the Eyedropper tool to pick up the color of your Web site background. This will be the color you matte your transparency to.

Select Existing image or layer transparency. Notice the faint white glow around the image on the right in the preview.

After selecting the matte color, you can see a faint blue outline around the letters in the preview on the right. Zoom in if necessary.

Under Partial Transparency, click the Blend Colors box to bring up the Color box. Enter the RGB values that you selected earlier.

6 Continuing to optimize the GIF, click the Colors tab and select **Optimized Median Cut**. Then reduce the number of colors. I used **8**.

7 Click **OK** and save your document.

Now the GIF graphic sits beautifully on the background with no harsh edges. It's easy to see why this is such an important step.

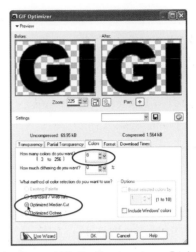

Select Optimized Median Cut, then choose 8 colors.

Question for the expert

Q: Why is there still a white halo showing on my text when my matte color is properly selected?

A: Chances are there is a stroke applied to the text. With the Pick tool selected and your original image opened (not the newly saved GIF image), double-click on your text to bring up the Vector Property box. Uncheck the Stroke box.

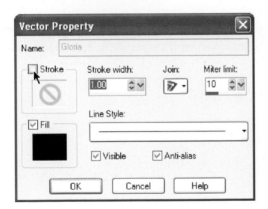

The blue matte blends perfectly with the Web site background.

If I did not select "Yes, blend with background color," the resulting image would have a very distracting ragged edge around the letters.

answers to cd and dvd storage questions

Q: How do you recommend backing up files? Is it OK to just back up several places on my hard drive?

A: Don't rely only on your hard drive for backup. Hard drives crash and die. Regardless if you use an external drive for a main backup, I also recommend backing up important documents and images onto CDs or DVDs. While these discs don't hold as much information as today's huge hard drives, that can be a good thing. If something happens to one disc, it won't mean your entire backup is gone. It's also a good idea to periodically check your backup CDs, to make sure they still open, and to be sure that the document can still be opened using your current software.

Q: Is one CD brand just as good as another?

A: Don't use the CDs and DVDs from the local business supply store that are a zillion for $20. They are fine for general short-term use, like distributing your images. But they're not good for long-term storage. You know the importance of using quality materials in your work—the same type of quality should be used in your storage materials. Look at archival-quality media such as Mitsui Archival CDs (www.mitsuicdr.com). These are universally accepted for their archival quality (estimated in excess of 100 years) with a patented formula that provides maximum resistance to environmental degradation.

Q: How should I label the CD?

A: Never write on a CD using a ball-point pen or a pencil. The sharp point can easily damage the CD surface, making it unreadable. And while a Sharpie-type marker's softer point will not damage the surface, the ink can eventually eat into the CD's protective coating, which can also make the CD unreadable. For long-term storage, use a marker with water-based permanent ink or one made specifically for writing on CDs. (Sniff your marker. A strong smell will tell you it's solvent-based.) Mitsui makes a water-based ink marker that sells for about $3. If you opt for paper labels, be sure the label adhesive does not contain any solvent that can damage your disc. Also, be sure to use thin labels that can be used on slot-loading readers (the drives on several Macintoshes and car stereos), since thicker labels can cause jams.

Q: Any other tips?

A: After you make your CD, verify that it works. Test it in other computers, if possible. When you clean the CD, clean it perpendicular to the tracks, as scratches across the disc are easier to correct than ones that follow the track. Use a lens cleaning cloth or CD cleaning fluid rather than a tissue or paper towel to clean your CD/DVD. Don't touch the recording surface of your CD—handle the CD by the edge. And store discs in jewel cases, DVD cases or Tyvek sleeves (away from sunlight).

chapter 16

batch processing images for the web

If you have several images to resize, you'll quickly learn that repeating the same steps over and over gets old fast. Imagine, for example: opening a file, resizing it, renaming it, changing the file type, saving it, then opening the next image and repeating all these steps again. Whether you resize images for your guild, for a show organization, or for use on your own Web site, learning to take full advantage of tools to handle repetitive tasks can speed up these tasks.

Generally batch processing works like this: you complete a form with information (such as which folder of images you'd like processed, the size you'd like the images, the file type, and where to store the new images. Once you click the "run" button, you can sit back and let the program do the work for you. If only everything else in life had batch commands!

📁 Quilt Images
　🖼 Blushing.jpg
　🖼 CirclePoint.jpg
　🖼 Opposing.jpg
　🖼 PinkFlower.jpg 　📁 Main Web Quilt Images
　🖼 PondFlowers.jpg 　🖼 Blushing_M.jpg
　🖼 SIllusions-5.jpg 　🖼 CirclePoint_M.jpg
📁 Thumbnail Quilt Images 🖼 Opposing_M.jpg
　🖼 Blushing_T.jpg 　🖼 PinkFlower_M.jpg
　🖼 CirclePoint_T.jpg 　🖼 PondFlowers_M.jpg
　🖼 Opposing_T.jpg 　🖼 SIllusions-5_M.jpg
　🖼 PinkFlower_T.jpg
　🖼 PondFlowers_T.jpg
　🖼 SIllusions-5_T.jpg

Saving Time with Batches

Some programs have all the functions you need to batch a folder of images and rename them right from the start. Others require you to create an **action** first. **An action is simply a way to record a series of operations**. For example, you start recording, go through the series of steps needed to complete a particular task, stop the recording, and save it. Then, when you need to do that same series of tasks again, you only need to click that particular action. Pretty nifty! An action can be applied to a single image, several, or a folder of images. Creating actions can be as easy or as complex as you desire.

Batch renaming of images is another time saver. If you import images from your digital camera, you know the names can be very unhelpful. Selecting your images and changing them from something such as DSC_9872.jpg to something like 2008-03-vacation.jpg is far more useful when it comes time to look for that series of vacation photos at a later date.

In this chapter I'll show how to start with one group of JPEGs and create a new set of JPEGs at 450 pixels in width, a good size for display on a Web page. (I am not concerned with the image height, since I will allow the program to calculate the correct height for me.) From this, I will describe how simple it will become to create a new set of images (in this example at 125 pixels in width, a good size for a Web site thumbnail image).

These are general settings, and describe one naming convention. Resize and rename your images however makes best sense to you. Additionally, once you understand these concepts, experiment with other settings that can make your work flow easier.

> **My setup:**
>
> The original images are in a folder called **Original Images**. A new folder called **Web Images** will be the destination file (where the new images will go). The naming convention is the **filename_M.jpg** for the main 450 pixel wide image and **filename_T.jpg** for the 125 pixel wide thumbnail image.

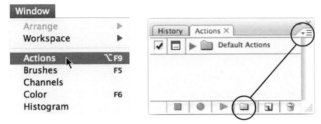

Click the Create a New Set button or select New Set from the fly-out menu to start a new set for your action.

Name the set Resize Images, or something specific to the actions you are about to make.

To start a new action, click the Create new action button or select New Action from the fly-out menu on the top-right.

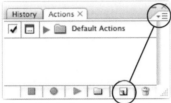

Name the action Resize 450 Width, or something specific to the action you are going to make.

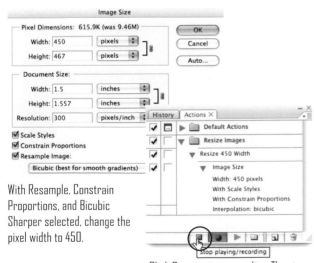

With Resample, Constrain Proportions, and Bicubic Sharper selected, change the pixel width to 450.

Click Stop to stop recording. The steps of your action display in the palette.

Recording an Action in Photoshop

Open a large JPEG image (larger than the size you want to resize your image to). Then:

1 Go to **Window > Actions**.

2 The Action palette appears.

3 Click **Create a New Set** (on the bottom of the Actions palette) or select **New Set** from the fly-out menu. Name the set: **Resize Images**. Click **OK**.

4 Click **Create New Action** (on the bottom of the Actions palette) or select **New Action** from the fly-out menu. Name the action: **Resize 450 width**. Click the **Record** button.

5 Go to **Image > Image Size**.

6 Make sure the **Resample** and **Constrain Proportions** boxes are checked. Select **Bicubic Sharper** since the images will be reduced in size. In the width box, insert **450 pixels**. Click **OK**.

7 Click **Stop Playing/Recording** (on the bottom of the Actions palette) or select **Stop Recording** from the fly-out menu. Expand the palette to see the steps in your action. You now have your action!

If you made a mistake, drag that action to the Actions trash and start again.

Modifying an Existing Action in Photoshop

You now have an action that resizes your image to 450 pixels in width. To create a new action to resize your images to 125 pixels in width (remember the goal was to create a folder of 450 pixel width images and 125 pixel width images), it's easiest to duplicate and modify the action you just created.

1 Go to **Window > Actions** to open the Actions palette.

2 Select the **Resize 450 Width** action. Select **Duplicate** from the fly-out menu.

3 Rename the action: **Resize 125 Width**.

4 Double-click on the **450 width** line to open the Image Size dialog box and change the width to 125. Click **OK**.

You now have a new action that will resize images to 125 pixels in width.

Click the small triangle in the upper-right corner to display the fly-out menu. Select Duplicate.

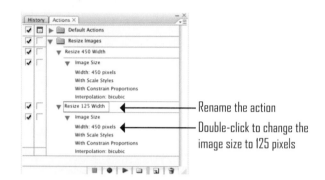

Rename the action

Double-click to change the image size to 125 pixels

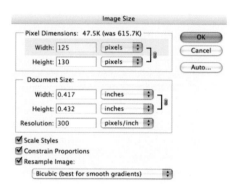

Change the pixel width to 125 then click OK.

Batch Resizing a Folder of Images in Photoshop

Now we will apply the newly created action to a folder of images.

1   Go to **File > Automate > Batch**.

2   In the Batch dialog, follow these instructions:

- In the **Play** fields, select **Resize Images**. For Action, select **Resize 450 Width**.
- In the **Source** fields, select **Folder**. Navigate to find the folder you created (in this case Original Images). Check **Suppress File Open Options Dialogs** and **Suppress Color Profile Warnings**.
- In the **Destination** fields, check **Folder**. Navigate to find the folder you created (in this case Web Images). Note that the entire path to the folder will appear in both instances.
- In **File Naming**, select **Document Name_M + extension**. (Select Document Name first, then add the _M.)
- For **Compatibility**, check **Windows**. (Select Windows even if you are creating the images on a Macintosh. A Mac can recognize the Windows format with ease, but not vice versa.)
- For **Errors**, select **Stop for Errors**.

3   Click **OK**. Magically, the program opens each of the images in your folder, resizes, and saves. What a time saver!

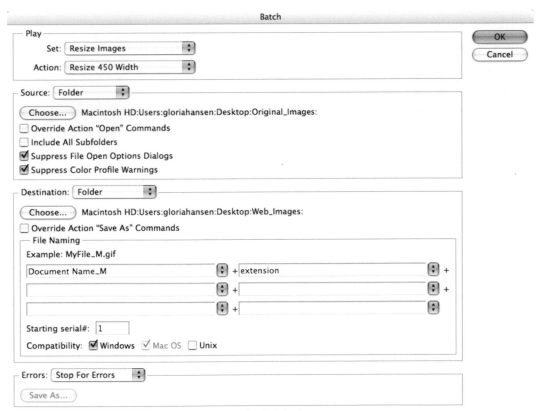

The Batch dialog box.

CREATING A SECOND SET OF IMAGES

The goal is to have two sets of Web images, a main image and a thumbnail. To create the second set, repeat the above process, except select the **125 pixel width** action instead of the 450. For Source, use the **Original Images** folder. For Destination, use the **Web Images** folder. For File Naming, use **Document Name_T + extension** (for thumbnails).

Batch Renaming of Images in Adobe® Bridge

The images that are resized are destined to be on my Web site. However, because I want to create another set of smaller images to use as thumbnails, I want to keep the same image name, but differentiate the two sets by adding an extension to the name.

If you're using Photoshop CS2 or CS3, you also have a program called Bridge, a picture management program. Here's how to change the name of your images in one swoop:

1   Open **Adobe Bridge**.

2   Navigate to find the folder of **Web Images** that you created (my Bridge display window is set so that you can see the images more clearly) and select all of them in the film strip. If you are using CS2, the first image will appear in your Preview pane. If you are using CS3, all of the selected images will appear in your Preview pane. The key is to select all of the images in the filmstrip.

3   Go to **Tools > Batch Rename**.

4   In the Batch Rename dialog, follow these instructions:

   •   In the **Destination** fields, select **Rename in Same Folder**.

   •   In the **New Filename** fields, select **Current Filename**, **Name**, **Original Case**. Click the + button to get a new line of options (or change the options if there is another line showing). Select **Text** and insert **_M**. That is my naming convention. You can use whatever naming convention you're comfortable with.

   •   In the **Options** field, check **Windows** compatibility.

   •   You'll see a **Preview** showing both the current name and new filename, so you can double-check to ensure the new file name will be as you planned.

   •   Click **Rename**.

5   Each image now has the **_M** annexed to the name.

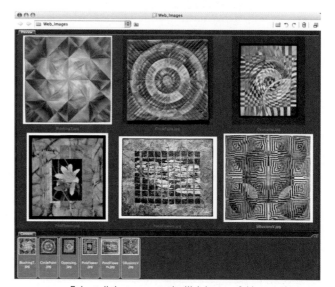

Select all the images in the Web Images folder.

Select Batch Rename to bring up the dialog.

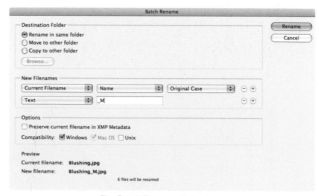

The Batch Rename dialog box.

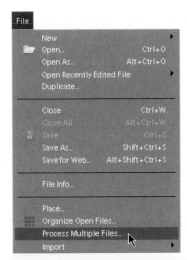

Select File > Process Multiple Files to set up the batch.

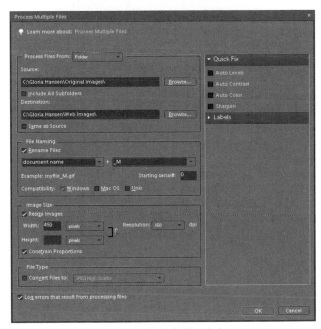

The Process Multiple Files dialog.

Batch Resizing and Renaming Images in Photoshop Elements

Photoshop Elements simplifies the entire process of resizing a folder of images by providing a Process Multiple Files dialog box that lets you resize and rename your images without having to first create an Action. (Elements does not include Actions.)

1   Go to **File > Process Multiple Files**.

2   In the **Process Multiple Files** dialog, follow these instructions:

- From the pop-up menu, select **Folder**.

- In the **Source** field, navigate to find the folder you created, in this case **Original Images**.

- In the **Destination** field, navigate to find the folder you created, in this case **Web Images**. Note that the entire path to the folder will appear in both instances.

- In **File Naming**, check **Rename Files**, then select **document name + _M**. (You must select **document name + None** first, then type in the **_M** in the field.)

- In the **Image Size**, check **Resize Images**, then insert **450 pixels**. Leave the resolution to whatever it defaults to. Check the **Constrain Proportions** box.

- Check **Log errors** that result for processing files so that you can review any problems after you process your images.

- Depending on the quality of your originals, you may consider checking a **Quick Fix** option. I suggest you first try it out on one image, and view the image at 100% to see how you like the results.

3   Click **OK**. Magically, the program opens each of the images in your folder, resizes, renames, and saves!

CREATING A SECOND SET OF IMAGES

Our goal is to have two sets of Web images, a main image and a thumbnail. To create the second set, repeat the above process except in Image Size field, insert **125 pixels**. For Source, use the **Original Images** folder. For Destination, use the **Web Images** folder. For File Naming, use **document name + _T** (for thumbnails).

NOTE TO WINDOWS USERS:

Add the **.jpg** extension if it's not in your file name. Some Windows users do not use their .jpg extension by default. Thus when renaming as described on page 173, you will still not have the extension. When adding images to the Web, you need the .jpg for the image to properly appear on all browsers. If you do not have the .jpg extension in your renamed files, do another batch name. Here's how.

1 Go to **File > Process Multiple Files**.

2 In the **Process Multiple Files** dialog, follow these instructions:

- From the pop-up menu, select **Folder**.

- In the **Source** field, navigate to find the folder with the resized Web images, in this case **Web Images**.

- In the **Destination** field, navigate and select the SAME folder, in this case **Web Images**. Note that the entire path to the folder will appear in both instances.

- In **File Naming**, check **Rename Files**, then select **document name + extension**.

- In **Image Size**, make sure **Resize Image** is underlined underscheck (since you already resized the images).

- Check **Log errors that result for processing files** so that you can review any problems after you process your images.

- Uncheck any **Quick Fix** on the right of the dialog box.

3 Click **OK**. Your files now have the .jpg extension.

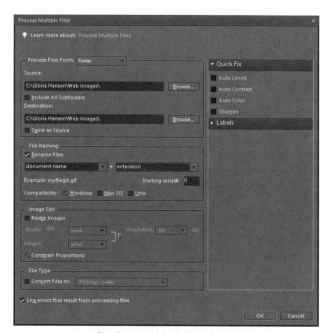

The Process Multiple Files dialog.

Q: How should files be named for the Web?

A: File names should only contain letters, numbers, hyphens, or underlines. They should not contain spaces because not all browsers, especially older ones, can read them. They should also not contain symbols. For example, if you include an @ symbol, the browser can ignore everything before that symbol. A forward or back slash within the image name can indicate a directory. The browser can search for that directory, which doesn't exist, and the search will result in a "not found" error message, a broken image icon or an X in a box symbol.

Batch Renaming Using Elements Organizer in Windows

You can also batch rename images inside of your Organizer. The naming convention isn't as flexible, but it is very useful when you want to rename images imported from your camera into Organizer. For example, instead of your images having unhelpful names such as DSC_9527.jpg, you can rename the images to something that makes more sense to you. To rename a series of images, do the following:

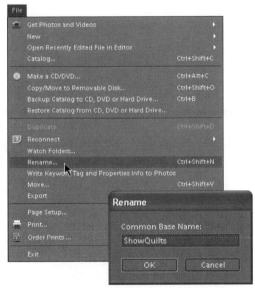

Choose a name that best describes your images.

1   Open the Organizer. To see your file names instead of only the date, go to **View > Show File Names**.

2   Select the images that you want to rename. (**Shift+click** to select a series of images; **Ctrl+click** to select non-adjacent images.)

3   Go to **File > Rename**. The Rename box appears. Whatever base name you use, the program will automatically include a number sequence so that each image has a unique name. <u>You only need to add the name, not a hyphen or a file format</u>; they also will be added automatically.

For example: If you use GrandCanyon as the base name, the resulting image names will be GrandCanyon-1.jpg, GrandCanyon-2.jpg., etc.

> **Tip:** If you go to **View > Show File Names** and find that the option is gray, being you cannot select it, check the **Details** box to the left of the Organize tab.

NOTE TO MACINTOSH USERS:

Macintosh Elements users also get Adobe Bridge. To access Bridge from within Elements, go to go to **File > Browse with Bridge**. This is very helpful should you use Bridge to import your digital images. Instead of images having unhelpful names such DSC_9527.jpg, select the images to rename, and follow the instructions above under Batch Renaming with Adobe Bridge.

Recording a Script in Paint Shop Pro

Open a large image (larger than the size you want to resize your image to). Then:

1 Go to **File > Script > Start Recording**.

2 Go to **Image > Resize**.

3 In the Resize dialog box, under Pixel Dimensions, insert **450 pixels** for the width. Ignore the Print information (remember that has no relevance to creating Web images). Click **Resample using Bilinear** (since the image is being reduced in size), and be sure the **Lock Aspect Ratio** button is checked. Click **OK**.

4 Go to **File > Script > Save Recording**.

5 The Save As dialog box will open and default to save in the Scripts-Restricted folder. This is correct. Name your file. I named it **Image Size 450 Pixels**. Click **Save**. You now have your first script.

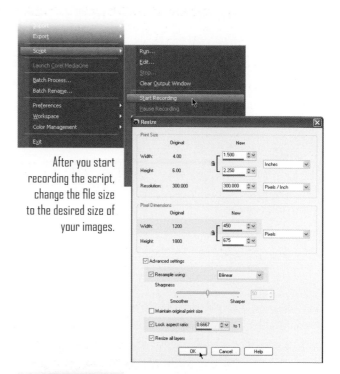

After you start recording the script, change the file size to the desired size of your images.

In addition to using File > Scripts to record and run scripts, you can do the same thing through the Scripts toolbar.

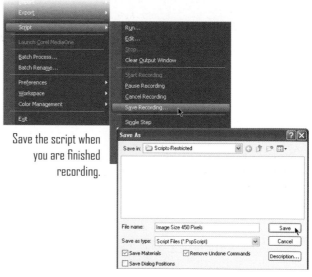

Save the script when you are finished recording.

To open your script, go to **View > Toolbars > Script**. In the drop-down menu you'll see the list of scripts included with the program, plus the new script, **Image Size 450 Pixels**, that was just made.

To make another script (to create a second file size, for example) repeat the above steps, but in the Image Resize box, use **125 pixels** in width instead of 450. When saving, call it **Image Size 125**. Then your 450 and 125 will be next to each other in the Scripts drop-down menu for easy batch filing of your Web images.

To open your script, go to View > Toolbars > Script.

Click File > Batch Process. Then navigate to the folder which holds your images and select all of them.

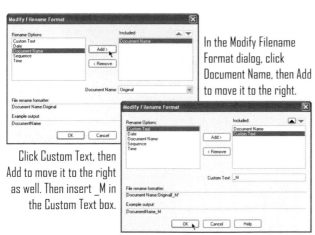

Check Use Script and select the script for resizing. Select Copy, then Browse and select the folder to save the copied files into. Click Modify.

In the Modify Filename Format dialog, click Document Name, then Add to move it to the right.

Click Custom Text, then Add to move it to the right as well. Then insert _M in the Custom Text box.

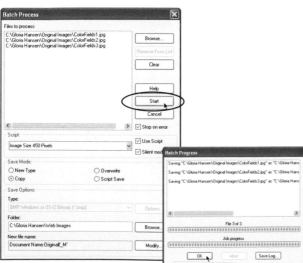

Click Start. The images will be processed.

Batch Resizing a Folder of Images in Paint Shop Pro

1. Go to **File > Batch Process**.

2. Click the **Browse** button on the top of the Batch Process dialog to navigate to the folder of images to resize. Select all of the images in the folder by clicking on the first image in the list and Shift+clicking on the last (which will also select everything in between). Click **Select**. The path to each selected image displays.

3. Under **Script**, check **Use Script**. Select one of the scripts you created on page 176 from the drop-down menu.

4. Under **Save Mode**, click **Copy**.

5. Under **Folder**, click the **Browse** button to navigate to the folder to save the copied files into. Select it and click **OK**.

6. Under **New File Name**, click the **Modify** button. This will bring up a Modify Filename Format dialog box. In the list on the left, click **Document Name** and click **Add**.

7. Click **Custom Text** on the left and click **Add**. In the Custom Text field, insert **_M**. Click **OK**.

8. Click **Start**. Each image will resize, rename, and save in your selected location!

Batch Renaming a Folder of Images in Paint Shop Pro

Make sure the .jpg extension is on your image names if they are destined for the Web. To add the .jpg:

1 Go to **File > Batch Rename**.

2 In the Batch Rename dialog box, click the **Browse** button on the top of the Batch Process dialog to locate the folder of images to add the .jpg extension to. Select all of the images in the folder by clicking on the first image in the list and Shift+clicking on the last (which will also select everything in between). Click **Select All**. The path to each selected file name displays in the Batch Rename box.

3 Click the **Modify** button to bring up the Modify Filename Format dialog box. Click **Document Name** in the left column and click the **Add** button.

4 Click **Custom Text** in the left column and click the **Add** button. In the Custom Text field, insert **.jpg**. Click **OK**.

5 In the Batch Rename box click **Start**. The images in the selected folder are now renamed.

Click File > Batch Rename. Then navigate to the folder which holds your images and select all of them.

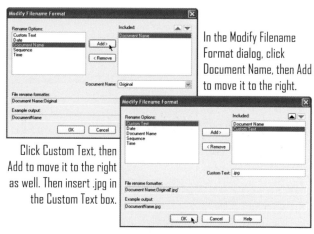

In the Batch Process dialog, select Copy. Then click Browse and select the folder to save the copied files into. Finally, click Modify.

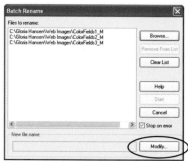

In the Modify Filename Format dialog, click Document Name, then Add to move it to the right.

Click Custom Text, then Add to move it to the right as well. Then insert .jpg in the Custom Text box.

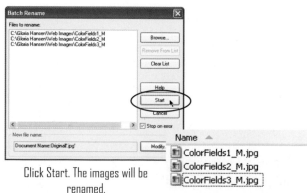

Click Start. The images will be renamed.

image protection—
can it be done?

How can I protect my images to prevent someone from downloading them from my Web site?

In short, you can't. There is nothing you can do to absolutely protect against Internet image theft. Once something is published on a Web site, it is fair game. If someone really wants an image, they will find a way to get it. But I'll suggest some ways to protect your images.

Protecting Your Web Site Images

Copyright Notice

Make it clear that you own the images on your Web site by adding a copyright note on the bottom of each Web page. Some people will still ignore this. But it may stop people who assume that if a page has no copyright notice, the images there are available for the taking.

Protect your Images from "Inlining"

Using images without permission is very common on the Web. Some people download an image, upload it to their site, and then republish it. Others do not download the image, but instead link to it. This is known as **"inlining"—displaying an image on one Web site that originates from another**. Inlining not only takes your image without permission, but steals your bandwidth, too! If you become aware of someone linking to your image, the easiest way to stop them is to change the name of your image.

If inlining becomes a real concern, you can also ask your Web host to configure its server to not serve your images to any third-party Web sites (or to particular Web sites). It's important to realize that allowing another site to link to your images can cost you. If it takes up enough of your site's bandwidth, your Internet host can charge you more money for that additional bandwidth.

Make Your Images Harder to Find

Many search engines allow people to search for images. So to safeguard yours, you can add code to your site to prevent your images from being listed. First, place all of your images in a folder. Then, use a robots.txt file placed in the root level of your Web site and include a reference as follows:

> User-Agent: *
> Disallow: /Images/

While this will stop the main search engines from indexing your images, it will not stop all. If you don't understand how to add such code to your site, ask your Web designer or programmer to do it for you.

Make Your Images Harder to Steal

You could disable the right-click function. (Right-clicking on an image brings up a menu allowing you to copy or save an image) This is done with a javascript. However, this is not recommended as it disables all right-clicking and can annoy your visitors. Besides, it would allow someone to simply drag the image to their desktop. So a better idea might be to put a transparent GIF image over your original image. Thus, when a user tries to drag an image or right-click on it, only the transparent image will be saved. Unfortunately, there are easy ways around this. The method that makes the most sense to me is to add a translucent watermark that appears on top of your image. There are two ways this can be done.

Add a Visible Watermark

One type of watermark is visible, that is with your text, logo, and/or copyright symbol placed directly on your image so it is visible for all to see. (You'll find the steps for adding a watermark below.) You can also use **iWatermark**, a low-cost program designed specifically for this purpose. It offers a variety of watermarking options and is available for the Mac or PC. See http://scriptsoftware.com/iwatermark for more information. The upside of adding a watermark is it signals clearly that your image is not for the taking. The downside is that the larger and less opaque the watermark is, the more it detracts from the image. But making the watermark smaller and less noticeable also makes it easier for a person skilled in image-editing to remove it.

ADDING A WATERMARK IN PHOTOSHOP AND PHOTOSHOP ELEMENTS

1   Open your image and the Layers palette.

2   Select **white** as your foreground color.

3   Select the **Type** tool from the toolbar palette.

4   In the Type options menu, select a plain font such as **Verdana**, a font size of **16**, and use **white** as the font color (unless your quilt is pale, then use black). In the Anti-alias drop-down, select **Sharp**. (Anti-alias is the double AA in the Type toolbar.) Elements users, click the **AA** anti-alias button to be sure it's on. A box will appear around it when on. You'll know it's off if the text has a ragged edge, or if it's smooth.

5   Click on your quilt to start typing. The type layer should be above the image.

6   Use the keyboard command **Ctrl+Alt+C** (Win) or **Option+G** (Mac) to create a copyright symbol, and add whatever copyright language you want to include. For example, **©2008 Gloria Hansen. All Rights Reserved.** Click the check in the options toolbar to accept the text. (If the keyboard command doesn't work on your PC, hold the **Alt** key and use the number keypad on the right side of your keyboard and type **0169**. Release the Alt key.)

7   Select the **Move** tool, then click the **type layer** in the Layers palette. In Photoshop, go to **Edit > Free Transform**. Hold the **Shift** key down to constrain the proportion and drag a corner handle outward to enlarge the text to cover the image to taste. (In Elements, go to **Image > Transform > Free Transform**. Make sure **Constrain Proportions** is checked in the top menu, then drag a corner handle outward to enlarge the text.) Click the **Enter** (Win) or **Return** (Mac) key to set the selection.

8   Lower the **opacity** of the type layer to taste. I used 55%. The opacity slider is located on the Layers palette.

ADDING A WATERMARK WITH A DROP SHADOW TO YOUR IMAGE

Adding translucent visual text onto your image is another form of watermarking. The translucent text is part of the image, appearing however large and wherever you place it. It will not prevent a person from taking your image, but it makes the image more difficult to use, since your ownership is clearly marked. Additionally, it can be an attractive way to unobtrusively add your information to the bottom of an image.

In Photoshop

When adding a watermark, the addition of a drop shadow to the text gives it a bit more definition without overpowering the letters or further distracting from the image.

1 Repeat steps 1-8 on page 181.

2 With the text layer selected, select **Drop Shadow** from the Layer Styles fly-out menu on the bottom of the Layers palette. (Or double-click on the layer.)

3 In the Drop Shadow dialog box, start with the settings **Opacity: 100**; **Distance: 6**; **Spread: 9**; **Size 9**. Then adjust the settings to taste. Click **OK**.

4 Lower the fill opacity (located under the opacity slider on the top of the Layers palette) to taste.

5 Save the document.

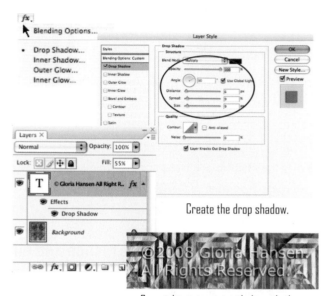

Create the drop shadow.

Copyright statement with drop shadow.

In Photoshop Elements

1 Repeat steps 1-8 on page 181.

2 Go to **Window > Effects**. Select the **Layer Styles** button at the top of the Effects palette.

3 The first effect is Bevel.

4 With the text layer selected, click the arrow next to Bevel to display the drop-down menu. Select **Drop Shadows**. Then, double-click on one of the drop shadow styles, or hit **Apply**, in the Effects palette to apply it to your text.

5 Double-click on the style icon (fx) on the right of the text layer.

6 Lower the opacity of the text layer to taste.

7 Save the document.

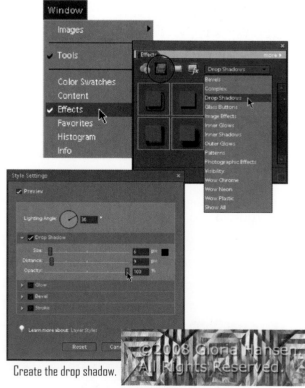

Create the drop shadow.

Copyright statement with drop shadow.

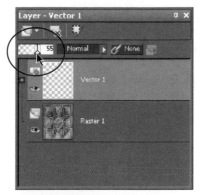

Using the Text tool, type your copyright statement so it's visible on your quilt.

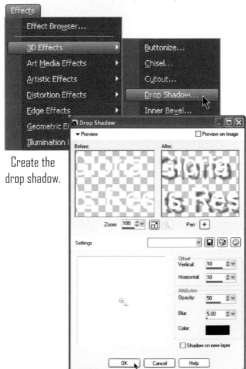

Lower the opacity of the layer.

Create the drop shadow.

Copyright statement with drop shadow.

In Paint Shop Pro

1   Open your image and the Layers palette.

2   Click the **Text** tool from the toolbar.

3   Set background/fill color to **white** (unless your quilt is pale, then set to black) and the stroke color to transparent. If the Materials palette is not displayed, go to **View > Palettes > Materials**.

4   On the Text tool palette, select **Vector**. Select a plain font, such as **Arial** with a font size of **16**. Under anti-alias select **Smooth**.

5   In the image window, click in the center of the quilt to indicate where the text will appear. If you want different placement, for example on the bottom of the quilt, click in that area. A Text Entry box will appear.

6   Type your information within the text box. Then click **Apply**.

7   The text will appear on your image. Move the text cursor towards the edge of the text until the text cross icon turns into a double-arrow cross. Grab a corner handle and drag the text outward to enlarge the text if you'd like.

8   Lower the opacity of the layer to taste. (The opacity slider is located on the Layers palette.)

9   Go to **Effect > 3D Effects > Drop Shadow**.

10 A box will appear telling you that the text layer needs to be converted to a raster layer. Be sure your text is spelled correctly. Once you rasterize the text, you will not be able to edit it. I suggest you keep this box set to **Prompt me before taking these actions**. Click **OK**.

11 A Drop Shadow dialog box will appear. Look at the before and after images and adjust the sliders to taste.

Add an Invisible Watermark

The second option is an invisible watermark embedded into the image. Depending on which level of protection you purchase, you can then track your images. If someone does take your images, you can learn which Web sites are displaying them. Digimarc is one such system that offers the technology which gives your digital image its own unique identity.

The higher-level package includes image tracking, meaning the invisible watermark is tracked. The program allows you to generate reports listing exactly which Web sites are displaying it. Knowing these sites, you can take steps to have the image removed. Usually a polite E-mail asking the site owner to remove the image is all that is required. It's surprising how many people think that if an image is on the Web, it's for the taking. If the unauthorized use continues, you can take additional steps while being able to prove the copyright violation.

Digimarc® (http://www.digimarc.com/register) works directly with several image-editing programs. First open an account with Digimarc, then to add the watermark:

- In Photoshop go to **Filter > Digimarc > Embed Watermark**.
- In Paint Shop Pro, go to **Image > Watermarking > Embed Watermark**.
- Photoshop Elements does not currently provide a direct tool that allows you to embed a watermark. However, Elements users can purchase an account directly with Digimarc and use its software.

You can see if a watermark is embedded in an image you are given. To do so in Photoshop or Photoshop Elements, go to **Filter > Digimarc > Read Watermark**. In Paint Shop Pro, go to **Image > Watermarking > Read Watermark**.

Registering your Work with the US Copyright Office

The single most important thing you can do for any work that is important to you is register it with the U.S. Copyright office. If you register before the work is published, or within three months of it being published, and if there is an infringement and if you decide to take legal action and win, you are entitled to attorney's fees and statutory damages from the infringer. If you register after three months of it being published and before a legal action, you are only covered from the date of registration rather than the first publication date. Registering is very straight forward. Look for Form VA for a Work of Visual Art. The PDF form is created in such a way that you can complete it online, clicking into each field and typing your information. From there you print and mail it in with the required documents. The current filing fee is $45. General copyright information is at www.copyright.gov. Information for registering a work of art is at www.copyright.gov/register/visual.html.

Question for the expert

Q: What if I'm looking for free images? Are there any out there?

A: There are some images that are free for the taking. Here's how to find them:

- **Open Clip Art** (www.openclipart.org)
  This site offers over 6,900 pieces of clip art, all free for the taking.

- **National Oceanic and Atmospheric Administration Photo Library** (www.photolib.noaa.gov)
  NOAA's site has over 20,000 images, including many higher resolution images.

- **PDPhoto.org** (www.PDPhoto.org)
  This site contains a large database of thousands of public domain photographs taken by Jon Sullivan. Jon offers his photographs "for anything, including commercial uses, other Web sites, school projects, articles, ads, whatever."

- **Creative Commons** (www.creativecommons.org)
  This non-profit organization offers "flexible copyright licenses for creative works."

- **Agricultural Research Service (ARS)** (http://www.ars.usda.gov/is/graphics/photos/)
  A complimentary source of high quality, royalty-free digital photographs available from the Agricultural Research Service Information Staff.

- **The National Park Services Digital Image Archives** (http://photo.itc.nps.gov/storage/images/index.html)
  This site provides links to public domain digital images of a variety of sites, including national parks, monuments, historic sites, and so on. All images posted on this site are free, and may be used without a copyright release (however, photo credit should go to the National Park Service).

- **The New York Public Library Digital Gallery** (http://digitalgallery.nypl.org/nypldigital/index.cfm)
  There are over 600,000 images in this collection!

- For more, visit Wikipedia's large collection of links to sites offering public domain images.
  http://en.wikipedia.org/wiki/Public_domain_image_resources. While they all say "free," and "royalty-free," always check the fine print to make sure you can use them how you intend.

chapter

the power of PDF files

I suspect that every quilt maker using a computer has at some time opened an Adobe® Reader® PDF file. The PDF—or **P**ortable **D**ocument **F**ormat—is amazing. It is the digital equivalent of a printed page. And it has become the worldwide standard for reliable distribution of documents.

Whatever you design on your computer can be saved as a PDF file. Depending on which PDF software you use, you can combine several documents into one. You can collaborate with someone, using marking tools such as sticky notes, pencil, and highlighter. You can even add a password or permissions to restrict who can print, save, copy, or modify the file.

Once you have a PDF Reader installed on your computer, you can open a PDF document, and it will display and print everything—fonts, layout, graphics—exactly as intended. PDF files work across platform, too. You can distribute a PDF on your Web site, on any type of digital media such as a CD, or as an E-mail attachment. With enough resolution in your images, you can even supply a PDF directly to your printer for high-quality output.

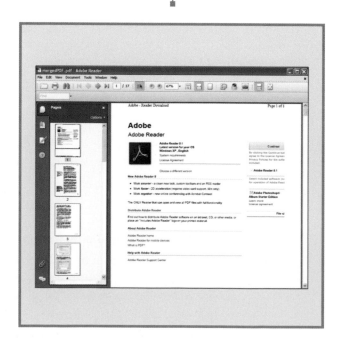

The PDF Format and Macintosh OS X

PDF is the "native" metafile format for the Macintosh OS X operating system. This gives the Mac OS X operating system some nice advantages over other operating systems. One of the biggest advantages is that **any application that supports the print command can automatically create a PDF document**—more on that later in the chapter. Another advantage is "PostScript" quality documents can be printed on all printers, even non-PostScript ones. That means your PDF will look great no matter what type of printer you use.

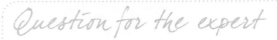

Q: What is a PostScript document?

A: PostScript is a vector-based language that describes the text, graphics, and layout of a printed page to a printer or image-setter hardware. It has become an industry standard for printing high-resolution documents. Printing to a PostScript device—something a commercial printer would generally do rather than a home user—creates a high-resolution bitmap of the page being printed at the output of the device.

A PDF also describes the text, graphics and layout as a vector file. This means you can print to any device without sacrificing quality. (Remember, vector files can be enlarged without sacrificing quality.) The bottom line? Being able to use PDF is a very good thing.

CAUTION! If the PDF contains bitmap images, these images will still degrade when enlarged. Embedding bitmap images in a PDF does not magically transform them from bitmap to vector files.

PDF Reader Utilities

To view a PDF file, you must have a PDF Reader installed on your computer. The two most popular choices are **Preview** and **Adobe Reader**. (The bulk of this chapter will focus on Adobe Reader.)

The Power of Preview in Leopard®

Preview, a program that comes preinstalled in the Applications folder on a Mac, has expanded its PDF features under the Leopard OS. You can now combine multiple PDFs, delete or add pages to a PDF, and rearrange pages in a PDF. This is incredibly useful. For example, you can organize your related PDFs into one document. Here's how:

1 Open the PDF in Preview.

2 Turn on the Sidebar. Either go to **View > Sidebarpdf**, OR click the **Sidebar** icon in the toolbar. The PDF will appear in the sidebar.

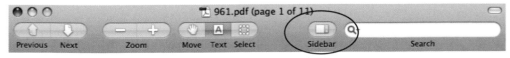

This opens your PDF with the pages in the document displayed as thumbnail images in a vertical column.

To Add a PDF to Another PDF Document:

1 Open PDF number one in Preview and turn on the Sidebar.

2 Open PDF number two in a second Preview window and turn on the Sidebar.

3 Select a page (or pages) from the Sidebar of one document and drag it (or them) directly into the Sidebar of the other document.

4 This can be done with multiple PDFs. Also, you can open more than one PDF into a single Preview window by selecting them and dragging them onto the Preview program icon in your Doc.

To Rearrange the Pages Within a PDF:

1 Select the page in the sidebar and drag it to towards its new location.

2 A red horizontal bar will appear indicating when you can release the mouse button to place the page into that location.

Use the Sidebar to rearrange pages within the PDF.

To Delete Pages from a PDF:

To delete a page from a PDF, select the page in the sidebar and hit the **Delete** key.

Adobe Reader

I'll use Adobe Reader in my examples because it is the standard. (It's often included on program installation CDs.) Adobe Reader is Adobe's free viewer application (formerly know as "Acrobat® Reader") available for PC and Macintosh users. You can generally download a free Adobe Reader here:

- **http://www.adobe.com/products/acrobat**
- Or go to **www.adobe.com** and look for the **Get Adobe Reader** icon.

Downloading Adobe Reader:

1 Click the **Get Adobe Reader** icon.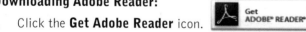

2 Follow the prompt to download the program appropriate for your computer; i.e. Windows Vista, Windows XP, Macintosh Intel, etc. **Note:** Unless you want the free additional software offered to Windows users such as the Google Toolbar, uncheck the option.

3 Once downloaded, follow the install directions.

Opening a PDF file:

- Double-click the file.
- Or, right-click on the file and select **Open with Adobe Reader**.
- Or, drag the PDF document directly to the program icon.
- Or, within Adobe Reader, click **File > Open**, then select the file to open. Use this method if you want to do anything with the PDF other than simply read or print it.

Setting Adobe as your Default PDF Reader

Generally, you'll have the option of selecting Adobe Reader as your default PDF reader after you install it and open it for the first time. If, however, another program opens, instead of Adobe Reader, here is how to change the settings:

Windows

In the Windows operating system, file name extensions are associated with specific programs. Opening a .pdf file should trigger Adobe Reader to open. However, if another program is opening and you want to make Adobe Reader the program associated with the .pdf format, the file association needs to be changed. Here are instructions for Windows XP. See Microsoft's site at http://support.microsoft.com for help with other operating systems.

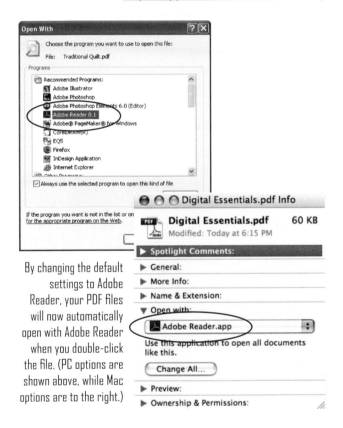

By changing the default settings to Adobe Reader, your PDF files will now automatically open with Adobe Reader when you double-click the file. (PC options are shown above, while Mac options are to the right.)

1 Right-click on a file with the .pdf extension.

2 Select **Open With** and select **Choose Program** on the bottom of the fly-out menu.

3 Click once on **Adobe Reader** in the list, to select it.

4 Check **Always use the selected program to open this kind of file**.

5 Click **OK**.

Macintosh

1 Select a PDF file.

2 In the Finder, go to **File > Get Info**.

3 In the document Get Info box, under Open with, select **Adobe Reader**.

4 Under "Use this application to open all documents like this," click **Change All** and then close the Get Info window.

Getting More from Adobe Reader

Most people tend to open a PDF, read it, or print it. But you can do so much more. Did you know you can also:

- Copy text to use in another document?
- Use a loupe to enlarge portions of text?
- Search for specific information?
- Print a booklet of your PDF?

Customize the Adobe Reader Toolbar

For easier access to these features, customize your toolbar. Here's how:

1 In Adobe Reader, go to **Tools > Customize Toolbar**.

2 Go through the list to select what will be helpful to you and deselect what you will not need. For example, I selected the Page Display and Navigation Toolbar, deselected the Send to FedEx Kinko's tool.

3 Click **OK**. Your toolbar is now customized with icons to make your PDF options easier to use.

If you don't see a tool you need, either right-click (**Control+click** on Mac) and select the tools you want to use, or go to **Tools > Customize Toolbar**, scroll down, and check off the various tools under the Select & Zoom toolbar.

With your toolbar customized, it's now easier to access some of the useful features in Adobe Reader.

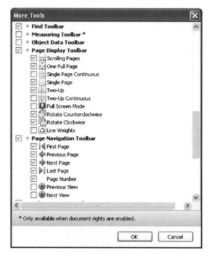

Put a check mark next to all the tools you want displayed on the toolbar. Click to remove check marks next to tools you don't want displayed.

The selected tools will be displayed on the toolbar.

Copying Text and Images

In the toolbar, click the **Select** tool. The pointer changes to an I-beam icon.

COPYING TEXT

- To select a word: double-click it.
- To select a line: triple-click it.
- To select a column: press the **Alt** key (Win) or **Command** key (Mac) as you drag a rectangle over the column.
- To select the entire page: go to **Edit > Select All**. OR, click <u>four times in the text</u>. This will select all of the text on the page no matter how it is displayed.

COPYING IMAGES

The pointer changes to a crosshair.

- Click the image. Or start at the upper-left of the image, and drag diagonally until the image is surrounded by a select box.
- Then either go to **Edit > Copy** (and then Edit > Paste into another open document) or right-click (**Control+click** on a Mac) and select the option to copy.

If you have the PDF document open and a second document open, most programs allow you to drag the selected image from the PDF into the open document. To deselect an image, click off of the image.

Copying All or Part of a Page

The **Snapshot** tool allows you to marquee off a section of the page, or the entire page, and copy it. The copy is an image that you can then place into another document.

In the toolbar, click the **Snapshot** tool. The pointer changes to a crosshair.

1 Start at the upper-left of the area you want to copy, and drag diagonally until the area is surrounded by a select box.

2 A prompt will display telling you that the selection has been copied. Click **OK**.

The Snapshot tool lets you copy all or part of a page.

Using the Zoom Tools

There are a variety of tools that change the magnification of the document. Remember, if you don't see all of the tools, either right-click (**Control+click** on Mac) and select the tools you want to use, or go to **Tools > Customize Toolbar**, scroll down, and check off the various tools under the Select & Zoom toolbar. There are icons to see the entire page (100% of the page), to have the document fill the width of the screen. I tend to use the increase and decrease buttons. Here are some options:

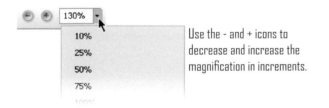

Use the - and + icons to decrease and increase the magnification in increments.

INCREASE AND DECREASE

Using the **-** and **+** icons on the toolbar decreases or increases the magnification with each click. Click and hold on the drop-down menu to the right of the + icon and select a particular magnification.

THE LOUPE TOOL

In the toolbar, click the **Loupe** tool. The pointer changes to a crosshair with a central square.

1 Click anywhere on your document to bring up a magnified portion of your document.

2 The slider bar on the bottom of the magnified portion allows you to zoom in and out on the selected area.

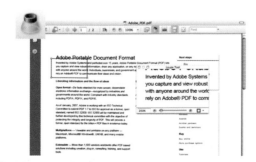

The Loupe tool magnifies a section of your document in the preview window for easier viewing.

PAN AND ZOOM

The Pan and Zoom tool is sort of the opposite of the Loupe Tool in that a small thumbnail of your document is in a small rectangle. The area of document magnification corresponds to the position of the red square in the thumbnail.

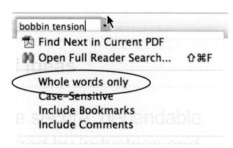

The Pan and Zoom tool magnifies the document based on the selection in the preview window.

Searching

The search feature is particularly handy when you are trying to find a specific piece of information in a large PDF. For example, if someone sends you a document on the basics of machine quilting, and you are looking for information on bobbin tension, you can type "bobbin tension" in the search window. Use the drop-down menu to the right of the search box and select **whole words only** to find every instance of "bobbin tension" in the opened PDF. Each time you hit the **Return/Enter** key, the next instance will appear.

OPEN FULL READER SEARCH

Another option is searching through several or even all PDFs in a selected area. In the drop-down menu to the right of the search menu, select **Open Full Reader Search**. A search box opens. Type in the search word or phrase, select **All PDF Documents in**, and use the drop-down menu to select the location of your PDFs. If you're like me and have many PDFs on your system, be sure to drag the relevant PDFs into their own folder and search in that folder rather than your entire system. Clicking on the **Use Advanced Search Options** on the bottom of the window gives you more searching options, including matching the exact word or phrase or any of the words.

Search for key words in your document.

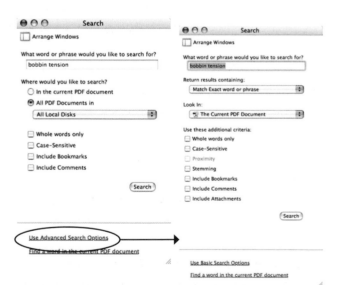

The Full Reader Search lets you search in several PDF documents at a time. Use the Advanced search to narrow your search parameters.

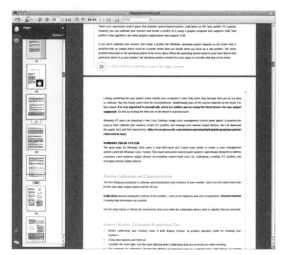

Displaying the thumbnail images of the pages in the PDF makes it easier to navigate through large documents.

Displaying Thumbnail Images

If you have a long PDF document, it's easier to navigate by first opening the thumbnail images window. Page thumbnails are a mini version of the pages displayed in a vertical filmstrip. By clicking on one of the thumbnails, the document jumps to that page.

To display the thumbnail view, click the page icon to the upper-left of your document. Or, go to **View > Navigation Panels > Pages** to display the Pages panel.

Printing

To print a PDF, either select the **Print** icon on the toolbar or go to **File > Print**.

As with any print dialog box, you can select the number of copies, if you want to print all pages, or certain pages. There are also options you can explore, including a printing tips button on the lower-left. Clicking this launches your browser and displays Printing Tips pages directly from Adobe's Web site.

PAGE SCALING

Paper scaling is a particularly useful feature. This option allows you to reduce, enlarge, or divide paper when printing. The default is None. Under the drop-down menu, you'll find the following options:

- **Fit to Printable Area:** This option will reduce or enlarge your PDF to fit on the selected paper size.
- **Shrink to Printable Area:** This option will reduce a PDF that is larger than your selected paper size, but it will not enlarge a PDF to the selected paper size.
- **Multiple Pages Per Sheet:** This handy option allows you to print more than one PDF page on the same piece of paper. The option provides settings for how many pages per sheet of paper, the page order, etc.
- **Booklet Printing:** For booklet printing to work, your printer must support printing on both sides of the paper. Printing on two sides is done in two print passes. That is, first the printer prints all even (or

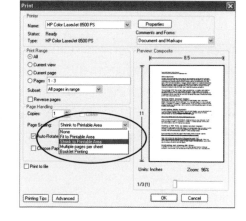

odd) pages. Then you flip the printed pages, insert them back into the printer, and the printer then prints the odd (or even) pages. Booklet printing allows you to print multiple PDF pages on the same piece of paper in the order needed so that when folded in half, the PDF reads correctly. This feature lets you create booklets of your favorite PDFs.

Creating a PDF

Macintosh

Unless you're using a pre-OS X Macintosh, any document that you can print can also be saved as a PDF. This is extremely handy, as you won't need anything more than the "Save to PDF" command included within the print dialog box.

After you create your document (be sure to save it), go to **File > Print**, to open the Print dialog box. Click the **Save as PDF** button on the bottom-left. Name the PDF, indicate where to save it, and click **Save**.

In the Print dialog box, you'll notice other PDF saving options. Two very useful ones are **Compress PDF** and **Encrypt PDF**.

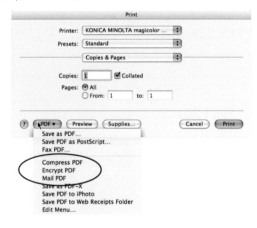

COMPRESS PDF

When selecting the Compress PDF option, the pages will first appear to print. However, in the toolbar, you'll see "Compress Images in PDF" to alert you that the document is compressing. After it is finished, a dialog box will appear. Name your document and indicate where to save it.

The Compress PDF option should be used when creating a PDF for the Web or for E-mail. You can select the Mail PDF option, which automatically attaches the compressed document to a draft E-mail.

Compress Images in PDF will display in the corner of your document to warn you that the file is compressing.

Notice the file size differences between the two files.

ENCRYPT PDF

The Encrypt PDF option allows you to assign a password to the PDF. This is very handy if you want to restrict who can open the document. The encryption process takes longer than normal printing, and you'll see the status of the encryption in the menu bar. If your document is long, be patient. When the process is finished, a dialog box prompts for a password. The Save dialog box then prompts for a name and location to save. When the document is opened, a Password dialog box will appear. Enter the password and click OK. The correct password must be inserted for the document to open.

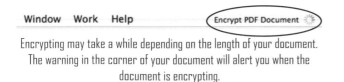

Encrypting may take a while depending on the length of your document. The warning in the corner of your document will alert you when the document is encrypting.

Now that you have encrypted the file, users will have to enter a password to access the file.

Two very useful Macintosh-only PDF programs for non-Leopard users (Leopard users see page 187 for using Preview)

YEP – www.yepthat.com

Like iTunes® for music or iPhoto® for images, Yep is designed to manage your PDFs. Unlike the other programs, Yep shows all of your PDF files based on where they are on your hard drive (meaning they can stay where they are). When Yep did a quick tag of the PDFs on one of my drives, 2054 PDF files came up! Try the program for 21 days free, and then it's $34.00. If you have a lot of PDFs and need to get them under control, it's worth it!

Skim PDF Reader —skim-app.sourcefore.net.

This handy program allows you to read, search, bookmark, add notes, highlight sections, and take "snapshots" for easy reference. It also allows you to give a full screen presentation of your PDF file. Best of all, it's free.

Windows

CREATING A PDF FROM MICROSOFT® WORD OR ANY 2007 MICROSOFT® OFFICE PROGRAM

Microsoft offers a free download from its Web site that allows you to save to the PDF format from any of the eight 2007 Microsoft Office programs, including Word.

Go to Microsoft's download page at http://www.microsoft.com/downloads.
In the Search window, select **Office** in the first field and search for "**As PDF or XPS Office Add-in**." Look for 2007 Microsoft Office Add-in: Microsoft Save as PDF or XPS.

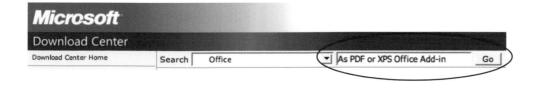

After clicking the link, click the **Continue** button (validation of your installed 2007 Office program is required). If you want to skip installing the Genuine Advantage Plug-in, scroll to the bottom of the page and click on Alternate Validation Method. Click the **Continue** button, follow the prompts, cut/paste the validation code into the box, and click **Validate**. Proceed to download and install the program.

After the program is installed, to save a document as a PDF click the **Microsoft Office** button on the upper-left. Select **Save As**. Then click **PDF** or **XPS**.

If you want to immediately look at the document, select **Open File after Publishing**. Name and select a location for the PDF.

> **Note:** If the document is for print, select Standard to the right of the Optimize for. If the document is for the Web, select Minimum size.

Click Save As to save your document as a PDF.

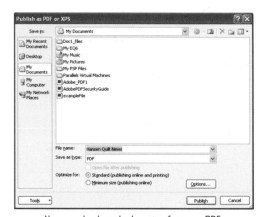

Name and select the location for your PDF.

Tips

ADDING PDF FILES TO YOUR WEB SITE

Adding PDFs to your Web site is a wonderful marketing tool. You can add your teaching contract, class supply list, or even free patterns. However, to keep the experience as good as possible for those who download from your site, remember that **file size is key**.

- Be sure your images are sized and optimized properly before placing them in your document.
- Do not use the image resize function in programs such as Microsoft Word. The feature does not actually reduce the file size but rather displays a smaller version of it.
- Consider adding security to a PDF such as your teaching contract. Allow printing but prevent editing.
- Be sure to use the compression features of your PDF creator to get the file size as low as you can.
- If your document is very long, consider breaking it into several PDF files. Or compress it using compression software such as ZipIt or StuffIt.
- Include a link to where to download Adobe Reader so that your readers can obtain a copy if needed.

Reference

Where Can I Find More Information On...

What Are the Main Differences Among Photoshop, Photoshop Elements, and Paint Shop Pro?

Elements is an excellent image-editing program that will fill the needs of a majority of quilt makers. It includes the core elements of Photoshop, hence its name. The program includes layers, adjustment layers, healing tools, automatic adjustment and selection tools, a large range of image filters for special effects, text, and vector shapes. It can also work with RAW files, albeit in a basic way. In all, the program does an excellent job at covering the basics and may be the best image-editing program for most quilt makers. It's a good value and very user-friendly.

The main difference between Elements 6 for the Windows and for the Mac is that the Windows version uses the "Organizer" to manage and tag images, and the Mac version uses the more powerful Bridge CS3.

Photoshop, however, expands on all of those features, offering more tools, filters, options, and far greater control over those tools and options. It also includes curve adjustments, layer masks, layer comps, and the ability to work with individual channels in the LAB color mode and in the CMYK color space. It has extensive color management, on-screen soft-proofing options, and 16-bit support. The RAW Camera support is far more powerful. Photoshop is the best image-editing program, but it costs far more, has a steeper learning curve, and is certainly not for everyone.

Paint Shop Pro is another excellent image-editing program. It has many of the same tools as Photoshop, but at the Elements price tag. Paint Shop Pro includes a learning center that guides one through a step-by-step process of completing a particular task. That's a great help to speed learning in those new to the program. Its tools for correcting color, lighting problems, and exposure are very good. My personal issues with it are that some tools are clumsy to use, such as working in a text box rather than directly on the document. It is also only available for the PC, which could be a reason why some creative professionals don't give it much weight. That being said, Paint Shop Pro has a wide range of features that can fill the needs of many quilt makers at an excellent price.

Want to Put Your PDF on Your Web Site?

Some people simply create a PDF meant for print, upload it and link the file to a Web page. The problem is that often these files are huge and can be problematic for those downloading or even when uploading. Thus, most important is keeping the file size of the PDF as low as possible.

Do this by using a Web quality resolution for all of the images contained within the PDF. Remember, since this is for the Web, you can keep the physical size of the image but lower the resolution. Refer to Chapter 6 (page 52) for more information on reducing the resolution of your graphics. Generally it's high resolution in graphics that create very large PDF file sizes.

Different programs also offer the option to reduce file size.
In Acrobat Professional, go to **Document > Reduce File Size**. The program does an excellent job at reducing the file size.

In InDesign, go to **File> Export**, select **Adobe PDF** from the Format drop-down menu. This will bring up a large Export Adobe PDF dialog box. Use these settings:
- In **General**: Select **Smallest File Size** from the Adobe PDF drop-down menu. Check **Optimize for Fast Web View** under Options.
- In **Compression**: Compress the color images, grayscale, and monochrome images to **96 ppi for images above 125 ppi**. Why 96? Simply because I find it generally works well. However, you may need to experiment to see what works.
- Then click **Export**.

Otherwise, if you're looking for an inexpensive program, do a Web search on "free programs to reduce PDF file size." You'll find a variety of free, shareware, and demo products.

When the Web version of your PDF is saved, it is ready for you to link to your site. Depending on which Web program you use or how you FTP your documents to your site, simply treat the PDF as you would any other item being linked to a page. If you do not understand how to link, ask the person who maintains your site to do it for you.

Useful Terms to Remember for Digital Applications

Additive Color: Red, green, blue (RGB) light combined in varying degrees to produce all of the colors in the visible spectrum. Mixing red, green, and blue in equal amounts produces white. (Page 41)

Anti-alias: Technique used to give the appearance of a smoother edge and higher resolution by rounding the pixels of a high contrast edge and its background up or down. (Pages 119 & 159)

Batch processing: A way to define a series of tasks (such as resizing an image and adding a name to it) and automate them so that a computer program executes them in one command. Using batch commands can be a tremendous time saver. (Page 168)

Bitmap: A graphic format that stores data for each pixel without any compression. A bitmap format is generally used for photo-realistic images. (Pages 10 & 18)

Color channel: The color components of a digital image based on the mode of the document. RGB has three channels (**r**ed, **g**reen, and **b**lue), CMYK has four channels (**c**yan, **m**agenta, **y**ellow, and black), and LAB has three channels (**l**ightness, **A**-magentas through greens, **B**-yellows through blues).

Color profile: A mathematically defined color space for a particular media device. For example, a color profile is often used for the goal of matching what you see on your monitor to what you see in your printed document. (Page 36)

Color space: A color model which generally includes the additive RGB colors, including sRGB, Adobe RGB, LAB (among other additive spaces), and the subtractive CMYK colors. (Pages 36-43)

- **Adobe RGB**: An additive color mode that has a larger range of colors than sRGB, includes an additive version of the colors that can be printed using CMYK inks, and those that a monitor can display. Adobe RGB is preferred for printed images.
- **CMYK**: A subtractive color mode using cyan, yellow, magenta, and black ink for printing.
- **LAB**: An additive color mode with three channels: L, the lightness or luminosity channel (it has no color information), and A and B which contain the color information. A runs between the magenta and green, and B between yellow and blue. Sharpening an image in the L channel of LAB is the preferred choice of many. This way the color information in the document is not changed, which avoids unwanted artifacts.

- **sRGB**: An additive color mode that uses standard **r**ed, **g**reen, and **b**lue (sRGB) that was designed to match an average color monitor. It is smaller than Adobe RGB and other color spaces, but is the preferred color space for Web Graphics.
- **RGB**: An additive color mode that produces the colors our eyes see.

Continuous tone images: Photographic images containing a large number of gray values or nearly all RGB colors in a continuous scale from dark to light and from unsaturated to saturated. (Page 13)

Curves: A powerful image editing adjustment tool that provides complete control over any point along the full 0-255 tonal range of a digital image. (Page 112)

DPI: Dots per inch. The DPI of an image describes how many dots of ink per square inch are used within a printed image. (Page 25)

Drawing software: A graphics program used for creating resolution independent two-dimensional images and shapes using vectors. A drawing program is also known as an illustration program. Examples are Adobe Illustrator and CorelDRAW. (Pages 11 & 18)

Histogram: A bar graph showing the tonal range of a digital image from the left, or darkest pixels, to the right showing the lightest pixels, with the mid-tones values in the center (0 being white and 255 being black). Tall bars indicate a tone that takes up a lot of space and short bars indicate a tone taking a small amount of space. A histogram that extends from the left to right generally indicates an image with a full ranges of tones. (Pages 100-102)

Image-editing software: A graphics program for modifying and transforming bitmap images, generally photographs. Higher-end image editors provide tools for editing in layers. Examples are Photoshop, Photoshop Elements, and Paint Shop Pro. (Pages 11 & 18)

Inkjet inks: (Page 28)
- **Dye-based**: A colored substance that is soluable in water, meaning it is not waterfast on most surfaces, including fabric. If using a dye-based ink to print on fabric, a pretreatment must be used, otherwise the ink will run off when wet. Dye-based ink has smaller molecules than pigment, meaning the ink will get absorbed into the fibers rather than sit on them. While many dye-based inks fade quickly in UV light, newer dye-based inks are developing with much greater UV resistance.

- **Pigment-based**: A colored substance that is insoluble in water, meaning it is waterfast on nearly all surfaces, including fabric. A pigment-based ink has larger molecules than a dye-based ink meaning it can better resist ultraviolet light and varying temperatures.

  Because of the larger molecules, pigment ink will sit on the fabric fibers rather than be absorbed into them. At one time the range of colors available in pigments was smaller than dyes and looked much duller. Today's pigment inks have a similar range of colors and can often look as good or better, plus they have the advantage of UV resistance.

Interpolation: A mathematical algorithm that creates new color pixels by blending the surrounding pixels. (Page 30 & 58)
- **Bicubic**: A type of nearest neighbor interpolation algorithm that uses a 4x4 range of known pixel values (16 pixels) surrounding the unknown pixel. Since the pixels are at different distances from the unknown pixel, it can product a sharper imager than a bicubic interpolation and is generally the standard default when resampling an image. Most image editing programs include options for "bicubic smoother" and "bicubic sharper" with smoother being the default of most applications and sharper being a good choice when downsampling an image.
- **Bilinear**: A type of nearest neighbor interpolation algorithm that uses the closest 2x2 range of known pixel values surrounding an unknown pixel and creates an interpolated value based on the average of the pixels. This helps to produce a smoother looking image. When downsampling an image, this interpolating can help produce a smoother looking image.

Levels: An image-editing adjustment tool that provides fives sliders to adjust three points of a digital image—the shadows, mid-tones, and highlights—and provides a histogram to let you see what is happening to your image based on the changes you make. A levels adjustment is a good way to correct the brightness and contrast of an image because adjusting the sliders does not change the entire image in equal amounts. (Page 101)

LPI: Lines per inch. A measurement of print resolution in systems that use a halftone screen. Halftone screens are used to commercially print complex images such as photographs. Specifically, it is a measure of how close together the lines in a halftone grid are. Higher LPI generally means greater detail and sharpness. Typical LPIs used range from 85 LPI for newsprint to 300 LPI for a very high quality color print.

Metafile: A general term for a file format that can store various types of data, including raster, vector, or text. (Page 10)

Paint program: A graphics program for creating resolution dependent two-dimensional images using bitmaps. Higher-end paint software often includes image-editing tools. Examples are Corel Painter and Paint Shop Pro.

Pixel: Short for **PIC**ture (or "pix") and **EL**ement, it is a single point, or smallest distinct element, in a digital document or digital display. (Pages 10 & 22)

- **Megapixel**: Short for one million pixels. This term commonly describes the maximum number of pixels a digital camera is capable of capturing.

- **Pixel density**: A measurement of the pixel resolution of a display (e.g. computer monitor), and the physical size of the display. Another example would be the dpi of a printed image and the size of the image. A high pixel density generally indicates a higher quality image (for example, the higher the pixel density of a flat screen TV, the better the picture quality).

PPI: Pixels per inch. A display resolution defined by pixel width by height and a method for defining how pixels should be interpreted in dots per inch when printing. (Pages 26 & 32)

Raster: An image described in pixels, also called a bitmap. Most digital images are raster images. (Page 10)

Resampling: A method of increasing or decreasing the number of pixels in a document. Increasing pixels is known as **up**sampling, and decreasing pixels is known as **down**sampling. (Page 57)

Resizing: A method of changing the print size of a digital document without changing the number of its pixels. (Page 54)

Resolution: The number of pixels in a digital file or digital device. It is measured by width and height, and stated in terms of that ratio, such as 800 x 600. (Page 22)

Subtractive color: Cyan, magenta and yellow (CMY) pigments that when combined in varying degrees produce a color depending on how the pigments on a surface absorb wave lengths of light. Equal amounts of cyan, magenta, and yellow produces black, although it's often a muddy gray rather than a pure black. For this reason, printed images use CMYK, or **c**yan, **m**agenta, **y**ellow, and black ink to create colors. (Page 41)

Unsharp mask: A technique that increases the contrast of a pixel's edge. (Page 140)

Vector: An object-orientated graphic file format, made from a series of mathematical geometric objects such as polygons and curves. (Pages 10 & 18)

Index

Symbols

A

B

C

D

DIGITAL ESSENTIALS: A Quilt Maker's Must-Have Guide to Images, Files, and More!